Bach and the Meanings of Counterpoint

In Bach's Germany musical counterpoint was an art involving much more than the sophisticated use of advanced compositional techniques. A range of theological, cultural, social, and political meanings attached themselves to the use of complex procedures such as canon and double counterpoint. This book explores the significance of Bach's counterpoint in a range of interrelated contexts: its use as a means of reflecting on death; its parallels with alchemy; its vexed status in the galant music culture of the first half of the eighteenth century; its value as a representation of political power; and its central importance in the creation of Bach's image in the nineteenth and twentieth centuries. Touching on a wide array of contemporary literary, philosophical, critical, and musical texts, the book includes new readings of many of Bach's late works in order to reevaluate the status and meaning of counterpoint in Bach's work and legacy.

DAVID YEARSLEY is an Assistant Professor at Cornell University. His scholarly work has appeared in the *Journal of the American Musicological Society, Early Music, Music & Letters*, and the *Journal of Seventeenth-Century Music*. His recordings of seventeenth- and eighteenth-century keyboard music are available on the Loft label.

New perspectives in music history and criticism

GENERAL EDITORS:
JEFFREY KALLBERG, ANTHONY NEWCOMB AND RUTH SOLIE

This series explores the conceptual frameworks that shape or have shaped the ways in which we understand music and its history, and aims to elaborate structures of explanation, interpretation, commentary, and criticism which make music intelligible and which provide a basis for argument about judgments of value. The intellectual scope of the series is broad. Some investigations will treat, for example, historiographical topics, others will apply cross-disciplinary methods to the criticism of music, and there will also be studies which consider music in its relation to society, culture, and politics. Overall, the series hopes to create a greater presence for music in the ongoing discourse among the human sciences.

Published titles

LESLIE C. DUNN AND NANCY A. JONES (eds.), *Embodied Voices: Representing Female Vocality in Western Culture*

DOWNING A. THOMAS, *Music and the Origins of Language: Theories from the French Enlightenment*

THOMAS S. GREY, *Wagner's Musical Prose*

DANIEL K. L. CHUA, *Absolute Music and the Construction of Meaning*

ADAM KRIMS, *Rap Music and the Poetics of Identity*

ANNETTE RICHARDS, *The Free Fantasia and the Musical Picturesque*

RICHARD WILL, *The Characteristic Symphony in the Age of Haydn and Beethoven*

CHRISTOPHER MORRIS, *Reading Opera Between the Lines: Orchestral Interludes and Cultural Meaning from Wagner to Berg*

EMMA DILLON, *Medieval Music-Making and the 'Roman de Fauvel'*

DAVID YEARSLEY, *Bach and the Meanings of Counterpoint*

Bach and the Meanings of Counterpoint

DAVID YEARSLEY

CAMBRIDGE
UNIVERSITY PRESS

CAMBRIDGE UNIVERSITY PRESS
Cambridge, New York, Melbourne, Madrid, Cape Town, Singapore, São Paulo, Delhi

Cambridge University Press
The Edinburgh Building, Cambridge CB2 8RU, UK

Published in the United States of America by Cambridge University Press, New York

www.cambridge.org
Information on this title: www.cambridge.org/9780521803465

© Cambridge University Press 2002

This publication is in copyright. Subject to statutory exception
and to the provisions of relevant collective licensing agreements,
no reproduction of any part may take place without the written
permission of Cambridge University Press.

First published 2002
Reprinted 2004 (twice)
This digitally printed version 2008

A catalogue record for this publication is available from the British Library

ISBN 978-0-521-80346-5 hardback
ISBN 978-0-521-09099-5 paperback

For my parents

CONTENTS

List of illustrations   *page* x
Preface   xiii
Acknowledgments   xv
List of abbreviations   xvi

1. *Vor deinen Thron tret ich* and the art of dying   1
2. The alchemy of Bach's canons   42
3. Bach's taste for pork or canary   93
4. The autocratic regimes of *A Musical Offering*   128
5. Bach the machine   173
6. Physiognomies of Bach's counterpoint   209

Bibliography   239
Index   251

ILLUSTRATIONS

1.1	*Vor deinen Thron tret ich*, BWV 668, manuscript fragment (courtesy of Staatsbibliothek, Berlin)	*page* 3
1.2	The battle with death, August Pfeiffer, *Liebes-Kuß* (1732) (courtesy of British Library)	9
1.3	Cruciform canon, Adam Gumpelzhaimer, *Compendium musicae latino-germanicum* (1625) (courtesy of Sibley Library, University of Rochester)	19
1.4	Frontispiece, depicting heavenly canon, Athanasius Kircher, *Musurgia universalis* (1650) (courtesy of Cornell University Library)	22
1.5	Frontispiece, based on Kircher, Johann Rist, *Sabbahtische Seelenlust* (1651) (courtesy of Yale University Library)	23
1.6	The Last Day and the resurrection of the dead, August Pfeiffer, *Liebes-Kuß* (1732) (courtesy of British Library)	27
1.7	Heavenly/earthly concert, August Pfeiffer, *Liebes-Kuß* (1732) (courtesy of British Library)	29
2.1	J. S. Bach, "Hudemann" canon (BWV 1074) as printed in *Der getreue Music-Meister* (1728) (courtesy of Staatsbibliothek, Berlin)	43
2.2	J. S. Bach, canon, *Fa Mi, et Mi Fa est tota Musica*, BWV 1078 (courtesy of Staatsbibliothek, Berlin)	61
2.3	Title-page, Johann Mattheson, *Der vollkommene Capellmeister* (1739)	63
2.4	Alchemist in his laboratory with musical instruments, Heinrich Khunrath, *Amphitheatrum sapientiae aeternae solius verae, Christiano-kabalisticum, divino-magicum . . . Tertriunum* (1609) (courtesy of Cornell University Library)	68
2.5	The *artifex* following Nature, Michael Maier, *Atalanta fugiens* (1618) (courtesy of British Library)	72
2.6	Johann Theile, *Musicalisches Kunstbuch*, no. 4 (copy by J. G. Walther) (courtesy of Staatsbibliothek, Berlin)	78

List of illustrations

2.7	Johann Theile, *Harmonischer Baum* (courtesy of Staatsbibliothek, Berlin)	85
2.8	*Arbor philosophica*, Samuel Norton, *Mercurius redivivus* (1630); reprinted in Vigilantius, *Dreyfaches Hermetisches Kleeblatt* (1667) (courtesy of British Library)	86
3.1	J. S. Bach, Duetto in F major (BWV 803), symmetrical layout	108
4.1	Title-page, G. P. Telemann, *Der getreue Music-Meister* (1728)	144
4.2	J. S. Bach, crab canon (no. 1) from *A Musical Offering*, BWV 1079, original print (courtesy of Staatsbibliothek, Berlin)	150
4.3	Scheme for a crab canon	152
5.1	Frontispiece, Jacques de Vaucanson, *Le mécanisme du fluteur automate* (1738) (courtesy of British Library)	177
5.2	Invertible Counterpoint "Device," C. P. E. Bach, *Einfall, einen doppelten Contrapunct in der Octave von 6 Tacten zu machen, ohne die Regeln davon zu wissen* as printed in F. W. Marpurg, *Historisch-kritische Beyträge zur Aufnahme der Musik*, vol. I (1755) (courtesy of Cornell University Library)	185
5.3	*Hauptcomposition/evolutio* scheme for Canons at the Tenth and Twelfth from *Art of Fugue*, BWV 1080/16 and BWV 1080/17	194
5.4	(a) and (b). Inversion tables for invertible counterpoint at the twelfth and tenth from Angelo Berardi, *Documenti armonici* (1687)	196
6.1	Bach's skull; photographs from Wilhelm His, *Bach: Forschungen über dessen Grabstätte, Gebeine und Antlitz* (1895)	213
6.2	Bach's skull dissected; photographs from His, "Anatomische Forschungen über Johann Sebastian Bach's Gebeine und Antlitz" (1895)	216
6.3	Bach's temporal bones, cross-sectioned; from His, "Anatomische Forschungen über Johann Sebastian Bach's Gebeine und Antlitz" (1895)	217
6.4	Bach's skull with "scientifically accurate" face; from His, *Forschungen über dessen Grabstätte, Gebeine und Antlitz* (1895)	219
6.5	Karl Seffner, Bust of Bach (1895)	221
6.6	Bach's skeleton; from His, "Anatomische Forschungen über Johann Sebastian Bach's Gebeine und Antlitz" (1895)	223
6.7	Bach portraits and skull; from Heinrich Besseler, *Fünf echte Bildnisse Johann Sebastian Bachs* (1956)	226

PREFACE

Abstract, recherché, arcane, speculative: this is the set of adjectives most often used by modern writers to describe Bach's strict contrapuntal music, a body of work encompassing canons, pieces in invertible counterpoint in which the voices are harmonically interchangeable, and more freely conceived works in which these techniques are employed with varying degrees of rigor. Consider canon, which, above all other genres, is often seen to create a closed musical system without reference beyond itself; it is an autonomous object uncomplicated – or perhaps untarnished – by "extra-musical" assumptions and attitudes. The more complex the canon the more self-contained. "Abstract" becomes another way of saying "devoid of broader meaning." As a result, strict counterpoint as a whole has been frequently depicted as an enterprise of isolated, unrelenting study divorced from the larger musical culture of the first half of the eighteenth century.

In this book I argue that the opposite is true: that in the first half of the eighteenth century no set of musical practices was richer in significance than strict counterpoint. Indeed, the minute, exacting, and seemingly esoteric world of canon could match the hermeneutic resonance of the most opulent of operas. No musical endeavor generated more polemical writing and more heated opinions during Bach's lifetime than did strict counterpoint; no set of techniques inspired greater devotion from its practitioners or more spirited antipathy from its detractors. Musicians literally wrestled over coveted books of contrapuntal knowledge; some guarded troves of contrapuntal treasure with almost mythic fervor; others consigned the long traditions of contrapuntal training to useless history. No mere abstraction would have inspired such intense and diverse reactions.

For a great many musicians of Bach's day counterpoint was saturated with meaning – social, theological, and political. Counterpoint could be used as a way of contemplating death and of investigating the hidden connections governing the universe. Canon could become a rite of passage into the musical elite or it could serve as a dubious mark of unquestioned obedience to antiquated values. The same techniques that were used to produce rarefied musical creations privately circulated among professionals could simultaneously be drawn on to create challenging musical puzzles for the delectation of amateurs. Strict counterpoint could represent a sublime quest for musical truth or be used to construct amusing games, mere diversions. Indeed, the same pieces could be viewed as priceless objects to be secreted away or as saleable commodities to be offered up to a nascent bourgeois consuming class. Canon could be likened to manure being shoveled around a barnyard or thought of as angelic music resounding through heaven.

That strict counterpoint could participate in these often contradictory impulses and that it could be so extensively battled over intellectually and even, on occasion, physically, speaks not only to its "extra-musical" power but to the turbulent musical climate of the first half of the eighteenth century. Bach produced most of his elaborate contrapuntal work during a period marked by a proliferation of accessible, journalistic criticism which helped create a public sphere for the discussion of musical issues; in these forums strict counterpoint was a perennial object of comment and controversy. But the shadowy margins, the spaces where counterpoint was put to private and particular use beyond the purview of critics, can be even more illuminating. To know something of the vitality of German musical life during Bach's lifetime requires an inquiry into both domains and the intersections between them – and into the meanings counterpoint found there.

ACKNOWLEDGMENTS

First I want to thank those people who nurtured my love for the music of J. S. Bach. At the head of that list are my parents, John and Karen Yearsley, to whom this book is dedicated. They are followed by Lucille Argenbright, Vicki Hoffman, Jerome Horowitz, Katherine Fowler, Michiko Miyamoto, Edward Hansen, Christa Rakich, William Porter, Harald Vogel, Jacques van Oortmerssen, Kimberly Marshall, and Robert Bates. Their presence is felt in these pages no less strongly than that of the many musicological colleagues who have helped this book in various and vital ways: Karol Berger, John Butt, Thomas Christensen, Laurence Dreyfus, Thomas Grey, Arthur Groos, Gregory Johnston, Jeffrey Kallberg, Ulrich Leisinger, Anthony Newcomb, Annette Richards, James Webster, and Neal Zaslaw. Portions of Chapters 1, 2, and 5 have appeared in *Music & Letters*, the *Journal of the American Musicological Society*, and the *Anderson Valley Advertiser*. I am indebted to the editors of all three for their comments and suggestions. Crucial support at an early phase of my research came in the form of a Wenner-Gren Foundation Fellowship at Gothenburg University. The Otto Kinkeldey Publication Endowment Fund of the American Musicological Society provided generous financial support. A grant from the Kennington Center for Eighteenth-Century Studies aided my work at the British Library. I am grateful to Diego Vega for copying the musical examples, and to Lenore Coral for helping me to secure far-flung bibliographic materials. Thanks are also due to Lucy Carolan for her indispensable editorial help, and to Penny Souster of Cambridge University Press for shepherding the project through from start to finish.

ABBREVIATIONS

BD   *Bach-Dokumente.* 4 vols. Ed. Werner Neumann and Hans-Joachim Schulze. Kassel, 1963–78.
BWV   *Bach-Werke-Verzeichnis.* Wolfgang Schmieder. *Thematisch-systematisches Verzeichnis der musikalischen Werke von Johann Sebastian Bach,* rev. and expanded edn. Wiesbaden, 1990.
NBR   *The New Bach Reader.* Ed. Christoph Wolff et al. New York, 1998.

1

Vor deinen Thron tret ich and the art of dying

We begin at the end, in July of 1750, with Bach on his deathbed. As was customary in the Lutheran rituals of death and dying, Bach was at home, probably on the second floor of the cantor's apartments in the Thomasschule, in his own bedroom above the Thomasplatz. A week before his death on July 28, Bach's condition had deteriorated quickly when he suffered a stroke which was soon followed by a "raging fever";[1] a pair of failed eye operations performed on him a few months earlier had left Bach blind, and lying in his bed he would not have been able to see the summer morning, early in his east-facing window. The hour of Bach's death was approaching. In these circumstances, the actions of the dying person and of the family members, friends, and clerics standing by were thoroughly ritualized. Those gathered around the deathbed would have comforted the dying man by praying and reading from the Bible, singing chorales, perhaps even playing them on a harpsichord or clavichord. But they were also there to watch for signs: at this critical juncture Bach's every action could give crucial information concerning the destiny of his soul, that is, the outcome of the final contest between good and evil, between heaven and hell. Even Martin Luther himself, when on his deathbed, had been repeatedly awakened by those around him so that they could confirm his faithfulness as near as possible to the actual moment of death. A pastor was the most reliable and resourceful interpreter of the actions of the dying, and during Bach's last week, his father confessor, Christoph Wolle, the archdeacon at the Thomaskirche, was summoned to the cantor's bedroom. Following his training in pastoral care, Wolle would have given Bach a final blessing, quoted

[1] *NBR*, 303; *BD* III, 85.

passages from scriptures, and read prayers, while commenting on the dying man's deportment in order to assure the family that his faith was unswerving. But however comforting father confessor and family may have been, in the last week of his life it was Bach alone who would determine the fate of his soul.

With this ultimate question to be decided over the course of Bach's last days, the composition or, as is more probable, the revision of his so-called deathbed chorale, *Vor deinen Thron tret ich hiermit*, would have played a crucial role in the domestic drama of his death. Bach's last piece is an elaborate demonstration of intricate contrapuntal technique used to treat a chorale text which both anticipates death and refers beyond it, to the arrival of the dead man in heaven:

> Vor deinen Thron tret ich hiermit
> o Gott, und dich demütig bitt
> wend dein genädig Angesicht
> von mir, dem armen Sünder nicht.
>
> Before your throne I now appear,
> O God, and humbly bid you,
> turn not your gracious face,
> away from me, poor sinner.

As one might expect of the dying musical utterances of a composer of Bach's stature, *Vor deinen Thron* is embedded in mystery and myth, fragments of truth often indistinguishable from the shapes of legend.

In the source Bach's deathbed chorale, which was copied by an anonymous scribe, is itself a fragment, breaking off after twenty-five measures (see Figure 1.1).[2] The scribe must have copied out the final chorale in its entirety but at some later date the second page was torn off and is now lost. The piece was first published posthumously in 1751, appended to the first edition of the *Art of Fugue* in order to make up, with its intrinsic finality, for the incompleteness of the collection's final contrapunctus. However, the version of the deathbed chorale that appears in the *Art of Fugue* print is provided with the penitential text more commonly associated with the melody *Wenn wir in höchsten Nöthen sein* (BWV 668a) and, consistent with the layout of the entire collection, is presented in open score rather than the organ format of *Vor deinen Thron*, which is written on two staves. The myth of finality is complicated further by the fact that *Vor deinen Thron* offers a few improvements to the printed version

---

[2] The chorale comes on the last page of one of the most important autograph collections of Bach's organ works, containing the Trio Sonatas (BWV 525–530), the *Canonic Variations* (BWV 769a) and the "Great Eighteen" Chorales (BWV 651–668). For a summary of scholarship on the source for BWV 668, see Russell Stinson, *J. S. Bach's Great Eighteen Organ Chorales* (Oxford, 2001), 33–38.

Figure 1.1 *Vor deinen Thron tret ich*, BWV 668, manuscript fragment

Example 1.1 Comparison of two versions of "deathbed" chorale: (a) BWV 668 and (b) BWV 668a, bar 10

appended to the *Art of Fugue*; for example the deceptive cadence found in m. 10 of BWV 668 provides a more satisfying reading than that offered by the authentic cadence at the same place in BWV 668a (Example 1.1). Here is a last word that, in its two versions, suggests a concern for careful revision. Yet in the note (Nachricht) which appeared on the reverse side of the title-page to the first edition of the *Art of Fugue* (1751), Carl Philipp Emanuel Bach claimed that shortly before his death his father had dictated the chorale extemporaneously (aus dem Stegereif) to an unnamed friend.[3]

C. P. E. Bach was not present in Leipzig at the time of his father's death, yet his account of the genesis of the last chorale was accepted

---

[3] *NBR*, 258, 260; *BD* III, 13.

without question by his contemporaries.[4] In the preface to the second edition of the *Art of Fugue* which appeared in 1752, the Berlin theorist F. W. Marpurg repeated the notion that Bach had extemporaneously dictated his final chorale. J. N. Forkel's 1802 biography of Bach, based in large part on information received from Carl Philipp Emanuel and Wilhelm Friedemann Bach, is somewhat more specific, asserting that the composer had dictated the piece to his son-in-law J. C. Altnikol "a few days before his death."[5] Although the early guardians of Bach's legacy presented the deathbed chorale as an inspired, unpremeditated creation, neither version of the piece could in fact have been dictated extemporaneously, at least not in its entirety, as Bach's myth-making heirs hoped to imply. Far from having been conjured up *ex nihilo* by the dying composer, this chorale is in fact an expansion of the short setting of *Wenn wir in höchsten Nöthen sein* (BWV 641) written around 1715 and transmitted in the *Orgelbüchlein*. The "deathbed" chorale strips the original of its elaborate ornamentation and introduces lengthy contrapuntal interludes thematically based on the chorale melody itself. What is remarkable, however – and this is what must have left a lasting impression on Bach's closest circle – is that even on his deathbed the composer was virtuosically engaged with the techniques of learned counterpoint, including melodic inversion, diminution, and stretto. It was complex counterpoint that had occupied Bach's last musical reflections.

While we should keep in mind that Bach did not compose the entire chorale in the last week of his life – a superhuman act thought by the heirs to be a suitably impressive yet devout summation of his genius – there is no reason to doubt that he was at work on an expanded version of the chorale while awaiting his death, perhaps even before the stroke on July 20. As far as his deathbed labors are concerned, Forkel's scenario seems plausible enough: Bach listened to someone play the piece, then dictated adjustments to an expanded, more contrapuntally complex, yet less elaborately ornamented version of the original *Orgelbüchlein* chorale. Altnikol, or some other family friend or relative, would have served as the amanuensis for these revisions, playing through the piece for the blind composer, who dictated the corrections while lying in what he clearly now knew was his deathbed. Could BWV 668a represent a slightly earlier version of this final chorale, and BWV 668 the last revisions? Given the debilitating illness which beset Bach in his last days, the slight differences between the two chorales might well approximate the level of composerly exertion the ailing man was then capable of.

---

[4] For an investigation into the myths surrounding the composition of *Vor deinen Thron* see Christoph Wolff, *Bach: Essays on his Life and Works* (Cambridge, Mass., 1991), 282–294.
[5] *NBR*, 466; J. N. Forkel, *Über Johann Sebastian Bachs Leben, Kunst und Kunstwerke* (Leipzig, 1802; reprint Berlin, 1968), 92.

In contrast to the claims of Bach's eighteenth-century devotees, *Vor deinen Thron* was probably singled out for revision by Bach from his backlog of chorale preludes before his last days and carefully chosen as the forum in which to utter his last musical statement. Just as Bach drew on his own library for what was to be the central musical work performed at his funeral, the double-choir motet *Lieber Herr Gott, wecke uns auf* by his kinsman Johann Christoph Bach, he also turned to his personal holdings for a piece that would both prepare him for death and serve as a kind of epitaph, the concluding measures of a musical life. That the final chorale is a set-piece takes nothing away from its legitimacy or significance as a final utterance, for such preparations for death were an integral part of personal religious activity for Lutheran believers of the middle of the eighteenth century, especially for someone of Bach's theological interests.

In his "Sermon on Preparing to Die," a foundational text of the evangelical *ars moriendi*, Martin Luther exhorted his followers to reflect early and often on their dying hour: "We should familiarize ourselves with death during our lifetime, inviting death into our presence when it is still at a distance."[6] Luther's sermon had a lasting influence on funerary homiletics of the seventeenth and eighteenth centuries, as well as on printed collections of funeral sermons such as Johann Heermann's widely-circulated "Schola Mortis: Todes-Schule" (School of Death) which promised to teach readers how "to die blessedly" (selig sterben). Many theologians and writers of popular religious books recommended personal improvement through the reading of and reflection on collections of funeral sermons like those contained in the appendix of Christoph Scheibler's *Aurifodina Theolog* (Frankfurt, 1664), a volume owned by Bach. The study of such sermons and the lives – and even more importantly the deaths – they described constituted a crucial aspect of the Lutheran pursuit of self-improvement and domestic spirituality.[7]

Bach appears to have been a model Lutheran in this respect: he amassed a large theological library, and given the importance of the *ars moriendi* to the Lutheran tradition it is not surprising that the topic of dying figures largely in his collection.[8] After the works of Luther,

---

[6] Martin Luther, "A Sermon on Preparing to Die," in *Luther's Works*, ed. Jaroslav Pelikan and Helmut Lehmann, 56 vols. (St. Louis and Philadelphia, 1955–76), XLII, 95–115, at p. 101.

[7] For more on exemplary Lutheran deaths see Rudolf Mohr, *Protestantische Theologie und Frömmigkeit im Angesicht des Todes während des Barockzeitalters hauptsächlich auf Grund hessischer Leichenpredigten* (Marburg, 1964), 229–308.

[8] For an annotated bibliography see Robin Leaver, *Bachs Theologische Bibliothek/Bach's Theological Library* (Neuhausen-Stuttgart, 1985). In all of the works of Müller and Pfeiffer referred to below it is not known which editions of the numerous printings were owned by Bach. My citations are of the editions that I have examined.

Vor deinen Thron tret ich *and the art of dying*

which made up the core of Bach's library, the Lübeck theologian and church superintendent August Pfeiffer (eight volumes), and the Rostock Superintendent Heinrich Müller's theological writings (five volumes) are the best represented there. The art of dying is a central theme in Müller's *Geistliche Erquickstunden*, first published in 1664 but reprinted often in the first half of the eighteenth century: "Help me, my God, that I be ever ready, and that everywhere I proceed with one foot in the grave and with the other in heaven."[9] The fundamental premise of earthly existence was that it would lead to death: "Above all things, know that you must die," wrote Müller in *Liebes-Kuß*, another of the books in Bach's collection advising constant preparation for the event.[10] Death was ubiquitous, neither isolated in hospitals nor unusual in the young and seemingly healthy. This much Bach's own life would have taught him painfully: orphaned at age ten, he went on to outlive twelve of his twenty children. The unexpected and arbitrary nature of death was brutally demonstrated to him in 1720 when he returned home to Cöthen after an extended trip to find that his wife, Maria Barbara, was dead and buried. She had been in fine health when he left.

Even for the devout, however, belief alone would not make the dying hours easy: although it was the door through which one entered eternity, death was plainly to be feared. The literature on dying typically includes admissions by authors, self-evidently pious, that they too fear death. In *Anti-melancholicus*, a book that belonged to Bach and one which contains a lengthy chapter on the final struggle with death (Todes Kampff), August Pfeiffer unleashed his most grimly descriptive language: "I take fright as well whenever I think that my limbs, which I so carefully nourished and clothed and so tenderly cared for in my lifetime and which did me such steadfast service, should moulder and rot in the earth, and become a stinking carcass, dung, and filth, and perhaps be carried off by a thousand worms or maggots."[11] For, as Bach would have learned on reading Pfeiffer, Müller and others, the hour of death (*Todes-Stunde*) brought with it an intensification of the devil's efforts, since there was little time left to win the damnation of the dying person's soul. The literature on death in Bach's library relished these opportunities to present harrowing pictures of this last pitched battle,

---

[9] Heinrich Müller, *Geistliche Erquickstunden* (Frankfurt, 1700), 600.
[10] Heinrich Müller, *Vermehrter und durchgehends verbesserter Himmlischer Liebes-Kuß oder Göttliche Liebes-Flamme* (Nuremberg, 1732), 677, 679.
[11] August Pfeiffer, *Anti-melancholicus, oder Melancholey-Vertreiber* (Leipzig, 1691). I include the German to give a better sense of its vehemence: "Ich erschrecke auch / wenn ich daran dencke wie diese mein Glieder die ich bey Lebzeit so sorgfältig ernehrt und bedecket die ich so zärtlich gehalten / die mir so viel treue Dienste gethan sollen in der Erden verwesen / verfaulen zum stinckenden Todten-Aas / Koth und Unflath und vielleicht von 1000. Würmern oder Maden verschleppt werden." Pfeiffer, *Anti-melancholicus*, 583.

particularly through negative example, that is, when the dying person had been godless during his or her life, or had lost the faith at the end: snapping lions, armies of demons, gnawing worms form the backdrop for this theatre of damnation. While such imagery was far from comforting, it was intended to channel the readers' energies towards preparedness, for only through unswerving efforts could the battle be won. Once equipped with the proper training to withstand any assault, the righteous were encouraged to treat death as a blessing: the saved were compared to babes in their mothers' arms, and the jubilation of angels dispersed the torment of demons (Figure 1.2).[12] On the one hand, unwavering preparations were necessary since the time of any individual death was kept hidden by God, and to be caught unawares could have catastrophic consequences. But these preparations were equally valuable in the event of a long drawn-out death such as that experienced by Bach. In the case of an extended battle, Pfeiffer offers the reader a potent mixture of fear and consolation to encourage him not to succumb to despair in the final days and hours, and in his chapter on the "Hour of Death" (Todes-Stunde) found in *Anti-melancholicus* he combines theological argument, linguistic analysis and metaphysical explanation with practical recommendations for prayer and methods of preparation that would allow one to remain faithful until the moment of death.[13]

Often fixating on the *Todes-Stunde* and the course of the final battle, funeral sermons frequently detailed the medical conditions that had led to the death of the person being eulogized.[14] Typical were the funerary homiletics of two leading figures of the Leipzig Orthodox tradition of the seventeenth century, Martin Geier and and his nephew Johann Benedict Carpzov, both of whom often included medical case histories of the deceased in their sermons – partly, it seems, to drive home the point that even the costly intervention of physicians could not prevent death when God so willed it. Such accounts also disabused believers of the enticing but errant notion that medical science could render death physically easy: even if one could afford the best physicians and medications, the final test would be dire and unrelenting. After recounting the physical demise that led up to death, funeral sermons invariably reported on the behavior of the person once he or she realized that death was unavoidable: after detailing the inevitable loss of the physical battle against the final illness, the preacher turned to the spiritual triumph of the deceased. In this respect Bach's own obituary, written by his son and two of his students, parallels contemporary funeral sermons in its recounting of the causes of death, the futile attempts of medical

---

[12] Müller, *Liebes-Kuß*, 672, 676.   [13] Pfeiffer, *Anti-melancholicus*, 608–609.
[14] Eberhard Winkler, *Die Leichenpredigt im deutschen Luthertum bis Spener* (Munich, 1967), 9.

Figure 1.2 The battle with death, August Pfeiffer, *Liebes-Kuß* (1732)

professions to help the dying man (Bach dies "despite every possible care given him by two of the most skillful physicians") and the final peaceful departure for the next life, even noting the exact time of his death, "on July 28, 1750, a little after a quarter past eight in the evening, in the sixty-sixth year of his life."[15]

---

[15] *NBR*, 303.

The formulas of redemption offered by sermons and also to be found in the contemporary literature of moral uplift were intended to provide concrete examples of pious deaths, models for others preparing for their own dying battles. Bach was certainly familiar with the content of Martin Geier's famous sermon preached at the 1672 Dresden funeral of Heinrich Schütz, since it had been glossed and quoted from in the introduction to the official Leipzig hymnal of 1730; the complete text of the sermon also circulated in a reprint edition published in Leipzig in 1687.[16] Schütz had suffered a final stroke that deprived him of the ability to speak; doctors were called in but yet again could provide no help; at last the father confessor was summoned and he read relevant scriptural passages. Geier makes sure to highlight the firmness of the dying man's belief even while beset by his final illness:

Several times the patient, with a nod of the head or a motion of the hands, indicated that he retained Jesus in his heart, whereupon the father confessor bestowed on him the last blessing. He lay asleep until finally the breath and pulse gradually declined and then ceased. The clock had struck four when he gently and blessedly departed this life without tremor, with the prayers and singing of those standing about.[17]

Thus the death of the leading Lutheran musician of the seventeenth century served as a model for successors such as Bach. Indeed, it would have been through the study of such examples that Bach prepared for his own death, and the scene portrayed by Geier – the confessor, the hymns, the search for signs of piety just prior to death – was likely quite similar to the final hours of Bach's life.

The study of texts – the Bible and chorales – played a central role in preparation for death. In *Liebes-Kuß*, Müller urged the believer "to choose several beautiful, comforting passages (*Trost-Sprüchlein*) with which to go to sleep,"[18] texts which were to be drawn from the basic lexicon of Lutheran thought, the Bible and the chorales. This is not simply recommendation for nightly prayer; Müller is also using "sleep" figuratively to refer to death, a common metaphor in Lutheran thought, and one we will return to later. According to Müller, the internalization of these passages is meant to provide a bulwark against temptation so that even the anguish of death will not distract the dying person from adhering to the content of these memorized words.

Indeed, last words were crucial not only to the dying, but to their survivors as well. For the former, the reiteration of individually chosen

---

[16] Robin Leaver, "The Funeral Sermon for Heinrich Schütz I: Introduction," *BACH* 4/4 (October, 1973): 3–17.
[17] Robin Leaver, "The Funeral Sermon for Heinrich Schütz, Part II, the Biographical Section," in *BACH* 5/1 (July, 1974): 13–20, at p. 19.
[18] Müller, *Liebes-Kuß*, 691–692.

passages anchored belief, while for the latter these final utterances provided proof that the deceased had triumphed over death by remaining true to God's word until the last; such a steadfast statement of belief consoled the mourners with evidence that the soul of the dead person was in heaven. Having the character of rehearsed epitaphs, these dying words were frequently included in funeral sermons. In *Gräber der Heiligen* Müller reported that the evidence that a certain man had been saved "was demonstrated by his last words" (zeiget an sein letztes Wort) which were drawn from a well-known chorale: "I will not leave my Jesus" (*Meinem Jesum laß ich nicht*).[19]

The usefulness of chorales in preparing for the final struggle is encapsulated in the work of the chorale commentator Gabriel Wimmer, a Lutheran cleric who published an exegesis of "Dearest Lord, when shall I die?" (*Liebster Gott, wenn werd ich sterben?*) in Leipzig in 1730. Bach had set the text and melody in his Cantata 8 for the sixteenth Sunday after Trinity, a moment in the liturgical year which elicited some of his most extended musical reflections on death.[20] Following the traditional formulations found in the Lutheran literature on death and dying, Wimmer's commentary praises the chorale as a beautiful and eminently practical way of contemplating death, and he sets out a far-reaching *ars moriendi* with a line-by-line theological interpretation of the chorale text. For Wimmer, a tireless interpreter of the rich body of chorale texts,[21] the cultivation of the art of dying could ensure redemption. Practice, which was to include the study of chorales, is decisive, and Wimmer describes "a daily dying Christian" (ein täglich sterbender Christ) – that is, one who takes seriously the *ars moriendi* – as "a good theologian" (ein guter Theologus). With their marriage of text and music, chorales allowed statements of belief to be deeply inscribed on the soul, just as Müller had envisioned when he recommended assembling a catalog of passages with which to face death.

By the beginning of the eighteenth century reflections on "last words" had developed into an identifiable genre of personal study and uplift. The Hersfeld theologian Conrad Mel originated the idea of delivering and then printing an entire year's worth of sermons devoted to the dying utterances of biblical figures, and he observed that the dying often gained the power "to deliver the quintessence of their best thoughts."[22]

---

[19] Quoted in Winkler, *Die Leichenpredigt*, 171. For another example of chorale singing at the deathbed, see Mohr, *Protestantische Theologie*, 288.

[20] Gottfried Wimmer, *Caspar Neumanns...Sterben-Lied* (Leipzig, 1730), 9; quoted in Martin-Christian Mautner, *Mach einmal mein Ende gut: Zur Sterbekunst in den Kantaten Johann Sebastian Bachs zum 16. Sonntag nach Trinitatis* (Frankfurt, 1997), 287.

[21] Gabriel Wimmer, *Ausführliche Liederklärung (wodurch die ältesten und gewöhnlichsten Gesänge der Evangelisch-Lutherischen Kirche...erläutert worden)* (Altenburg, 1749).

[22] Conrad Mel, *Die letzte Reden der Sterbenden*, 3rd edn., preface, quoted in Winfried Zeller, *Theologie und Frömmigkeit*, ed. Bernd Jaspert, 2 vols. (Marburg, 1971–78), II, 31.

Similarly, Pfeiffer noted in *Anti-melancholicus* that "in the final hour of death, when all physical powers have fallen away, one often hears with astonishment how such people... speak completely rationally of high and heavenly matters."[23] Last words and actions were not simply a matter of piety, however; rather, they allowed those surrounding the deathbed a passing glimpse of transcendence, of heavenly life as seen through the eyes of the dying. If Bach adhered to the teachings on dying so amply collected in his library, he would necessarily have prepared some kind of final statement, knowing that a chorale could provide a focus for the forthright contemplation of, and preparation for, death. The final corrections to the preexisting, and perhaps already revised, chorale that resulted in *Vor deinen Thron tret ich hiermit* were thus a last devout utterance in the lofty musical discourse that would be worthy of a saved man – the quintessence of Bach's best thoughts. Manipulating complex counterpoint provided a way for Bach to guide his reflections, to resist the devil's temptation; the result confirmed for the family that having died a pious death, Bach's soul was destined for heaven.

It was not uncommon for Lutheran composers of the seventeenth and early eighteenth centuries to respond in music to the admonitions of contemporary preachers that they prepare themselves for death. In 1683, following an outbreak of the plague in Erfurt which claimed his wife and child, Johann Pachelbel published his *Musicalische Sterbens-Gedancken*, a collection of four extended variation sets on well-known chorale tunes associated with death and dying.[24] A decade later, the organist Christian Flor published a work of learned counterpoint with the striking title *Todesgedanken in dem Liede: "Auf meinen lieben Gott," mit umgekehrtem Contrapuncte fürs Clavier sehr künstlich gesetzt und gedruckt zu Hamburg 1692* (Thoughts on death in the song "On My Beloved God," in invertible counterpoint very artfully set for the clavier and printed in Hamburg 1692).[25] The teenage Bach was a chorister in Lüneburg where he came into contact with Christian Flor's son Johann Georg, and it is perhaps through him that Bach gained his knowledge of some of the elder Flor's music. Whether or not Bach actually saw the elder Flor's *Todesgedanken*, he could have read a reference to this work in Walther's *Lexicon*. The titles used by Pachelbel and Flor refer to the category of personal study and death preparation found so frequently in contemporary books on the *ars moriendi* such as those by Müller,

---

[23] Pfeiffer, *Anti-melancholicus*, 589.
[24] Johann Gottfried Walther, *Musicalisches Lexicon* (Leipzig, 1732; reprint, Kassel, 1953), 458.
[25] Ibid., 249. This piece is also cited by Walther. The striking association of death with contrapuntal music was first noticed by Friedrich Riedel; see his *Quellenkundliche Beiträge zur Geschichte der Musik für Tasteninstrumente in der zweiten Hälfte des 17. Jahrhunderts* (Munich, 1990), 70, 182.

Pfeiffer and Wimmer, which continually press the reader to entertain *Sterbens-Gedanken, Todes-Gedanken,* and *Todes-Andachten*.[26]

But it is the highly self-conscious use of strict counterpoint, elaborately described in the title itself, which distinguishes Flor's volume from that of Pachelbel, and, in turn, links it with a north German practice of commemorating death through elaborate contrapuntal techniques – a practice that extended through to Bach's dying hours. An outstanding example of this tradition is presented by Dieterich Buxtehude's *Mit Fried und Freud ich fahr dahin* (BuxWV 76), a setting in invertible counterpoint of Luther's burial hymn which was performed at the funeral of Buxtehude's father, Johannes, in 1674. This was not the first time Buxtehude had written strictly contrapuntal funeral music; three years earlier, he had composed and published a learned work for the funeral of the former Lübeck superintendent, Meno Hanneken the elder.[27] Only the music for Johannes Buxtehude's burial survives, and the piece shows just how exacting his son made his counterpoint for this deeply meaningful funerary context. Buxtehude's 1674 setting of *Mit Fried und Freud* is made up of four movements grouped into two pairs, each made up of a *contrapunctus* and its harmonic inversion, called an *evolutio*. The first pair inverts the arrangement of the voices, the second pair introduces melodic as well as harmonic inversion (see Example 1.2).[28]

In 1704 Bach's relation and Weimar colleague Johann Gottfried Walther had traveled to Halberstadt to visit the noted theorist and organist Andreas Werckmeister; the two carried on a regular correspondence, and Walther received from Werckmeister a large number of keyboard works by Buxtehude and others; included among these must have been Buxtehude's *Mit Fried und Freud*, because Walther discussed particulars of the piece's use of inversion in his composition treatise, *Praecepta der musicalischen Composition* – a work completed in 1708, the year of Bach's arrival in Weimar.[29] Bach would likely have seen the *Praecepta* as well as Buxtehude's counterpoints on *Mit Fried und Freud*. For his part,

---

[26] See, for example, Müller, *Liebes-Kuß*, 680–681; and Pfeiffer, *Anti-melancholicus*, 595. See also the anonymous *Evangelische-Todesgedancken* (Gotha, 1675).

[27] That Buxtehude reused Hanneken's 1671 funeral music for his own father's burial is assumed by Kerala J. Snyder in *Dieterich Buxtehude: Organist in Lübeck* (New York, 1987), 214; this conclusion is based on the fact that the surviving title-pages of both works describe their respective contents as both consisting of "two counterpoints." The claim for the identity of the two works is contested by Dietrich Kilian in *Das Vokalwerk Dietrich Buxtehudes* (Berlin, 1956), 79, and Norbert Bolin, "Sterben ist mein Gewinn": Ein Beitrag zur Evangelischen Funeral-Komposition des Barock (Kassel, 1989), 261.

[28] For a more detailed analysis of BuxWV 76 see David Yearsley, "Towards an Allegorical Interpretation of Buxtehude's Funerary Counterpoints," *Music & Letters* 80/2 (May 1999): 183–206.

[29] Walther, *Praecepta der musicalischen Composition*, ed. Peter Benary (Leipzig, 1955). Walther claimed to own more than 200 pieces by Buxtehude and Bach; those by Buxtehude, many of which he claimed were autographs, had been passed on to him by the aged Werckmeister. He mentions his acquisition of Werckmeister's collection

Example 1.2   Dieterich Buxtehude, *Mit Fried und Freud ich fahr dahin*, BuxWV 76/1: *Contrapunctus I–Evolutio I; Contrapunctus II–Evolutio II*, mm. 1–3 in each

Walther had tried to emulate Buxtehude's contrapuntal procedures in the second and third verses of his setting of the chorale melody *Herr Jesu Christ, wahr' Mensch und Gott* which features two counterpoints and their harmonic inversions, employing the same inversion scheme as that of Buxtehude's *Mit Fried und Freud*. (The first *evolutio* of the second verse is simply a slightly decorated version of the second *evolutio* [Example 1.3].) Given that Bach and Walther shared many of their ideas and interests during their years together in Weimar, it is hard to imagine that Bach would not have been aware of Buxtehude's celebrated funerary piece; moreover, Bach himself had visited Lübeck to study with Buxtehude for four months in 1705–06. His musical activities there included attendance at – or, more likely, participation in – the *Castrum doloris*, the enormous semi-theatrical spectacle presented in the Marienkirche in Lübeck to

of Buxtehude manuscripts in two letters to Heinrich Bokemeyer: August 6, 1729 and October 3, 1729. See J. G. Walther, *Briefe*, ed. Klaus Beckmann and Hans-Joachim Schulze (Leipzig, 1987), 62–83, esp. 70. See also Snyder, *Dieterich Buxtehude*, 126–128.

Vor deinen Thron tret ich *and the art of dying*

Example 1.2 *(cont.)*

mark the death of Emperor Leopold I.[30] Through this direct contact and his later study of Buxtehude's funerary works, Bach would have familiarized himself with the full range of musical approaches to death, from the monumental *Castrum doloris* to the contained and controlled *Mit Fried und Freud*.

Just as Walther had constructed a piece of learned counterpoint using Buxtehude's *Mit Fried und Freud* as a model, Buxtehude had based his own effort directly on *Prudentia prudentiana* by Christoph Bernhard, onetime director of music in Hamburg (a city well within Buxtehude's musical orbit). Also descended from *Prudentia prudentiana* or perhaps, more directly, from Buxtehude's *Mit Fried und Freud* is a work by the Copenhagen organist Martin Radek entitled *Jesus Christus unser Heylandt, in ordinari und doppelten Contrapunt gesetzt* (Jesus Christ our Savior, set in ordinary and double counterpoint), which survives in a copy by Walther.[31] For his contribution to the art of writing in

---

[30] Only the libretto of this massive production survives.
[31] This work is found in Staatsbibliothek zu Berlin, Mus. ms. 6473M. See Harald Kümmerling, *Katalog der Sammlung Bokemeyer* (Kassel, 1970), 11–12. For a modern

Example 1.3 J. G. Walther, *Herr Jesu Christ, wahr' Mensch und Gott*: *Versus 2–Evolutio 1/Evolutio 2; Versus 3–Evolutio*; mm. 1–3 in each

double counterpoint, Radek treated the well-known communion chorale, which was also sung on Maundy Thursday and was associated with the passion and death of Christ.

In 1685 Nicolaus Adam Strungk, whose peripatetic career took him as far north as Hamburg and as far south as Rome, composed his extraordinary *Ricercar Sopra la Morte della mia carissima Madre Catharina Maria Stubenrauen*. Strungk reflects on the death of his mother in a long and complex contrapuntal essay, one which begins as a *fuga contraria riversa*

edition of the work see Martin Radek, *Jesus Christus, unser Heiland: Koralvariationen*, ed. Bo Lundgren (Copenhagen, 1957).

Vor deinen Thron tret ich *and the art of dying*

Example 1.3 *(cont.)*

Example 1.4 N. A. Strungk, *Ricercar sopra la Morte della mia carissima Madre*, mm. 1–7

where the fugal subject is answered by its exact melodic inversion, and culminates in a section combining the opening theme with three countersubjects (Example 1.4). Walther singled out the piece among Strungk's keyboard works; C. P. E. Bach listed Strungk as one of his father's influences, and it would seem unlikely that this, perhaps Strungk's most famous keyboard piece, would have remained unknown to Bach. Though more flamboyant than Bach's *Vor deinen Thron* in its use of counterpoint, Strungk's *Ricercar* would have offered Bach the chance to play

Bach and the meanings of counterpoint

and to study one of the most powerful reflections on death composed in the seventeenth century.³²

The practice of using counterpoint as a means of contemplating death, as represented in this group of interrelated pieces, may have grown out of a still earlier tradition. A century before Bach's birth, the south German editor and composer Adam Gumpelshaimer published his *Compendium musicae latino-germanicum*, a mainstay of the Latin school system in Lutheran Germany that included numerous pedagogical canons intended to help train students to sing polyphony. The volume was reprinted more than a dozen times in the seventeenth century and was likely encountered by Bach in the musical education he received in his native Thuringia or in the northern city of Lüneburg. The frontispiece to Gumpelshaimer's collection is an engraving of the cross made up of a six-part retrograde canon, an allegorical image which links the crucifixion with learned counterpoint – the most universal of deaths here bound to the most elaborate of compositional techniques (Figure 1.3).³³ Canon, of course, was by no means specific to death-commemorative genres; but given his interest in the work of the late seventeenth-century composers who drew on associations between death and learned counterpoint, it is little wonder that Bach explored these same connections in *Vor deinen Thron* during the long hours of his dying.

What was it that gave the associations between death and counterpoint their resonance? For an answer to this question, we must turn to the music theory of the late seventeenth and early eighteenth centuries. One of the most prolific and influential theorists of the period was the central German organist Andreas Werckmeister, whose 1702 composition treatise *Harmonologia musica* included two laudatory poems by Buxtehude.³⁴ By 1702, the year the *Harmonologia* appeared, Werckmeister had probably already acquired his large collection of Buxtehude's music, including the funerary settings of *Mit Fried und Freud*. Buxtehude's contrapuntal essay may even have been in Werckmeister's thoughts when he wrote in the *Harmonologia musica* of the "curious (*wunderlich*)

---

[32] For a discussion of the musical sources – including music by Strungk – that Bach studied and made manuscript copies of as a youth see Robert Hill, " 'Der Himmel weiß, wo diese Sachen hingekommen sind': Reconstructing the Lost Keyboard Notebooks of the Young Bach and Handel," in *Bach, Handel, Scarlatti: Tercentenary Essays*, ed. Peter Williams (Cambridge, 1985), 161–172.

[33] Adam Gumpelzhaimer, *Compendium musicae latino-germanicum*, 9th edn. (Augsburg, 1632). This canon is taken from Pietro Cerone's *El melopeo* (Naples, 1613), 1130–1131. See Denis Brian Collins, "Canon in Music Theory from c. 1550 to c. 1800" (Ph.D. diss., Stanford University, 1992), 324–328. For a solution to the canon see Wil Dekker, "Ein Karfreitagsrätselkanon aus Adam Gumpelzhaimers *Compendium musicae* (1532)," *Die Musikforschung* 27/3 (1974): 323–332.

[34] For these poems, along with English translations, see Snyder, *Dieterich Buxtehude*, 127.

Figure 1.3   Cruciform canon, Adam Gumpelzhaimer, *Compendium musicae latino-germanicum* (1625)

harmonies" of double counterpoint and its mysterious properties which were "nearly beyond the understanding (*Verstand*) of men" – a sentiment he repeats in his other writings regarding double counterpoint and canon.[35] Werckmeister is not only astounded by the properties of double counterpoint and canon, but he attempts to account for them through allegory. One such interpretive move in the *Harmonologia* hinges on a comparison between the movement of voices in invertible counterpoint and the motion of planets, where cosmology and harmony are manifestations of the same universal principle:

> The heavens are now revolving and circulating steadily so that one (body) now goes up but in another time it changes again and comes down... We also have this mirror of heaven and nature [*Himmels- und Natur-Spiegel*] in musical harmony, because a certain voice can be the highest voice, but can become the lowest or middle voice, and the lowest and middle can again become the highest. One voice can become all other voices and no other voice must be added, and at the very least... four voices can be transformed in different ways in good harmony.[36]

In a lengthy appendix to the *Harmonologia*, Werckmeister again ponders the relationship between the cosmological order and invertible counterpoint, stating that a piece in invertible counterpoint can reach its perfection in its "inversion" (*replica*) and is therefore "A mirror of nature and God's order" (ein Spiegel der Natur und Ordnung Gottes).[37] Werckmeister gives musical form to this allegorical conception in a four-part setting of the chorale *Vater unser im Himmelreich* employing invertible counterpoint at the octave and twelfth, presenting ten of the possible permutations; he does not conclude the piece but simply writes "and so forth" (u.s.w.), suggesting that these combinations could be continued until the musical system returns to its original configuration, the progression of the voices recreating in microcosm the cycles of the planets.[38] The constant motion of the heavens is thus analogous to the perpetual revolution of the parts in a well-constructed piece of double counterpoint, whose inversions mirror the perfection of heaven and provide earthly beings with a glimpse of God's unending order, a prelude to the heavenly concert.

But the relationship between these phenomena was more than simply one of likeness: the mechanics of the heavens were not simply allegorized by double counterpoint, they were manifested in its workings. Bernhard's choice of the word *revolutio* for the contrapuntally inverted verses of *Prudentia prudentiana* is suggestive of this same celestial

---

[35] Andreas Werckmeister, *Harmonologia musica* (Quedlinburg, 1707; reprint, Hildesheim, 1970), 89. See also Werckmeister, *Musicae mathematicae hodegus curiosus* (Frankfurt and Leipzig, 1687; reprint, Hildesheim, 1972), 108; see also 137–138.
[36] Werckmeister, *Harmonologia musica*, dedication, [v].   [37] Ibid., 101.
[38] Ibid., 90–93. There are 24 possible configurations of the four voices.

Vor deinen Thron tret ich *and the art of dying*

metaphor. Thus microsom was inextricably linked to macrocosm, counterpoint and the heavens governed by the same fundamental principles. As the Jesuit Athanasius Kircher put it in his *Musurgia universalis* of 1650, a book known to virtually all German music theorists of the seventeenth and eighteenth centuries, God was "a taskmaster (*Zuchtmeister*) of order, the guiding principle of everything."[39] And since God was concerned primarily with order in disposing of the universe then it was entirely appropriate that the heavens should resound with the most orderly of music – strict counterpoint – as the frontispiece to the *Musurgia* so extravagantly shows. In heaven – high above the underworld and the earth – two angels carry a banner displaying a thirty-six-voice perpetual canon for nine choruses of four voices. Seated in the lower left-hand corner is Pythagoras, the discoverer of the proportions of the universe and the most successful researcher into God's order. The canon – a majestic, if static, elaboration of a major triad in infinite consonance – is given in the center of the banner, with nine choirs of angels singing above it (Figure 1.4).[40] The *Musurgia* frontispiece provided the model for that of Johann Rist's *Sabbahtische Seelenlust*, a book of devotional poetry with melodies supplied by the Hamburg cantor Thomas Selle; the volume appeared in 1651 in Lüneburg, only a year after the publication of the *Musurgia* (Figure 1.5).[41] C. P. E. Bach owned a copy of the *Sabbahtische Seelenlust*, possibly inherited from his father, who bequeathed to him a substantial part of his musical library, or perhaps acquired after his arrival in Hamburg in 1767 to become one of Selle's successors as the city's director of music.[42] J. S. Bach could well have known Rist's collection from his time in Lüneburg, and he certainly would have seen Kircher's *Musurgia universalis*.

The allegorical potential of double counterpoint and its close companion canon was a theme frequently taken up by a circle of important seventeenth-century composers and theorists, many of whom had studied with Buxtehude's friend Johann Theile.[43] For Georg Österreich, collector of Buxtehude's vocal music and student of Theile in the 1680s,

---

[39] Athanasius Kircher, *Musurgia universalis* (Rome, 1650; reprint, Hildesheim, 1970); trans. Andreas Hirsch, *Germaniae redonatus: sive artis magnae de consono et dissono ars minor* (Schwäbisch Hall, 1662), i.

[40] The engraving is by F. Baronius after Paul Schor.

[41] Johann Rist, *Sabbahtische Seelenlust* (Lüneburg, 1651). Kathi Meyer-Baer discusses both frontispieces in her *Music of the Spheres, The Harmony of the Spheres and the Dance of Death* (Princeton, 1970), 210–212.

[42] Ulrich Leisinger, "Die 'Bachsche Auction' von 1789," *Bach-Jahrbuch* 77 (1991): 97–126, at p. 122. C. P. E. Bach copied out a thirty-six-voice solution to the frontispiece canon in magnificent full score and falsely attributed it to Selle. Daniel Melamed, "A Thirty-Six-Voice Canon in the Hand of C. P. E. Bach," in *Bach Studies* 2, ed. Melamed (Cambridge, 1995), 107–118.

[43] Jacob Adlung, *Anleitung zu der musikalischen Gelahrtheit* (Erfurt, 1758; reprint, Kassel, 1953), 184.

Figure 1.4 Frontispiece, depicting heavenly canon, Athanasius Kircher, *Musurgia universalis* (1650)

Vor deinen Thron tret ich *and the art of dying*

Figure 1.5 Frontispiece, based on Kircher, Johann Rist, *Sabbahtische Seelenlust* (1651)

double counterpoint and canon were concrete manifestations of the "order of God" (Ordnung Gottes), and their elaboration revealed the inexplicable essence of God's creation, not merely as a metaphor for God's order, but as a concrete realization of that order.[44] For another of Theile's followers, Johann Philipp Förtsch, learned counterpoint was a profoundly meaningful distillate of musical practice, a purifed form in which "the unfathomability of music" (die Unergründlichkeit der Music) was most clearly to be perceived.[45] Österreich's student and Bach's contemporary, the Wolfenbüttel cantor Heinrich Bokemeyer, who inherited his teacher's library of counterpoint treatises and music (including works by Buxtehude), believed that canon and double counterpoint addressed most directly the ineffable "mystery of harmony" (*mysterium harmonicum*).[46]

In Bokemeyer's view perpetual canon was not only the apogee of musical accomplishment, it was also a metaphor for God's original creation of the universe and of the heavenly harmony. In a passage which illustrates the persistent allegorical power of strict counterpoint well into the eighteenth century, Bokemeyer mythologizes the moment of revelation when the archetypal contrapuntist discovers the first infinite and invertible canon:

> There he finds the beginning and end bound together and has discovered the perpetual canon in order to remind himself of the eternal unending origins, as well as the harmony, of all eternity (*die in alle Ewigkeit bestehenden Harmonie*) as a rule of nature of the most perfect example of his artistic work.[47]

Bokemeyer's frequent correspondent Walther also recognized the vital metaphorical dimension of canon and double counterpoint, and the proof value they offered.[48] The Gotha organist Gottfried Heinrich Stölzel, who joined Lorenz Mizler's Society in 1739 (the same year as Bokemeyer, and some eight years before Bach) was keenly interested in counterpoint and was the author of a treatise on canon, which appeared in 1725.[49] Like Bokemeyer, Stölzel recommended the study of learned counterpoint and applauded its allegorical reach: "Since God gave mortals the most beloved music for great and high purpose... we will,

---

[44] Georg Österreich, Untitled manuscript, Staatsbibliothek zu Berlin, Mus. ms. theor. 1038, fol. 35r.

[45] Johann Philipp Förtsch, *Musicalischer Compositions Tractat*, Staatsbibliothek zu Berlin, Mus. ms. theor., 300, fol. 33r.

[46] Heinrich Bokemeyer in *Critica musica*, ed. Johann Mattheson, 2 vols. (Hamburg, 1722–25), I, 328.

[47] Ibid., 342–343.

[48] Walther to Bokemeyer, April 4, 1729, in Walther, *Briefe*, 32–34. The canon he is referring to is *Keüscheste Flammen brennt ewiglich fort!*, the text of which describes eternal flames (see p. 52 below).

[49] G. H. Stölzel, *Practischer Beweis / wie aus einem nach dem wahren Fundamente solcher Noten-Künsteleyen Canone Perpetuo... zu machen seyn* (n.p., 1725).

indeed we must, hear of other miracles of music, of which canons are one, particularly when they can be shifted, inverted, and mingled in a thousand ways."[50] Examining the profusion of unending combinations (undendliche Verbindungen) so enduringly ordered by God was a wondrous and rewarding pursuit.[51] The contrapuntal research of Bach's *Vor deinen Thron*, with its melodic inversions and ingenious examination of the permutational possibilities of the chorale melody itself, is no less committed an investigation into the mysterious principles of God's order, an order manifested so perfectly in heaven and its music.

While for many counterpoint functioned as a harbinger of the heavenly music, the nature, and even the very existence, of this divine concert spawned a lively debate that continued to exercise Lutheran theologians, music theorists, and musicians during Bach's last years. The point of departure for many of these inquiries was the metaphysics of the soul, its destiny after death and the conditions to be anticipated in heaven. Luther himself had upheld the traditional definition of biological death as the separation of the soul from the body; in contrast to his seventeenth-century successors, however, Luther did not believe that the soul would enjoy immediate rapture after the demise of the body. Rather, death was akin to sleep, with the soul remaining in a suspended state until being roused on the Last Day. "Death has become my sleep" (Tod ist mein Schlaf worden), as Luther himself put it in the last line of *Mit Fried und Freud*, which he included in the first collection of funerary chorales to be published after the Reformation (1542) and which was so masterfully set by Buxtehude for his father's burial. While sleep continued to provide a useful metaphor for death into the eighteenth century, most seventeenth-century Lutheran theologians held that immediately after dying the soul left the body and, if saved, ascended eagerly to heaven. This view became a mainstay of Lutheran Orthodoxy, promising immediate reward for true believers, in contrast to the delayed judgment of Roman Catholic purgatory. As Heinrich Müller put it in a funeral sermon from a volume published in 1675, "the moment in which the soul [leaves] the body is exactly the moment that it travels to heavenly bliss (*himmlische Seligkeit*)."[52] Now death could be more readily accepted, even embraced.

But what of the body, whose defilement inspired such horrifying descriptions in the literature on dying familiar to Bach? This is where

---

[50] Stölzel, *Practischer Beweis*, paragraph 46.
[51] Stölzel, quoted in Friedrich Wilhelm Marpurg, *Abhandlung von der Fuge*, 2 vols. (Berlin, 1753–54; reprint, Hildesheim, 1970), II, 82. This passage apparently comes from the expanded edition, and was added after paragraph 42 of the surviving copy of Stölzel's treatise.
[52] Heinrich Müller, *Gräber der Heiligen* (Frankfurt, 1675), 100. Quoted in Winkler, *Die Leichenpredigt*, 164.

Luther's notion that death was a kind of sleep retained particular value for later theologians. While the "empty and worm-eaten body" (nichtige wurmichte Gebeine), as Müller put it, was to be left behind by the soul, this separation was temporary and the remains of the dead would not be forgotten by God: "The Lord will preserve for the righteous (der Gerechte) all his bones, so that not one will be lost."[53] Lutheran theology construed graves as resting places (Dormitoria) from which the dead would be raised up at the Last Judgment (Figure 1.6).[54] On that day, the decomposing body would be transformed, so that in heaven the faithfully departed could look forward to an existence devoid of physical strains and sinful desires, in a place where there would be "no old age, no weaknesses... no debilitation (Leibes Schwachheit), but instead nothing but eternal youth, enduring beauty, everlasting strength and health."[55] In the preface to his 1542 edition of burial hymns, Luther explained his admonitions against excessive mourning with the promise of the non-physical human form which the saved will have in heaven:

[St. Paul] bans from his sight every ugly aspect of death in our mortal body and brings to the fore a wholly delightful and joyous picture of life when he says:... it is sown [i.e., buried] a natural body, it is raised a spiritual body.[56]

It was this Pauline concept of bodily resurrection and transfiguration which allowed Luther and the orthodox theologians of the next century to promise their followers the complete metaphysical transcendence of their sin-racked, earthly existence.

These doctrines concerning the body and soul had crucial consequences for both theologians and music theorists inquiring into the nature of heavenly existence and its music. During the same years that Bach was turning to a more intense reflection on his own death and the life to come, Mattheson was also considering these topics, most extensively in his 1747 book *Behauptung der himmlischen Musik*. (The book was dedicated to Ludewig Friedrich Hudemann, to whom Bach also dedicated his most famous canon, BWV 1074, which I will discuss in Chapter 2.) The music of heaven had been a lifelong concern of Mattheson; from his first book, *Das neu-eröffnete*

---

[53] Müller, *Liebes-Kuß*, 760.

[54] The title of the fourth volume of Johann Heermann's series of funeral sermons reflects this conception of the graves of the blessed: *Dormitoria: Etlicher frommer Christen Schlaff-Häuslein. Das ist Christlicher Leich-Predigten Vierdter Theil* (Rostock, 1650).

[55] Johann Heermann, *Christianae Euthanasias Statutae* (Leipzig, 1630), 262; quoted in Winkler, *Die Leichenpredigt*, 149.

[56] Martin Luther, "Preface to the Burial Hymns (1542)," in *Luther's Works*, ed. Jaroslav Pelikan and Helmut Lehmann, 56 vols. (St. Louis and Philadelphia), LIII, 326. Luther makes this same distinction between the physical and spiritual body in "Two Funeral Sermons, 1532," in *Works*, LI, 238.

Vor deinen Thron tret ich *and the art of dying*

Figure 1.6   The Last Day and the resurrection of the dead, August Pfeiffer, *Liebes-Kuß* (1732)

Orchestre of 1713, a volume marked by its vehement resistance to many of the received truths of music theory, Mattheson had nonetheless embraced the long-cherished notion that there was a heavenly harmony. Mattheson respectfully concurred with the assertion of the seventeenth-century theorist J. A. Herbst that the music of heaven "will be performed in the angelic, heavenly choir, with the highest perfection... in all eternity to the praise and glory of God."[57] This heavenly performance was also a favorite topic for preachers and theologians, and in the *Behauptung der himmlischen Musik* Mattheson asserts that he is in the mainstream of religious thought in describing the heavenly music as "truly excellent" (vortrefflich) and comprised of "the most perfect harmony" (die vollkommenste Harmonie).[58] The writers represented in Bach's theological library certainly would have concurred with Mattheson's views. Müller, for example, concludes the first volume of the *Liebes-Kuß* with a chapter on the nature of eternal life, a discussion which includes ecstatic treatment of the "most blessed music" (die holdseligste Musica) and our participation in it.[59] Indeed, the heavenly music provides for Müller one of the most powerful incentives for embracing death. Again, music offers not only a glimpse of heavenly life, but a tool with which to focus one's thoughts about death. Müller closes the chapter, and the book, with his own lyric paraphrase of the chorale *Mit Fried und Freud ich fahr dahin*, which he directs to be sung to the powerfully uplifting major-mode melody of the burial hymn *Alle Menschen müssen sterben*, thus neatly combining in words and music the central themes of the *ars moriendi* – the inevitability of death and the peaceful, joyful departure of the soul for heaven. Music, the chorale in particular, serves as both a preparation for dying and an evocation of heaven.

That there were undeniable parallels between the music of heaven and earth was a commonplace of the religious literature of Bach's time. In an engraving from a 1732 edition of *Liebes-Kuß* both realms are joined in synchronic concert, and the final line of the caption emphasizes the transformative power of human song and, as the image makes clear, its instrumental accompaniment: "The heavens praise you, the earth [praises] heaven/So that when I praise you, I become angelic" (Figure 1.7).[60] Mattheson agreed that the greatest value of music was that it provided "the strongest idea of eternal life," a "foretaste" of the heavenly concert.[61] For this reason, he, like Luther, accorded music a status nearly equal to that of theological investigation. While there would be similarities between musical life on earth and in heaven, there would also be crucial differences. In eternity music would reflect only essential truths, and would be set free from aesthetic and critical concerns, aspects of tuning and the calculation of intervals, that is, those issues that had so

---

[57] Johann Mattheson, *Behauptung der himmlischen Musik* (Hamburg, 1747), 70, 77.
[58] Ibid., 78, 72. [59] Müller, *Liebes-Kuß*, 543. [60] Ibid., 759.
[61] Johann Mattheson, *Das neu-eröffnete Orchestre* (Hamburg, 1713; reprint, Hildesheim, 1993), 303.

Vor deinen Thron tret ich *and the art of dying*

Figure 1.7   Heavenly/earthly concert, August Pfeiffer, *Liebes-Kuß* (1732)

involved Mattheson throughout his long, productive life. Instead there would be nothing but "eternally pure sounding harmony."[62]

Since the uplifting variety of earthly music was a prelude to that of eternity, many writers assumed that there would be instrumental music

[62] Johann Mattheson, *Bewahrte Panacea* (Hamburg, 1750), 157.

in heaven. In response to the question as to how it would be possible for the transfigured, non-physical body to play a real instrument, Mattheson answered matter-of-factly that if God could transform the flesh he could just as well make a "transfigured instrument" (verklärtes Werkzeug).[63] It therefore seemed perfectly plausible that musicians should be able to use their specific talents in heaven, though all the saved would also be able to join in the eternal concert. Therefore, one might encounter "a gifted boy" (ein geschickter Knabe) playing the harpsichord (Flügel) in heaven; having died young, like Bach's gifted but ne'er-do-well son Bernhard, his ability would not be forgotten or wasted in heaven.[64] Indeed, the promise of participation in the heavenly ensemble was a particularly alluring prospect for musicians, and the idea that the great figures of Lutheran music would join in with the angelic symphony was a widely used obituary trope. One of many examples of this can be found in H. J. Sivers' 1730 disquisition on the accomplishments of learned Lutheran cantors, in which the author describes the deceased Johann Kuhnau, Bach's predecessor in Leipzig, as having "finally, on June 25, 1722... exchanged earthly music for that of heaven."[65] Similarly, the music theorist Martin Fuhrmann, who heard Bach play in Leipzig in the late 1720s and lavished praise on him for his mastery of the keyboard, believed that musicians could look forward to joining in the heavenly concert after their deaths. For Fuhrmann the eternal symphony would certainly be polyphonic, and the unsurpassable richness of these celestial sonorities would make the terrestrial music recently left behind by the newly arriving musicians seem monophonic by comparison.[66] What joy could be anticipated by the aged Mattheson, having given up active music-making long before owing to his own deafness; with his transfigured body and his newly acquired heavenly ears, he would experience again the bliss of music in pure and unending ecstasy, leaving the critical debates of his earthly life behind forever. The same metaphysical rewards awaited the blind and ailing Bach on his deathbed.

Eventual participation in the heavenly concert would, of course, have had particular appeal for composers, and it is just this kind of instant, heavenly gratification through music that is depicted in the lyric Buxtehude himself supplied for his *Klag-Lied* of 1674, the companion piece to his contrapuntal setting of *Mit Fried und Freud ich fahr dahin*, both of which were performed and published on the occasion of his

---

[63] Mattheson, *Behauptung der himmlischen Musik*, 4.
[64] Mattheson, *Bewahrte Panacea*, 162.
[65] H. J. Sivers, *Dissertatio ex historia litteraria, sistens cantorum eruditorum decades duas* in *Opuscula academica quibus variae dissertationes* (Altona and Lübeck, 1730), 14.
[66] Martin Heinrich Fuhrmann, *Die an der Kirchen Gottes gebauete Satans-Capelle* (Cologne, 1729), 19–20.

Vor deinen Thron tret ich *and the art of dying*

father's funeral in Lübeck. Johannes Buxtehude had been an organist, and the first half of the sixth (and final) stanza depicts the musical afterlife of the recently deceased:

Er spielt nun die Freuden-Lieder	He is now playing songs of joy
Auf des Himmels-Lust-Clavier,	on the happy heavenly keyboard,
da die Engel hin und wieder	where the angels from time to time
Singen ein mit süszer Zier.	join in singing with sweet ornament.

Crucially, Buxtehude's poetic reference to the heavenly concert contrasts sharply with the music to which the words are actually set. The *Klag-Lied*, a piece in the modern style, laden with dissonance and keening tremolo strings, opposes the sorrows of those left behind to the heavenly joy of the deceased; the heavenly concert in which Johannes Buxtehude is engaged is clearly not the music we hear, but rather the reassuring eternal counterpoint heard already in *Mit Fried und Freud*.

Like Kircher, Mattheson believed that the eternal concert would consist exclusively of the Sanctus, and in his book *Bewahrte Panacea* of 1750 he presents an inspiring account of its performance: in heaven "we will all join unceasingly together, the one still better than the other both playing and singing in the incomparable immensity of Holy, holy, holy, Lord God of Hosts."[67] An occasional critic of Kircher, and certainly familiar with the *Musurgia*, Mattheson does not say whether old age had brought him to the belief that learned counterpoint, rather than the less complex musical style he favored on earth, would constitute the heavenly concert's musical text. However, his former antagonist the Erfurt organist Heinrich Buttstett specified this music's stylistic particulars: although earthly music gave only the vaguest notion of the heavenly concert, it was clear to him that one would certainly hear the nine choirs of angels resounding in canonic splendor just as Kircher had anticipated in the *Musurgia*. For Buttstett the music of heaven would be strict counterpoint, and he ends his book with the prayer that he and all blessed Christians be called to this eternal concert when they die: "God help me and all your good Christians to this incomparable heavenly harmony and everlasting pleasure (*unvergängliche Vergnüglichkeit*)."[68] These were the very real hopes of good Lutherans, but especially of musicians.

While the theological and musical literature of the middle of the eighteenth century overwhelmingly endorsed the idea of the heavenly music, some remained sceptical. In his *Gedancken von dem Zustande der Seele nach dem Tode* (Thoughts on the State of the Soul after Death), the Halle professor of philosophy G. F. Meier challenged Mattheson's claims

---

[67] Mattheson, *Bewahrte Panacea*, 157–158.
[68] Johann Heinrich Buttstett, *Ut, mi, sol, re, fa, la tota musica et harmonia aeterna* (Erfurt, [1715]), 176.

regarding the heavenly music, arguing that it was impossible to ascertain what the state of the posthumous soul would be; thus Mattheson's arguments concerning the metaphysics of the soul and body, and therefore, too, his descriptions of the heavenly music were "nothing more than mere conjectures."[69] Indeed, Mattheson's views only confirmed Meier's opinion that "each person constructs heaven according to his own fancy (*nach seinem eigenen Gefallen*)."[70] An unsparing opponent of dogmatism except when he himself was being dogmatic, Mattheson baldly asserted in response that to deny the heavenly music was a damnable sin.[71]

Meier's skepticism had been anticipated by Bach's student and supporter Lorenz Mizler, a professed follower of the secularized philosophy of Christian Wolff, Meier's sometime colleague at the University of Halle. Mizler argued that for there to be music in heaven the same physical conditions would have to prevail as those found on earth. Therefore to verify the existence of heavenly music Mizler argued that

> One must first declare that there is air in eternal life. One must have investigated the powers and peculiarities of this same air. One must prove that the nature of the ear will not have changed along with the transfiguration (*Verklärung*) of the body. Simply because this is impossible, one also cannot say that there will be music in heaven.[72]

True to his rationalist outlook, Mizler would not be drawn into the metaphysical complexities of transfiguration and the possibilities it promised. Mattheson was most likely referring to Mizler in the *Behauptung der himmlischen Musik*, when he gainsaid arguments against heavenly music as "altogether too mathematical" (*gar zu mathematisch*), criticizing such beliefs because they did not glorify God.[73]

---

[69] G. F. Meier, *Gedanken von dem Zustande der Seele nach dem Tode*, 2nd edn. (Halle, 1749), 18. The second edition of Meier's book appeared in 1749, the first edition in 1746, before the publication of Mattheson's *Behauptung*, and thus Meier is actually referring to views expressed elsewhere – where exactly is unclear – than in Mattheson's main book on the subject.

[70] Ibid., 18.   [71] Mattheson, *Behauptung der himmlischen Musik*, 18.

[72] Lorenz Christoph Mizler, *Neu eröffnete musikalische Bibliothek* (Leipzig, 1739–54; reprint, Hildesheim, 1970), I, part 2, 30. In 1747 Mizler also reprinted – with his own extensive commentary – an essay by his student G. L. Schneider entitled "Beweis, daß eine zukunftige Musik im ewigen Leben höchstunwahrscheinlich sey" (proof that it is highly unlikely that there will be music in eternal life; *Neu eröffnete musikalische Bibliothek*, III, 585–691). The article was solicited by Mizler in response to a short essay entitled "Gründlicher Beweis, daß im ewigen Leben wirklich eine vortreffliche Musik sey" (Fundamental proof that there will truly be splendid music in eternal life) by J. C. Ammon printed first in a Regensburg weekly; Ammon's discussion, known to both Meier and Mattheson, was itself a response to Mizler's initial attempt to dismantle the ideology of heavenly music. As these interlocking references demonstrate, the debate concerning the music of eternity was a contentious one.

[73] Mattheson, *Behauptung der himmlischen Musik*, 2.

Vor deinen Thron tret ich *and the art of dying*

Reflections such as these on the state of the soul and the heavenly music figured in the early reception of Bach's *Vor deinen Thron*. The theologian Johann Michael Schmidt, who probably had also studied with Bach in Leipzig, argued for the existence of music "in eternal life" (im ewigen Leben) in his 1754 book *Musico-Theologia* because "God will not change our entire nature when we enter his kingdom, only our imperfect traits."[74] Accordingly, "The soul ... will also receive certain pleasures through the nourishment of its transfigured body there [in heaven], including those which come through the ear."[75] Music, then, was to be one of the main delights of eternity. For Schmidt, who admiringly cited Mattheson's work on the heavenly music in his own book, irrefutable proof of the immateriality of the soul, and therefore of its immortality, was "the chorale which Bach dictated in his blindness to the pen of another: *Wenn wir in höchsten Nöthen seyn*." Schmidt's comments on the piece should be understood not only as a tribute to Bach's genius and a rebuttal of materialist tenets (a matter we will return to in Chapter 5), but also as part of a broader defense of heavenly music, which, of course, presupposes the immortality of the soul. Without a soul there can be no appreciation or understanding of this music; but beyond that, the soul is articulated through music, that glorious gift of God and foretaste of heaven. It is no coincidence that Schmidt describes Bach's admittance into the heavenly concert with reference to one of his most complex contrapuntal creations, "the engraved and published chorale of Bach, who has now been taken up into the choir of angels: *Vom Himmel hoch da komm ich her*."[76] Instead of appealing to the sensations and emotions of the earthly body, it is the intellectual complexity contained in the essential and enduring contrapuntal relationships, understood and appreciated only by the higher faculties, that mark this music as eternal.

As much as he subscribed to prevailing theological opinion on the subject, the dying Bach, thinking about and preparing for death through the intricately constructed counterpoint of his last organ chorale, would have anticipated the flight of his soul from his pained body and its immediate participation in the heavenly concert, joining in with so many of his predecessors, colleagues, and Bach family musicians in heaven. Following the obituary jointly authored by C. P. E. Bach, J. F. Agricola, and Mizler published in the *Musikalische Bibliothek*, Mizler printed a "Singgedicht" by the Breslau pastor Georg Wenzky, an avid defender of heavenly music whom Mattheson had cited in his own work.[77] The final recitative of Wenzky's poem is in Bach's voice, singing to his friends

---

[74] J. M. Schmidt, *Musico-Theologia* (Bayreuth, 1754), 219. Schmidt may have studied with Bach when he was a student at Leipzig University beginning in 1749.
[75] Ibid.   [76] NBR, 361; BD III, 73.
[77] Mattheson, *Behauptung der himmlischen Musik*, 72.

and admirers still living on earth, assuring them from heaven that he is experiencing for the first time a music of infinite bliss:

> O that you could hear the pure tones,
> That our choir sings in praise of God,
> O that you could hear the music-making
> that has no end.[78]

> O köntet ihr die reinen Töne hören,
> Die unser Chor zu Gottes Lob anstimmt,
> O köntet ihr das Musiciren hören,
> Das hier kein Ende nimmt!

Wenzky concludes the recitative with Bach's last words to his friends and family:

> Therefore console yourselves.
> And follow me. That music which you have lost with me
> is heard even more excellently within these gates.
> Nothing, nothing, equals these singers.
> Therefore console yourselves.

> Drum tröstet euch
> Und folget mir. Was man an mir verloren
> Das hört man treflicher in unsern Toren.
> Nichts, nichts ist diesen Sängern gleich.
> Drum tröstet euch.

Like the text of *Vor deinen Thron* the trope employed here by Wenzky is *prosopopoeia*, a common rhetorical figure used in Lutheran funeral sermons and burial music, whose purpose was to give the impression that the soul of the departed was speaking through the preacher – or singer or choir – directly to the congregation. This effect was given dramaturgical power through the common practice of placing the coffin directly below the pulpit, so that in the case of the funeral sermon, the assembled mourners would hear "the deceased himself preaching through *prosopopoeia* directly from the coffin."[79] It is certainly possible that *Vor deinen Thron* could have been performed at Bach's funeral, just as Walther claimed that Buxtehude's *Mit Fried und Freud* was an organ piece, and that it had been heard at his father's funeral. The use of *prosopopoeia* in *Vor deinen Thron* (this rhetorical device was not employed in the alternate text *Wenn wir in höchsten Nöthen sein*) would have

---

[78] Georg Wenzky, "Singgedicht" in *Neu eröffnete musicalische Bibliothek*, IV, 173–176.
[79] Caspar Titius, *Loci Theologi Historici* (1684), 1290. Quoted in Winfried Zeller, "Leichenpredigt und Erbauungsliteratur," in *Theologie und Frömmigkeit*, ed. Bernd Jaspert, 2 vols. (Marburg, 1971–78), II, 23–34, at p. 24, 67. See also Gregory Johnston, "Rhetorical Personification of the Dead in 17th-Century German Funeral Music: Heinrich Schütz's *Musikalische Exequien* (1636) and Three Works by Michael Wiedemann (1693)," *Journal of Musicology* 9/2 (1991): 186–213.

Vor deinen Thron tret ich *and the art of dying*

Example 1.5   J. S. Bach, *Wenn wir in höchsten Nöthen sein*, BWV 641

powerfully engaged the imaginations of the gathered mourners, who would have heard Bach "speaking" to them from heaven about his appearance before God. The stark presentation of the melody and the lengthy and involved contrapuntal episodes provided comfort to the survivors and offered proof that the dead man's diligent *Todesgedanken* had reaped for him his eternal reward.

However clearly Bach expressed his own beliefs concerning the itinerary of his soul after death in his choice of text for his final chorale, his concept of the relationship between the soul and the body is brought further into focus by a comparison of the death-bed chorale with the piece it was based on, the *Orgelbüchlein* setting of *Wenn wir in höchsten Nöthen sein* composed some thirty-five years earlier. This earlier chorale prelude is a model of concision, its fourteen measures marked by elaborate coloratura writing in the soprano part, to be played, as the rubric makes clear, on a second manual (Example 1.5). Even for Bach's sometime critic Johann Adolph Scheibe, Bach was "a particularly great master" of just this kind of lavish ornamentation, which Scheibe assigned to a category he called "florid expression" (verblühmter Ausdruck). Although he criticized Bach elsewhere for writing out too many ornaments, Scheibe claimed that Bach's mastery of this kind of expression surpassed even Scheibe's musical heroes, the preeminent moderns Hasse, Graun, and Telemann.[80] For Scheibe the great merit of expressive

---

[80] *NBR*, 332, 338.

ornamention was its appeal to the senses, and the *Orgelbüchlein* chorale is literally filled up with ornament, with the superficial, the sensual.

The opposition between the sensual and sin-racked earthly existence, and non-physical, transfigured eternity was a standard topic of funeral sermons and music. Bach would have seen this dichotomy powerfully represented in Buxtehude's 1674 funeral music for his father, in which the transcendent counterpoints on *Mit Fried und Freud* are followed by the cathartic *Klag-Lied*. Such emotion-laden music acknowledged Luther's assertion that the expression of grief was a necessary part of coming to terms with death, since he disparaged complete stoicism at the loss of a friend or family member as an "artificial virtue and a fabricated strength."[81] In its embrace of the sensual, Bach's *Orgelbüchlein* chorale on *Wenn wir in höchsten Nöthen sein*, like the *Klag-Lied*, is music of the body, of painful suffering. In short, it is earthly music.

The separation of the soul from the body, release from the travails of earthly existence, the transfigured body in heaven – these tenets of Lutheran eschatology were well known to Bach. He even underlined a lengthy passage on these themes in a copy of Luther's German translation of the Bible with commentary by the seventeenth-century theologian and editor Abraham Calov: "Afflict to the limit these old bodies of ours so long as we may obtain others not sinful, as these, not given to iniquity and disobedience; bodies that can never know illness, persecution or death; bodies delivered from all physical and spiritual distress and made like unto Thine own glorified body, dear Lord Jesus Christ" (Bach's underlining).[82] Here is a glimpse of Bach at biblical study, practicing the *ars moriendi*. The transformation, or better, transfiguration, of the *Orgelbüchlein* version of *Wenn wir in höchsten Nöthen sein* to the death-bed chorale parallels this move away from the body and towards the spiritual. Bach's paring away of the sensual exterior, the lavish ornamentation, of the *Orgelbüchlein* chorale, and his expansion of the piece in anticipation of his own death with intensely reflective counterpoint is a project of purification, of orienting the piece towards heaven.

Indeed, the "narrative" embedded in *Vor deinen Thron* itself parallels the journey towards physical release, for as the piece progresses it becomes increasingly intellectual, moving ever farther from the body and into the domain of the spirit: it is in this way a representation of the act of dying. Thus the complexity of the contrapuntal voices grows with each imitative section interspersed between the entrances of the *cantus firmus* (i.e., those sections of the piece taken from the *Orgelbüchlein* version). The first contrapuntal section (Example 1.6, mm. 1–7) opens with

---

[81] Luther, "Two Funeral Sermons, 1532," 232.
[82] Robin Leaver, *J. S. Bach and Scripture* (St. Louis, 1985), 138–139.

Vor deinen Thron tret ich *and the art of dying*

Example 1.6 J. S. Bach, *Wenn wir in höchsten Nöten sein*, BWV 668 (complete version of "deathbed" chorale from original print of *Art of Fugue*)

two voices in melodic inversion, widely spaced, but with some overlap; the second section (mm. 11–19) has a closer stretto with quicker entry of the third voice and a chromatic counter-subject; in section 3 (mm. 22–28) the third voice of the complex (the bass) enters more quickly, and the contrapuntal density is increased in mm. 27–29 with an ingenious and elegant stretto just before the entry of the chorale. But most

Example 1.6 (cont.)

extraordinary is the final section, which is made up of two contrapuntal complexes and presents a rather extended contrapuntal summation that prepares the final entry of the *cantus firmus*. The first (last beat of m. 32 to the end of m. 34) introduces the *rectus* version of the chorale in long note values, with the two remaining voices imitating in diminution and melodic inversion. The second complex (second beat of m. 38 in the bass to the third beat of m. 40) presents the longer note values in melodic inversion with the quicker, imitating voices right-side-up, and in even closer stretto; the alto follows the tenor entry after just two beats in mm. 38–39, instead of the spacing of a full measure between alto and bass in mm. 33–34. Thus the harmonic reconfiguration in this last section of fore-imitation presents a sort of miniature *contrapunctus* and *evolutio* pair. Bach further enriches the contrapuntal texture in m. 40 by bringing in the motive in the tenor, anticipating the *cantus firmus* at the octave below, in diminution and continuing for half a bar in stretto.

If this flurry of inventive insight – or even its refinement – is truly the work of a dying man then it is a remarkable reflection of the kind of elevated thinking described by pastoral witnesses to death scenes. Bach was not only writing a final, personal statement; with his dying actions he was adhering to, even surpassing, the finest exemplars of the genre of last words. The focused consideration and faithful resolve in the face of death reflected in Bach's final revision of the chorale is an exemplary articulation of the *ars moriendi*. His use of learned counterpoint follows a practice studied from north German sources, and is based on the combinatorial possibilities not of thematic material of his own devising (as, for example, in the *Art of Fugue*) but of the chorale itself, the foundation of Lutheran church music. The resulting piece, and the act of producing it, anticipated the perpetual celebration of the risen, purified spirit, and offered a prelude to the unimaginable joys of the transfigured body. It was chorale prelude not to congregational singing, but to eternal life.

While much of Bach's music and especially his final chorale represents the kind of unsparing contemplation of death encouraged by the literature on the topic in Bach's possession, a profound transformation in the culture of death and dying in Germany was taking place in Bach's last years. Mattheson, for whom no corner of humanistic thought was beyond critical purview, was yet again one of the most important voices of change, launching an attack on the traditional *ars moriendi*. In his 1747 book *Inimici mortis verdächtiger Todes-Freund* (Enemies of Death, Suspicious Friend of Death), he criticized the yearning for death so evident in much of the popular literature on the subject.[83] Then in 1752 and 1753, Mattheson published his two-volume *Freuden-Akademie*, which can be read in large part as a lengthy critique of the Lutheran fascination with death. Here are the lineaments of the modern rejection of the art of dying, the concentration on life rather than death. Where Müller and the other authors known to Bach rebuked those who ignored the fact of their own eventual deaths, believing that faith alone, rather than concrete preparation, would see them through to heaven,

---

[83] Johann Mattheson, *Inimici mortis verdächtiger Todes-Freund* (Hamburg, 1747), preface, 1–12.

Mattheson urged his readers to embrace earthly life to the last moment. While conceding that "assiduous thinking about death without fear doubtless brings about circumspection and intelligence," Mattheson cautioned against such meditations, since they often inspired only "fear and trepidation" (Angst und Furcht).[84] The indefatigable Hamburg author, who in 1761 described himself at the age of eighty as full of "all liveliness" (alle Munterkeit) and constantly busy with "useful work,"[85] claimed that undue fascination with death encouraged a distemper with the world, a moral fatigue that contravened God's imperatives towards life: "Whoever is tired of the world, no longer enjoys living as he should."[86] Talk of earthly misery and complaints about physical maladies and pain were to be suppressed. As the modern cliché would have it, life was to be lived to the fullest right until the end. As in so many of the other topics on which he wrote, Mattheson's views were prophetic. By 1769 Gotthold Ephraim Lessing was conceiving of death as the border of life, and showed little concern with what came after. Obliquely polemicizing against the Lutheran *ars moriendi*, a practice predicated on a robust fear of dying, Lessing claimed that a religion in which "natural death was considered the wages of sin must infinitely augment the horror of death."[87] Hoping to return to what he saw as the ancients' view of death as sleep, Lessing proclaimed that dying should no longer be feared, nor should death be dwelled upon. Preparation was unnecessary, reflection self-defeating. Once death was purged of these frightening associations, the *ars moriendi* would itself die.

But for Bach death was to be feared and then prepared for. Thus his last creative efforts brought *Vor deinen Thron* into a form that could be claimed as one of the most enduring expressions of the Lutheran art of dying. Not simply an allegory of the eternal concert, *Vor deinen Thron* was a real prelude to the music of heaven, a bridge from this world to the next. As a dying musical utterance it was not the grand, spontaneous creation claimed by his heirs, but a small, meaningful gesture of faith. It was the most important act of Bach's entire life, for contemporary Lutheran believers would have recognized that the final battle had been won. Living in an earthly world of total darkness, Bach had listened

---

[84] Johann Mattheson, *Die neuangelegte Freuden-Akademie*, 2 vols. (Hamburg, 1751–53), II, [a3].

[85] John Mainwaring, *Georg Friedrich Händels Lebensbeschreibung*, trans. Johann Mattheson (Hamburg, 1761), 25. These are marginal comments rebutting what Mattheson sees as the false claims made by Mainwaring regarding the youthful altercation between Mattheson and Handel outside the Hamburg opera. Ever vigilant, Mattheson was still fiercely patrolling the publishing world for errors, particularly ones that miscast his own role in history.

[86] Mattheson, *Die neuangelegte Freuden-Akademie*, II, [b].

[87] G. E. Lessing, *Wie die Alten den Tod gebildet*, ed. Ludwig Uhlig (Stuttgart, 1984), 64. See also Mautner, *Mach einmal mein Ende gut*, 26.

Vor deinen Thron tret ich *and the art of dying*

to his own reflections on death in the form of an involved contrapuntal elaboration of a timeless chorale melody. Continuing his musical "Todes-Gedancken" from his bed, he faithfully and fervently awaited admission to the eternal perfection of the heavenly concert, anticipating escape from his own blindness into the brilliant light of heavenly vision, listening as his own *Vor deinen Thron* was overwhelmed by the infinite music of the angels.

2

The alchemy of Bach's canons

In January of 1738 Johann Gottfried Walther sent a letter to his longtime correspondent Heinrich Bokemeyer, the Wolfenbüttel cantor. Along with the letter came a precious piece of paper – a written-out resolution of one to Bach's canons in the composer's own hand.[1] Although this autograph page is now lost, it is likely that the piece in question was the so-called Hudemann canon, BWV 1074, named for its dedicatee, a jurist and learned amateur in music; by 1738 the canon was already a celebrated miniature of strict counterpoint. A decade earlier the Hudemann canon had first appeared in print in *Der getreue Music-Meister*, a bi-weekly music serial emanating from Hamburg and edited by Bach's friend G. P. Telemann. The version of Bach's canon published in *Der getreue Music-Meister* was presented in enigmatic notation, the only clue to its proper resolution lying in the jumble of clefs arrayed on either end of the staff (Figure 2.1). Another resident of Hamburg, Johann Mattheson, also saw a copy of the canon around that time, even noting for his readers the exact day that the piece had arrived – August 18, 1727 – during one of his lectures before the students of his composition class; Mattheson immediately instructed his students to set about trying to solve the puzzle, and after a while two of the pupils lighted on the same solution. This is presumably the one that Mattheson published a dozen years later in *Der vollkommene Capellmeister* (Example 2.1).

Given the popularity of *Der getreue Music-Meister* and *Der vollkommene Capellmeister* among music professionals and enthusiasts it is probably fair to say that in the first half of the eighteenth century the Hudemann

---

[1] Walther to Bokemeyer, January 24, 1738, in Johann Gottfried Walther, *Briefe*, ed. Klaus Beckmann and Hans-Joachim Schulze (Leipzig, 1987), 209–212.

The alchemy of Bach's canons

Figure 2.1 J. S. Bach, "Hudemann" canon (BWV 1074) as printed in *Der getreue Music-Meister* (1728)

Example 2.1 J. S. Bach, "Hudemann" canon, BWV 1074, resolution

canon was Bach's most famous piece. As it appeared in these widely circulating publications, the canon was a very public display of Bach's command of counterpoint at its most pure, an art still marveled at by some, respected by many, and scorned by more than a few. In its ten sphinx-like notes the Hudemann canon was, as Mattheson put it, an invitation to extended "reflection," a challenge both to experts like Walther and Bokemeyer, and to amateurs like those who subscribed to *Der getreue Music-Meister*. Indeed, Walther himself had apparently first seen the Hudemann canon in Telemann's serial and in 1735 forwarded to Bokemeyer a solution that had previously been sent to him by a certain Doctor Syrbio from Jena.[2] It seems that the canon was gaining a welcome reception in a number of contexts, and in Walther's correspondence we

---

[2] Walther to Bokemeyer, August 3, 1735, in *Walther Briefe*, 185–188.

gain a glimpse of amateurs (Syrbio) and professionals (Walther and Bokemeyer) alike indulging their fascination with the piece. Flaunting its complexity through the use of cryptic notation, Bach presented the canon as a mystery to be unveiled: the version for public consumption was a purposely obscure representation of the mournful majesty to be heard in the sounding piece locked within.

The large readership of *Der getreue Music-Meister* and *Der vollkommene Capellmeister* would have had to confront these mysteries with no word of advice or assurance from the oracle himself. Unlike Mattheson, who would remain unsure, though not terribly troubled, about the correctness of his solution, both Walther and Bokemeyer later had the opportunity to see Bach's own answer to the riddle. Away from the venues of bourgeois music culture – the publications of Mattheson and Telemann – Bach was apparently willing to let his intentions be known: the cultivation of public inscrutability gave way to the restricted sharing of knowledge, a collegial traffic in ideas conducted under implicit rules about the safeguarding of secrets. Only the initiated and truly appreciative would be treated to the master's explanation of his own most complex thoughts.

Indeed, in the same letter with which he passed on to Bokemeyer Bach's own solution to the Hudemann canon, Walther also mentioned his own failed efforts at unraveling a retrograde canon by the Dresden church composer J. D. Zelenka which had also appeared in *Der getreue Music-Meister*. For the moment at least this piece, which according to its rubric allowed for fourteen inversions (Verkehrungen), remained for Walther "a very dark secret" (ein sehr dunckeles Räthsel).[3] In fact, Zelenka had, unbeknownst to Walther, based his contribution to the *Music-Meister* directly on a canon from Angelo Berardi's 1687 *Documenti armonici* where the fourteen solutions Zelenka had in mind are listed.[4] The great mystery turns out to be nothing more than a gimmick in which the different solutions consist of various routes for the upper two voices – those involved in the canon – through their parts; for example, reading normally from left to right; changing direction at the central pause and proceeding back to the beginning (simply another way of achieving the retrograde); switching the upper two parts at the pause, and so on. But failing the slightest of clues from Zelenka, Walther would perhaps remain in the dark, puzzling over what was nothing more than a simple permutational exercise – not, as he apparently thought, a complex and obscure set of contrapuntal relationships.

In contrast to such distant silence, Bach's own solution to his most famous canon was a welcome and valuable gift. In another 1735 letter

[3] Ibid.
[4] Angelo Berardi, *Documenti armonici* (Bologna, 1687; reprint, Bologna, 1970), Book I, 59–60.

to Bokemeyer, Walther included an anonymous poem written for Bach's birthday:

> O day, come often! Joyous day return
> When GOD gave you to us, and Bach was born!
> We thank Him, praying that He long your life may spare,
> For seldom does the World receive a gift so rare.[5]

Clearly, Bach's accomplishments as a composer were highly respected by Bokemeyer and Walther, both of whom would have been honored by their initiation into the secret of the Hudemann canon.

Even to those outside this circle, the canon was an enticing mystery, intimating a profound insight into essential contrapuntal truths discernible from the spare melody itself. Any reasonably well-informed musician or music-lover would recognize at the opening of the canon that Bach intended to exploit the fact that the rising fourth is one of the most attractive ways of harmonizing a descending third. This by no means trivial piece of information was imparted to students by virtually all contrapuntal treatises from Zarlino to Walther, who in his *Praecepta* (see p. 13 above) cited this as a particularly good use of contrary motion.[6] Bach had already investigated the properties of rising fourths followed by falling thirds in the A major fugue from the *Well-Tempered Clavier* Book I (see Example 2.2). In m. 4 of the piece, Bach uses this chain to create an ephemeral canon illustrating just one of the ways in which these alternating intervals combine like clockwork: at the second (ninth) at the distance of a dotted quarter note. At m. 6 he presents another possibility: imitation at the upper fifth at the distance of a quarter note. Yet one more combination is demonstrated in m. 9, with the second voice (the bass) entering at the sixth below and at the distance of a dotted quarter. In these examples the voices move from one consonance to the next in contrary motion; Bach also lays out the obvious combinations in which the voices move in parallel, as at m. 21. These fleeting canonic bursts exploit the friction between the scansion of the subject and the natural hierarchies of the meter of the piece; the delightful ambiguity of interlocking fourths ascending pairwise but as triplets is amplified by the combinatorial potential of the fourth–third chain, a potential which must have been crucial to the invention of the subject in the first place. That the Hudemann canon and the A major fugue occupy opposite poles on a stylistic and affective continuum ranging from contemplative grandeur to unbridled insouciance only goes to confirm the universal contrapuntal value of fourths and thirds in alternation.

---

[5] *NBR*, 312.
[6] Walther, *Praecepta der musicalischen Composition*, ed. Peter Benary (Leipzig, 1955), 124–125.

Example 2.2 J. S. Bach, Fugue in A major, BWV 864 from *Well-Tempered Clavier* Book I, treatment of interlocking fourths

After opening with an ascending fourth, the Hudemann canon then refers its students to another contrapuntal verity: that a succession of falling thirds and rising seconds meshes perfectly, not only in note-against-note motion but in the kind of syncopation resulting from Bach's alternation of half and whole notes – i.e., in oblique motion and at various intervallic and temporal levels (Example 2.3). Clearly, given the upside-down clefs to the right of the staff in the Hudemann canon these contrapuntal facts remain valid in melodic inversion. The same elemental realities inherent in a rising fourth followed by a falling chain of thirds and seconds were investigated at incredible length by Bach's contemporary Christoph Graupner, the Darmstadt Kapellmeister, who along with Bach was an applicant for the Leipzig cantorate in 1722. Using a theme whose outline is strikingly similar to that of the Hudemann

Example 2.3   Interlocking thirds and seconds in canon

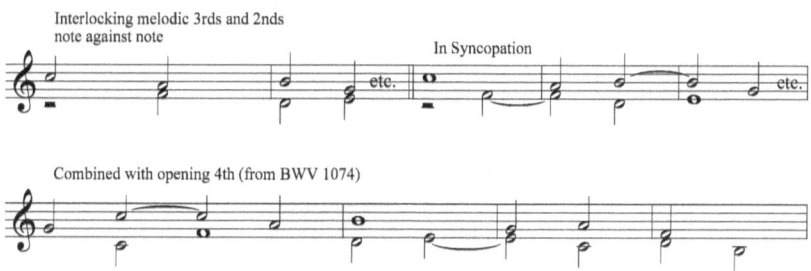

canon, Graupner wrote out 5,625 of the permutational possibilities in a sisyphean labor of *ars combinatoria*.[7] That these sequences could sustain this kind of extended elaboration and scrutiny was proof of their value. In the Hudemann canon, then, Bach takes hold of these and other basics of contrapuntal combination – material taught to beginning students of counterpoint – and creates from them a priceless treasure to be held, turned over, looked at from different angles, a creation to be contemplated and enjoyed by distant admirers and close friends. In its derivation from contrapuntal essentials the piece has an ineluctable yet strangely paradoxical power: it transforms the axiomatic into something unique, the particular into something universal.

By 1738, the year he sent Bach's Hudemann solution to Bokemeyer, Walther had known Bach for some thirty years. They had become colleagues when Bach had arrived in Weimar to become court organist in 1708, the year after Walther had taken up his post as organist at the Stadtkirche, a position he would hold until his death in 1748. Walther's command of music theory can be judged by his *Praecepta der musicalischen Composition*, a treatise he completed the year before Bach arrived in Weimar. Dedicated to Weimar's music-loving duke, the young Johann Ernst, the *Praecepta* concludes with chapters on canon and double counterpoint featuring many examples of highly intricate contrapuntal procedures. By the time Walther and Bach became colleagues it was Walther who had already been studying the discipline of learned counterpoint and the kinds of complex musical problems that would so occupy Bach in his last decade. Their meeting in Weimar was certainly significant to Bach's continuing musical education. Walther's library of treatises, built through his correspondence with Werckmeister and others, would also have been an important resource for the eminently practical Bach in his initial encounter with the esoterica of learned counterpoint. Together they appear to have been the first composers to treat a *cantus firmus*

---

[7] See Peter Cahn, "Christoph Graupners 'Kanons' als Versuch einer systematischen Imitationslehre," *Musiktheorie* 1/2 (1986): 130–136.

itself in canon in organ chorale preludes. The degree of cooperation, even friendly competition, that existed between the two men is suggested by the fact that Walther and Bach set three of the same melodies in this way.[8]

It was also during his Weimar years and his association with Walther that Bach wrote his earliest surviving speculative canon, BWV 1073; it is in four parts and the unknown dedicatee is perhaps Walther himself.[9] Thus the two musicians cultivated, almost in tandem, both short dedicatory canons and practical, but no less artful, chorale preludes; just as important for Bach's development in general, but more specifically with respect to strict counterpoint, he and Walther shared an interest in the study and preservation of the music of the previous generation. Given Walther's continuing interest in Bach and his counterpoint, an interest of which the exchange of the Hudemann canon likely gives only a partial view, Walther is a particularly good gauge of the reception of Bach's work among his colleagues. As we have seen, the commemoration and contemplation of death was one purpose to which strict counterpoint was put, and the hermeneutic richness of Bach's final setting of *Vor deinen Thron* would certainly not have been lost on his Weimar relation. But counterpoint had other meanings, other resonances that referred beyond itself, and one of these was an association with alchemy.

In the summer of 1730, near the beginning of their correspondence, Bokemeyer had received a letter from Walther relating a curious encounter.[10] On Wednesday July 19, Walther had made one of his customary visits to the Ducal Library in Weimar, perhaps on his way to do some research for his *Musicalisches Lexicon*, which he would publish two years later. He found the library closed, but the elderly curator of the adjacent ducal *Kunst-Kammer* saw Walther waiting outside and invited him in to look at the collection's numerous scientific instruments.[11] On entering this museum of natural history and technology, Walther noticed a barometer and asked the *Kunst-Kämmerer* if it gave accurate readings. The old man replied that the device was not air-tight and as a result the mercury in it was not active. Much to Walther's surprise, the curator then launched into a lengthy monologue on the nature of mercury, claiming that whoever knew how to treat this substance with the "philosophical fire" (*philosophisches Feuer*) and "the sun" (i.e., gold) could become very

---

[8] Russell Stinson, *Bach: The Orgelbüchlein* (New York, 1996), 73–74.
[9] *NBR*, 65.
[10] Walther to Bokemeyer, August 3, 1730, in *Walther Briefe*, 122–124.
[11] The Weimar *Kunst-Kammer* was founded in 1700 by Duke Wilhelm Ernst, who would later be J. S. Bach's employer. This reference comes from Goethe, who would later spend a good deal of time in the *Kunst-Kammer* himself. See Johann Wolfgang Goethe, *Werke* LV (Stuttgart and Tübingen, 1833), 157.

lucky, even rich. In response to Walther's question as to the nature of this philosophical fire (not real flames but a metaphor for an alchemical reaction) the old man described an elaborate machine he had seen some thirty years earlier that had been constructed using twenty-four glasses which ground metal to a fine grey powder – an alchemical process called calcination. According to the curator, this powder had unfortunately consisted only of "mere mercury," that is, it did not contain any of the rare, philosophical (i.e., alchemically active) mercury that could produce a true philosophical fire, and as a result the process had not yielded any gold. The ducal librarian had in the meantime arrived, and Walther excused himself to make his visit to the library, but this chance meeting with the *Kunst-Kämmerer* and the discovery that he was also an alchemist left a lasting impression on Walther; two weeks later he wrote to Bokemeyer to ask him about the viability of constructing a grinding machine, such as that described by the Weimar *Kunst-Kämmerer*.[12] Could such a contraption be constructed so as to produce a purified substance that could then be transformed into gold?

This vignette is just one example of the lengthy and numerous musings on hermetic science to be found in Walther's letters to Bokemeyer. These provide a record of an interest in the occult that has been a source of some discomfort for post-Enlightenment scholars. Various strategies have been adopted for explaining away Walther's fascination with the occult, all of them tacitly implying that alchemy had no real bearing on eighteenth-century thought.[13] One was to assert that Walther was naturally gullible, and so became momentarily misled by Bokemeyer's alchemical obsessions;[14] another has been simply to ignore the issue altogether, and in this way insulate the leading German music encyclopedist of Bach's time, author of the *Musicalisches Lexicon*, from the irrational, and other interests that might weaken his credibility as a historical source.[15] In evasions such as these, an unwillingness to investigate the potential correspondences between music and alchemy in Walther's thought succeeded in preventing hermetic ideas from coming dangerously close to J. S. Bach.

Musicological attempts to deny the possible cogency of Walther's hermeticism and to cast Bokemeyer as a purveyor of useless, even

---

[12] Walther mentioned this same *Kunst-Kämmerer* in a letter to Bokemeyer written exactly one year later, remarking that he had unfortunately not spoken with the elderly curator again. Walther to Bokemeyer, August 3, 1731, *Walther Briefe*, 141.

[13] Only Werner Braun, in a 1969 article, made a passing guess that there might have been a connection between Bokemeyer's fascination with alchemy and his views on music. Werner Braun, "Bachs Stellung im Kanonstreit," in *Bach-Interpretationen* (Göttingen, 1969), 106–111.

[14] Georg Schünemann, "J. G. Walther und H. Bokemeyer," *Bach-Jahrbuch* 30 (1933): 86–118, esp. 117.

[15] Klaus Beckmann and Hans-Joachim Schulze, "Vorwort" to *Walther Briefe*, 11.

unhinged modes of knowledge parallel efforts by historians of science to suppress the importance of alchemy for many of the leading figures of seventeenth- and early eighteenth-century rationalism, most famously Newton and Leibniz.[16] Over the past twenty years, however, scholars have begun to investigate the significance, even centrality, of alchemy in the mature thought of Newton and Leibniz, both of whom were committed alchemists, and much has been done to correct the general tendency to suppress the role of the occult in the work of figures who have become for us symbols of scientific progress.[17] Even an Enlightened leader such as Frederick the Great encouraged extensive scientific research in the Prussian Academy while retaining an avid interest in alchemical projects.[18] Instead of explaining away the tenacity of alchemy in the eighteenth century, scholars have begun to show how occult and religious elements shaped Newton's own work on optics and gravitation, as well as Leibniz's monadology. The penetration of occult beliefs and practices into rationalist programs is increasingly coming to be seen less as an embarrassing contradiction than as a rich mingling of ideas.

Indeed, the relevance of alchemy to eighteenth-century musical thought cannot be easily rejected. Walther's own correspondence hints at the links between music and hermetic science. He first discusses alchemy in a letter to Bokemeyer, the longest that survives, dated March 10, 1729. After a colorful account of his life, Walther apparently responds to earlier alchemical questions from Bokemeyer, explaining that he possessed "only a superficial knowledge" (nur eine *superficielle Wißenschaft*) of the discipline; however, he goes on to list the considerable contents of his own hermetic library (at least twelve bound volumes, some containing a number of works), and writes of his fascination with the intricacies and obscurities of the theory and practice of alchemy since his school days.[19] Walther claims that, unlike others, he has never doubted the validity of this "supreme and most beautiful art"

---

[16] For the case against the importance of alchemy in Newton's thought see I. Bernard Cohen, "The *Principia*, Universal Gravitation, and the 'Newtonian Style,' in Relation to the Newtonian Revolution in Science: Notes on the Occasion of the 250th Anniversary of Newton's Death," in *Contemporary Newtonian Research*, ed. Zev Bechler (Dordrecht, 1982), 21–108. For a typically off-hand dismissal of Leibniz's interest in alchemy see Roger Ariew, "G. W. Leibniz: Life and Works," in *The Cambridge Companion to Leibniz*, ed. Nicholas Jolley (Cambridge, 1995), 18–42, esp. 21.

[17] Betty Jo Teeter Dobbs and Margaret C. Jacob, *Newton and the Culture of Newtonianism* (Atlantic Highlands, NJ, 1995), esp. 21–27; Betty Jo Teeter Dobbs, *The Janus Faces of Genius: the Role of Alchemy in Newton's Thought* (Cambridge, 1991); Allison P. Coudert, *Leibniz and the Kabbalah* (Dordrecht, 1995), esp. 7, 95–97. As for Leibniz, he was keen to make his fortune in alchemy and invested frequently in alchemical ventures; he was an easy mark for alchemists in search of money. Leibniz's dying words concerned a report that gold had been transmuted from iron nails with the aid of a spring. G. MacDonald Ross, *Leibniz* (Oxford, 1984), 5.

[18] Robert Asprey, *Frederick the Great: The Magnificent Enigma* (New York, 1986), 359.

[19] Walther to Bokemeyer, March 10, 1729, in *Walther Briefe*, 65–83, esp. 76.

(allerhöchste und schönste Kunst).[20] Alchemy and music also appear alongside one another in the lengthy postscript to the letter, where he writes that

> just as you [went] through the ciphers (*Schlüßel*) 1 through 7 of occult philosophy, so have I come to understand, through the contemplation of the numbers 1, 2, 3, 4, 5, 6, 7, and 8, the instruction on canon (*Lehre der Consequenzen*) so extensively discussed by Zarlino, of which the aforementioned author proclaims that (with respect to judgment) canon is the highest level of composition.[21]

The connection between Walther's own attempts at numerological exegesis – which of course has a long tradition within occult philosophy – and Zarlino's discussion of canon is not entirely clear, but beyond his intimations of hidden links between the numbers and their referents, the language itself is suggestive. Just as Walther, presumably following Bokemeyer's lead, described alchemy as the "highest and most beautiful art," so too Zarlino and his eighteenth-century German followers saw canon as the "highest level of composition."[22] As Walther himself would have recognized, this description of counterpoint evoked the ubiquitous references in the hermetic discourse to alchemy as "an art above all other arts, the noblest."[23] Both disciplines occupied the place of honor in their respective branches of knowledge: alchemy was, for the devotees of hermetic knowledge, preeminent in philosophy while canon was, for enthusiasts of counterpoint, the pinnacle of music.

Although none of Bokemeyer's letters to Walther survive it is clear from Walther's correspondence that his friend was an "adept," a skilled and widely read alchemist. Bokemeyer appears to have owned a considerable collection of hermetic tracts, although Walther sometimes provided his colleague with bibliographic information about various alchemical books he had seen (perhaps in the Weimar library), works in his own collection, or treatises he was trying to acquire. The two musicians had a lengthy and lively exchange concerning the hermetic sciences, which continued until January of 1732 when Walther offered a solicitous reply

---

[20] Ibid., 76.
[21] Ibid., 81. This is probably a reference to the seven precepts of the prolific occult writer and physician Paracelsus (1493–1541). Walther himself owned several volumes by Paracelsus, including the *Coelum Philosophorum*, which contains these seven *Schlüßel* of the metals.
[22] Gioseffo Zarlino, *The Art of Counterpoint*, trans. Guy A. Marco and Claude V. Palisca (New Haven, 1968), 126. For a German paraphrase of Zarlino's description of canon that would have been known to Walther see Christoph Bernhard, *Tractatus compositionis augmentatus*, ed. Joseph Müller-Blattau in *Die Kompositionslehre Heinrich Schützens in der Fassung seines Schülers Christoph Bernhard*, 2nd edn. (Kassel, 1963), 112.
[23] Ulrich Poyselius, "Spiegel der Alchemie," in *Aureum vellus, oder Guldin Schatz und Kunstkammer* (Hamburg, 1718), 214–229, esp. 214. Walther knew Poyselius' treatise. See Walther to Bokemeyer, August 3, 1731, in *Walther Briefe*, 138–148, esp. 143.

to the news – conveyed in a now-lost letter – that Bokemeyer had momentarily put aside his alchemical experiments.[24] Nevertheless, neither man gave up his interest in alchemy or, apparently, his belief in its value.

Along with his second letter to Bokemeyer, written in April of 1729, Walther sent his friend one of his own cantatas which contained an aria on the text "Keüscheste Flammen brennt ewiglich fort" (Chastest flames, shine forth eternally!), set as a six-voice perpetual canon. Walther noted that since it was impossible for the voices to stop all at once, his canon could "represent a kind of infinity" (ein *typum* der Unendlichkeit darstellen können). He went on to mention that he had sent the cantata to Johann Mattheson, who had judged the piece favorably; Walther stressed that the noted critic's approval had extended to the canonic aria. Hoping that Bokemeyer "had not given up all consideration of the study of canon," Walther also sent his Wolfenbüttel colleague some other pieces which would further demonstrate that canonic writing was not merely to be undertaken as a school exercise but could still be used effectively in church music.[25]

One senses that Walther is choosing his words carefully here: along with musicians across Germany, he had followed the closely watched dispute between Bokemeyer and Mattheson over the merits of canon, entitled (by Mattheson) "Die canonische Anatomie" and conducted throughout 1723 and into 1724 in the pages of Mattheson's music periodical *Critica musica*, the first such publication to appear in Germany. Bokemeyer was certainly well equipped to engage Mattheson publicly on this contentious issue, since he had amassed one of the most impressive collections of treatises on learned counterpoint compiled from German and Italian sources.[26] Although he himself composed Italianate music and, like Mattheson, had learned to sing in the modern Italian style as a youth, Bokemeyer upheld the conservative belief in both the importance of canon to musical pedagogy and its inherent aesthetic primacy, a notion based on Zarlino's claim that canon represented the "highest level of composition."[27]

The polemical arguments put forth by Bokemeyer and Mattheson in "Die canonische Anatomie" often reflected extreme positions of the

---

[24] Walther to Bokemeyer, January 25, 1732, in *Walther Briefe*, 152–154.

[25] Walther to Bokemeyer, April 4, 1729, in *Walther Briefe*, 33.

[26] The Italian theorists whose teachings are represented in the collection include Carissimi, Penna, Berardi, and Bononcini. For an inventory of these holdings see Harald Kümmerling, *Katalog der Sammlung Bokemeyer* (Kassel, 1970), 11.
In describing canon and its frequent companion double counterpoint as "learned counterpoint" I follow Kerala Snyder, who examines the use of these procedures as intellectual tributes to colleagues in late seventeenth-century north Germany. See Kerala J. Snyder, "Dietrich Buxtehude's Studies in Learned Counterpoint," *Journal of the American Musicological Society* 23 (1980): 544–564.

[27] Zarlino, *The Art of Counterpoint*, 126.

The alchemy of Bach's canons

most vehement members of the music profession. By the first decades of the eighteenth century in Germany, canon and double counterpoint had come to epitomize for many the conflict between theory and practice in composition, and the role of the senses versus that of the intellect in musical judgment. In his highly esteemed *Musikalische Diskurse* completed in the 1690s but not published until 1719, Johann Beer cited canon and the related device double counterpoint in order to summarise the debate: "daily experience demonstrates that many orderly canons as well as [pieces of] double counterpoint which follow the rules seldom sound good, although they are not dissonant."[28] Even if grammatically constructed, these pieces were often unconvincing rhetorically. But Beer was no enemy of learned counterpoint and he cautioned against condemning such procedures outright, since they could, when properly handled, be pleasing to the ear; further, knowledge of these strictest forms of counterpoint was required of a composer, and would help him develop his musical faculties. Beer's position represents the moderate, and probably most widely held, view on the matter during the first part of the eighteenth century.

A radical departure from this middle ground was taken by Mattheson in his 1717 book, *Das beschützte Orchestre*, the second volume of his *Orchestre* trilogy, just one of Mattheson's works that were objectionable to musical conservatives of Bokemeyer's persuasion. In *Das beschützte Orchestre*, Mattheson's penchant for polemic found him reducing to a silly diversion what had been for Zarlino, and continued to be for many musicians of Mattheson's own day, the very symbol of compositional mastery:

One goes in for jocular apothegms (*scherzhaffte Apophthegmata*) while drinking a glass of wine or on a boring journey, inventing canons and singing them for fun in order to pass the time. Indeed, these pieces are very artful but of little use.[29]

In his typically offhand manner, Mattheson argues that the effort spent in creating sophisticated canonic compositions is largely wasted since the modern style has little room for such intricacies. A dogged advocate of the natural, Mattheson at his most polemical cast the complexity of canon as an aesthetic evil in general, although he admitted its use within church music.

In the same year that *Das beschützte Orchestre* appeared Mattheson published and edited the third part of *Die musicalische Handleitung* by the

---

[28] Johann Beer, *Musicalische Diskurse* (Nuremberg, 1719; reprint, Leipzig, 1982), 34; see also pp. 95, 100. Mattheson cited this passage in "Die canonische Anatomie" (p. 310; see n. 32 below), but in typically selective fashion, he did not mention the more complimentary views on double counterpoint to be found in Beer's book.

[29] Johann Mattheson, *Das beschützte Orchestre* (Hamburg, 1717; reprint, Leipzig, 1981), 139.

Copenhagen organist Friedrich Erhard Niedt, who had died nine years earlier. With a seemingly single-minded desire to enrage musical conservatives (and probably moderates as well), Niedt repeatedly lampooned learned counterpoint and its practitioners:

> Many an honest bore (*Saalbader*) has spent many an hour of his life trying to excel at canons... We should let be what these old [Canon Masters] out of childish ignorance believe to be good, for one must make allowances for old age.[30]

As editor, Mattheson now stood responsible for a text packed with invective. Heinrich Bokemeyer, for one, failed to appreciate Niedt's humor, and stepped up to defend the honor of counterpoint, writing a letter to Mattheson championing canon as the apex of musical achievement. At Bokemeyer's request, Mattheson printed the letter, interspersing his own responses in "Die canonische Anatomie"; a second exchange followed and the article was extended to four installments.[31]

In the dispute, Bokemeyer repeated the old claims for the exalted status of canon as an essential part of compositional training; canon possessed "the very greatest use in music," and to master canon was to climb the art's highest peak.[32] Since canon was the most difficult musical technique, argued Bokemeyer, it provided the "foundation" for success in all other genres, including fugue, imitation, double counterpoint, the church style, and even modern Italianate vocal music. Mattheson, in his response to Bokemeyer, took a more considered approach to canon than had Niedt: "To be sure, I would want to advise the musical student (*Studioso melopoetico*) to practice this genre of composition [i. e., canon] to the extent that it is applicable to other genres."[33] But Mattheson went on to attack what he saw as the undue importance given to a procedure of little relevance to contemporary musical practice and one that prevented the invention of free-flowing, natural melody:

> As soon as the ear notices that the composer has used more harmonic artificiality (*harmonische Künsteley*) than the melodious Natural, more fugal, canonic limitations and pedantic subtleties (*Finessen*), than free, expressive modulations, it perceives a certain tiresome inclination, which deprives it of all pleasure and freedom, denying free rein to the affections.[34]

As editor of *Critica musica*, Mattheson took the liberty of allotting himself ample space for detailed refutations of Bokemeyer's arguments and peppered his opponent's essays with his own withering footnotes. In the end Bokemeyer was unable to withstand this relentless polemic,

---

[30] F. E. Niedt, *Die musicalische Handleitung dritter und letzter Theil*, ed. Johann Mattheson (Hamburg, 1717), preface; translation in F. E. Niedt, *The Musical Guide*, trans. Pamela L. Poulin and Irmgard C. Taylor (Oxford, 1989), 27.

[31] "Die canonische Anatomie" is printed in *Critica musica*, 2 vols. (Hamburg, 1722–25; reprint Amsterdam, 1964), I, 236–368.

[32] Ibid., 240–241.   [33] Ibid., 238.   [34] Ibid., 248–249.

and Mattheson relished the opportunity to conclude "Die canonische Anatomie" with a final letter from Bokemeyer in which the defeated combatant performs a complete reversal, retracting his former statement and repudiating the centrality of canon in contemporary musical practice. Indeed, Bokemeyer explains how, as a result of Mattheson's enlightening arguments, he has realized the marginal role of the art he had once so vehemently espoused:

> But now I (and undoubtedly many others with me) have the unanticipated good fortune to have been led by Your Honorable Sir to melody – and at the same time from the periphery to the center [of musical thought] – as the correct and only source of truly musical art. Accordingly, I think of my defeat as a great triumph over my previous ignorance in this respect, and I am not ashamed to acknowledge it publicly.[35]

In a letter to Mattheson written in 1725, nearly two years after the publication of "Die canonische Anatomie," Bokemeyer was abject: "When I look at my old ideas (*retroacta*) I am filled with the greatest disgust... The longer I look, the more [I believe] that the harmonic [i.e., contrapuntal] arts have up to now hindered the true goal [of music]."[36]

The argument between Mattheson and Bokemeyer in "Die canonische Anatomie" was anything but an arcane debate. As was his custom in these controversies, Mattheson solicited the opinions of other leading musicians, and he received replies in support of his position, though with varying degrees of enthusiasm, from Georg Philipp Telemann, Johann David Heinichen, and Reinhard Keiser, all of which he printed at the end of "Die canonische Anatomie."[37] When Gotha organist Gottfried Heinrich Stölzel published his own treatise on canon in 1725, he acknowledged Mattheson's arguments, hoping that his declared awareness of the dispute would be enough to protect him from the suspicion that he believed canons to be the ultimate in musical accomplishment.[38] "Die canonische Anatomie" had apparently set out the parameters for aesthetic discussion of learned counterpoint.

Although Bokemeyer's defeat marked a key moment in the waning of canon's status, learned counterpoint continued to serve as a favorite target for progressive music critics. Among the most vociferous was the Dresden Kapellmeister Heinichen, who, in his seminal treatise *Der General-Bass in der Composition* of 1728, likened learned counterpoint to the worst superstitions of an irrational world. Heinichen

---

[35] Ibid., 362. Bokemeyer and Mattheson did have another go-round over theories of melody in later installments of the same journal. See "Der melodische Vorhof" in Mattheson, *Critica musica* II, 289–380.

[36] Bokemeyer to Mattheson, June 18, 1725, printed in Mattheson, *Critica musica* II, 294.

[37] The letters are printed in "Die canonische Anatomie," 356–360.

[38] Gottfried Heinrich Stölzel, *Practischer Beweis wie aus einem nach dem wahren Fundamente solcher Noten-Künsteleyen gesetzten Canone Perpetuo ... Theils an Melodie, Theils auch nur an Harmonie ... zu machen seyn) ...* (n.p., 1725), paragraph 44.

depicted enthusiasts of counterpoint as deceitful fanatics who wrapped canonic practice in a shroud of complexity, making bogus claims for its almost magical powers. Heinichen derided "the excessive cult of counterpoint" (der *excessive Cultus* der *Contrapuncte*) and compared the making of canons to a kind of witchcraft.[39] In typically Enlightened fashion, Heinichen, like Mattheson, urged an intrepid encyclopedist to research, codify and explain all the devices of learned counterpoint, and thereby remove from the discipline its undeserved mystique:

> Our music would certainly be well served by a capable man, who would, as far as possible, collect his own musical secrets as well as the others circulating around the world ... diligently search for the key to puzzles to which he does not know the answer, and forthrightly discover all similar musical concepts (*Kunstgriffe*). Such [an undertaking] would greatly lessen the general wonderment at these kinds of paper witcheries, and contain the abuse of excessive counterpoint, and we would learn to apply our musical reason to more important things.[40]

Without such research, canon would continue to flummox and fascinate gullible musicians. In "Die canonische Anatomie," Mattheson insisted that "a composer (*ein* Melopoeta) must diligently reflect on this secret [canon] and investigate it, otherwise he gropes in the dark with all canons."[41] Neither Mattheson nor Heinichen favored the complete abandonment of canon and double counterpoint; rather, they asserted that these techniques could no longer claim a privileged aesthetic position. Mattheson would later include chapters on both procedures in his *Vollkommener Capellmeister* of 1739,[42] in which he repudiated the scurrilous Niedt's outlandish attack on canon. When engaging in polemics, both Mattheson and Heinichen invariably characterized learned counterpoint as the product of an irrational and antiquated musical culture epitomized by, among others, Heinrich Bokemeyer. What they objected to more than the constricting effect of contrapuntal artifice on free-flowing melody was the culture of obscurantism and secrecy which surrounded such music.

That Heinichen, and especially Mattheson, could expend so much of their polemical energies on demystifying, even "enlightening" music theory bears witness to the persistent influence of the occult and magical in musical thought well into the eighteenth century. This influence

---

[39] Johann David Heinichen, *Der General-Bass in der Composition* (Dresden, 1728; reprint, Hildesheim, 1969), 9, 936.
[40] Heinichen, *Der General-Bass*, 936. This connection of canon with witchcraft brings to mind Haydn's string quartet Op. 76, no. 2: the third movement is entitled "Hexenmenuette" and is a two-voice canon doubled at the octave.
[41] "Die canonische Anatomie," 264. For a thorough description of the multifarious types of canons (a modern answer, perhaps, to Heinichen's request), see Denis Collins, "Canon in Music Theory from c. 1550 to c. 1800" (Ph.D. diss., Stanford University, 1992).
[42] Johann Mattheson, *Der vollkommene Capellmeister* (Hamburg, 1739; reprint, Kassel, 1954), 393–427.

figures prominently in the writings of Andreas Werckmeister, a frequent target of Mattheson's attempts at rationalizing music theory. As we have seen, Werckmeister subscribed to the Neoplatonist notion that music replicates the layout of the heavens and can work its powerful effect on man because he too is a microcosm of the universe.[43] In *Musicae mathematicae hodegus curiosus* of 1687, Werckmeister explained how his method of fabricating canons is based on the principle of contrary motion, and that this scheme is derived from the fundamental properties of the monochord, whose division into intervals reflects the ordering of the cosmos. His investigations into the nature of counterpoint were not merely for the practical benefit of musicians; more than that, they revealed both the ethical and occult working of music. There was for Werckmeister "something secret and of much good"[44] hidden in the astronomical principles which themselves provided "the key [*Schlüssel*] to all kinds of canons and double, triple, and quadruple counterpoint."[45]

Although Werckmeister preferred to cite Christian scripture in support of his Neoplatonist views on music and its sympathy with the cosmological order, he also adduced the writings of occult authors, most notably the early sixteenth-century hermetic doctor and medical reformer Paracelsus, and his contemporary Henry Cornelius Agrippa, whose *De occulta philosophia* (Cologne, 1533) circulated widely among theorists into the eighteenth century.[46] A believer in the efficacy of natural magic, Werckmeister had read the other great renaissance magi as well – Marsilio Ficino, Pico della Mirandola, and Giordano Bruno – and his views on music owe much to the hermetic tradition.[47] For the renaissance magus, and the seventeenth- and early eighteenth-century musicians who shared many of Werckmeister's views, the world was ordered hierarchically, and the composer could both exploit music's sympathy with the higher powers and gain greater understanding of the structure of the universe through music itself.[48]

No one knew better – or resented more deeply – the pervasiveness of the occult in musical thought than did Mattheson. In the opening pages of his first book, *Das neu-eröffnete Orchestre* of 1713, Mattheson had

---

[43] One of Werckmeister's most widely cited and influential efforts in disseminating these Neoplatonist ideas was his translation of Agostino Steffani's *Quanta certezza habbia da suoi principii la musica* which had appeared in Amsterdam in 1695. Steffani was Kapellmeister at Hanover during the first part of Leibniz's tenure there as court librarian from 1676 until his death in 1716. Andreas Werckmeister, *Musicalisches Sendschreiben* (Quedlinburg, 1699; reprint, Hildesheim, 1970).

[44] Ibid., 82.   [45] Werckmeister, *Harmonologia musica*, 102.

[46] Werckmeister, *Musicalische Paradoxal-Discourse* (Quedlinburg, 1707; reprint, Hildesheim, 1970), 12, 21–22. Walther and Bokemeyer both owned the works of Paracelsus.

[47] For Werckmeister's sources see Rolf Dammann, "Zur Musiklehre des Andreas Werckmeister," *Archiv für Musikwissenschaft* 11 (1954): 206–37.

[48] Gary Tomlinson, *Music in Renaissance Magic* (Chicago, 1993), 45–46. See also Michel Foucault, *The Order of Things* (New York, 1971), 17–77.

attacked not only the pedantry of music theory but also its reliance on obscure mystical ideas inherited from antiquity and the renaissance.[49] To illustrate the tenacity of what he considered to be a network of irrational and counterproductive beliefs, Mattheson describes how he lent his copy of Kircher's *Musurgia universalis* to a man who, on returning the volume, recounted how he had conjured up a ghost while reading through the book. Mattheson relates how the man cited Agrippa and one or another writer on magic (Zauber-*Autore*) as proof that such a thing could happen.[50] The fervent Neoplatonist Heinrich Buttstett objected to this seemingly casual, but nonetheless breathtaking, assault on the venerable Kircher;[51] Mattheson responded by comparing the occult teachings found in the "magic books" of Agrippa, Kircher and others to the words of barbarians, and alleged that the "highly-praised learning (*hochgerühmte Gelehrsahmkeit*) of the otherwise industrious Jesuit [Kircher]" was full of "mediocre ideas" (mittelmäßige Gedancken).[52] That Mattheson would begin *Das neu-eröffnete Orchestre* with an attack on Kircher and the nimbus of magic that surrounded music theory, speaks both to the popularity of these beliefs and Mattheson's commitment to eradicating them.

Where Bach stood in all this can only be guessed at, but that he knew of the arguments in play and their implications for his own work seems certain. He acted as Leipzig agent for Heinichen's *Der General-Bass in der Composition*, and may have been the "musician" whom a visitor to the 1729 Leipzig Easter Fair heard voicing his admiration for the newest

---

[49] A similar distrust of the occult can be found in seventeenth-century writings on music theory. Michael Praetorius' *De Organographia* begins with a wonderfully ironic attack on those who had criticized him for publishing a scholarly book in German instead of Latin, in which the author satirizes such high-minded secrecy with a disparaging comparison between the hoarding of musical and alchemical knowledge, sardonically pleading that his book should not be thought of as "a great philosopher's stone, which the authors of Secret Philosophy hold to be such a mystery." Michael Praetorius, *Syntagma musicum* II: *De Organographia* (Wolfenbüttel, 1619; reprint, Kassel, 1958), 5. Similarly, in *Der musicalische Quacksalber*, Heinichen's teacher Johann Kuhnau ridicules his novel's main character, the musical charlatan Caraffa, by comparing him to an alchemist who loudly claims to have found the philosopher's stone, but has nonetheless not produced any gold. Kuhnau, *Der musicalische Quacksalber* (Dresden, 1700; reprint, Bern, 1992), chapter 36. Mattheson, *Das neu-eröffnete Orchestre* (Hamburg, 1713; reprint, Hildesheim, 1993), 5.

[50] Mattheson, *Das neu-eröffnete Orchestre*, 5. Kircher himself was a leading writer on hermetic and occult philosophy. See Frances Yates, *Giordano Bruno and the Hermetic Tradition* (London, 1964), 416ff., and Yates, *The Rosicrucian Enlightenment* (London, 1972), 230.

[51] Heinrich Buttstett, *Ut, mi, sol, re, fa, la, tota musica et harmonia aeterna* (Erfurt, [1717]), 8. Among the magical beliefs found in the book is Buttstett's claim that music has occult medical powers to heal sickness (pp. 15–16). For antecedents in renaissance magic see Tomlinson, *Music in Renaissance Magic*, 78–81, 132.

[52] Mattheson, *Das beschützte Orchestre*, 49. Werckmeister, *Musicalisches Paradoxal-Discourse*, 26–27.

works by both Mattheson and Heinichen.[53] And given the number of references to "Die canonische Anatomie" in contemporary sources, it is hard to imagine that Bach did not follow the dispute, or at least have some sense of the issues at stake. Indeed, it has been suggested that the Hudemann canon might have been a demonstration of Bach's support for Bokemeyer's views, or at least a defense of the merits of canon more generally.[54] Two of Bach's most elaborate canons might also suggest links to, or at least an awareness of, Mattheson's writings and the controversies aired in *Critica musica*. Bach's so-called Faber canon is one of these; although the canon survives only in a later copy by his student J. P. Kirnberger and was apparently dedicated to the Leipzig medical student B. G. Faber in 1749, Bach seems to have drawn on a collection of his canons for commemorative purposes, in this case Faber's successful completion of his inaugural disputation. It is possible, then, that the piece might date back to the 1720s, when the debate over solmization was at its peak. The title of Bach's canon, *Fa Mi, et Mi Fa est tota Musica*, refers to a commonplace – increasingly challenged by progressive theorists – of early eighteenth-century music theory. What was being challenged, however, was not that the semitone, as the smallest indivisible unit of tonal organization, was the foundation of music, but rather the use of medieval solmization syllables to describe it. Indeed, the title of Bach's canon could be taken as a reference to the debate over solmization printed in Mattheson's *Critica musica* in 1724. Once again using his journal as a forum for the reform of music theory, Mattheson canvassed leading musicians regarding the validity of arguments in favor of retaining solmization put forth by Buttstett in his 1717 treatise, *Ut, mi, sol, re, fa, la tota musica et harmonia aeterna...*, itself a response to Mattheson's treatment of the subject in *Das neu-eröffnete Orchestre* of 1713. Both Buttstett's title and Bach's refer to the solmization syllables as *tota musica*.

Those who sent Mattheson their opinions regarding the solmization controversy ranged from the amateur – the soldier/musician General Georg von Bertouch, a man with connections to the Bach family and one who was familiar with some of J. S. Bach's music – to professionals of high standing, including Saxon Kapellmeisters J. C. Schmidt and Heinichen, and the Imperial Kapellmeister J. J. Fux. But it is elements of the letter of Christian Ritter, former Kapellmeister of the Royal Swedish Court, along with Mattheson's rejoinder to it, that were perhaps echoed most clearly in the Faber canon. In his letter Ritter wrote

---

[53] See George Stauffer, "Johann Mattheson and J. S. Bach: The Hamburg Connection," in *New Mattheson Studies*, ed. George J. Buelow and Hans Joachim Marx (Cambridge, 1983), 353–368, at p. 360.

[54] Braun, "Bach's Stellung in Kanonstreit." In printing the canon and its solution in *Der vollkommene Capellmeister*, Mattheson wryly noted that he didn't believe it was worth spending too much effort in studying such pieces. *Der vollkommene Capellmeister*, 412–413.

that the semitone (*mi fa*) is the quintessence of musica, and that "the *Musicus* who truly understands the sense of the *mi* and *fa*... is a true *FAmulus* and Servant of God and His Church, and a *MIrum quid* who knows the Son."⁵⁵ Mattheson discounted Ritter's play on words as a useless exercise, and flatly asserted that designating the semitone with *mi/fa* was confusing, worthless, even inane. Indeed, in the title page of *Das beschützte Orchestre*, Mattheson's initial refutation of Buttstett, the Hamburg critic had indulged in his own wordplay, distorting the phrase *tota musica* into "todte musice" (dead/killed music). Ritter's capitalization of the syllables FA and MI in this passage parallels Bach's orthographic play in the Faber canon which highlights these syllables in a similar way (Figure 2.2). Rather than pronouncing the venerable *mi fa* solmization pair dead, Bach forcefully resuscitates them, restoring their primacy as *tota musica*, and aligning himself with traditionalists such as Fux, Ritter, and Schmidt.

And what of the curious fact that the title of Bach's *Concordia discors* canon, BWV 1086 (Example 2.4) is an inversion of Mattheson's personal motto *Discordia concors*, which appears on the frontispiece of *Der vollkommene Capellmeister* (Figure 2.3)? The title of the canon refers to its use of contrary motion, and it is perhaps possible that the piece is in part Bach's musical commentary on contemporary critical conflicts, especially that concerning strict counterpoint in which Mattheson was the central figure. By adopting the contrapuntal technique of inversion Bach cleverly represents in musical form his grammatical inversion of the *Vollkommener Capellmeister* epigram. The canon's prevailing step-wise motion and simple, natural affect adopts Mattheson's own rules for melody making; eminently capable of tortured and dissonant writing, even in the highly structured framework of a canon, Bach goes out of his way in this piece to achieve complete harmoniousness in order, of course, to allegorize the consensus that can result even from voices seemingly working at cross purposes. If the Hudemann canon is Bach's contribution to "Die canonische Anatomie" then perhaps BWV 1086 is an ingenious appropriation of Mattheson's own rhetoric to respond to the Hamburg critic's often tendentious treatment of counterpoint. Of course it would be a mistake to construe the meaning of both the Faber and *Concordia discors* canons too narrowly as private responses to Mattheson; but in their appropriation of the specific language of ongoing aesthetic debates and their relevance to topics under critical consideration in the public arena, the Faber canon and *Concordia discors* tantalizingly imply Bach's awareness of these issues and his willingness to engage with them.

---

⁵⁵ Ritter in Mattheson, *Critica musica*, II, 257–259. Walter Schenkman, "Portrait of Mattheson, the Editor together with His Correspondents," *BACH* 9/4 (October 1978): 2–9, at pp. 2–4.

The alchemy of Bach's canons

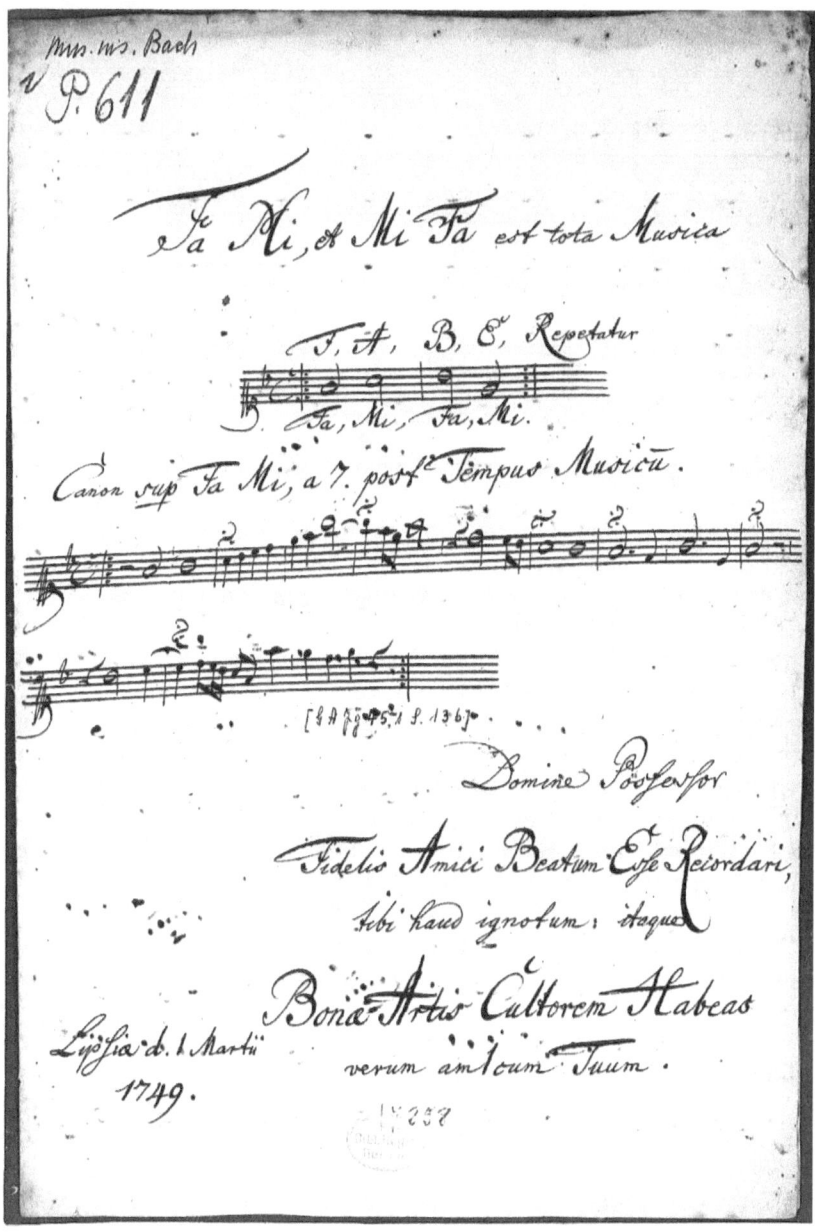

Figure 2.2 J. S. Bach, canon, *Fa Mi, et Mi Fa est tota Musica*, BWV 1078

Example 2.4 J. S. Bach, *Concordia discors* canon, BWV 1086

Bach's relation to hermeticism is even more difficult to judge. In 1741 he returned a number of canons with notes on their resolution to Johann Wilhelm Koch, Cantor in Ronnenburg, friend of the family and godfather to one of the Bach daughters. The accompanying letter written by Bach's nephew and then secretary, Johann Elias Bach, thanks Koch for sending the pieces and goes on to say that "There is no magic (*Hexerei*) involved here, as he [Bach] put it, and he has written a comment on the large ones."[56] It is unclear whether or not this constitutes an explicit rejection of the occultist trappings that had for so long accompanied the cultivation of canon, or whether it was simply a stock phrase to which Bach attached no particular meaning. In either case, the letter offers another instance of Bach's involvement in the private exchange of contrapuntal puzzles: his reputation had clearly been augmented by the wide circulation accorded his Hudemann canon, and his was now one of the most coveted opinions on matters of counterpoint.

Alchemy itself was of course widespread in Bach's time: from the Weimar *Kunst-Kämmerer* to Frederick the Great, "rationalists" and neoplatonists – a false dichotomy to be sure – were equally likely to be interested in reaping the rewards of discovering the philosopher's stone. Bach's student and ardent defender Lorenz Mizler was in many respects an archetypal Enlightened figure, who, for example, reprinted Euler's mathematical inquiries into perception in his journal, and, as we have seen, was skeptical of traditional beliefs about the heavenly concert. Yet Mizler himself had more than a passing interest in alchemy, and claimed to have once been in possession of many "chemical [i.e. alchemical] secrets" (*chymischen Geheimnissen*), one of which involved turning tin into silver through the utterance of certain magical sentences. After many unsuccessful attempts at effecting alchemical transformations,

---

[56] *NBR*, 210.

Figure 2.3 Title-page, Johann Mattheson, *Der vollkommene Capellmeister* (1739)

however, Mizler came to see the search for the philosopher's stone as futile and foolish.[57] But for many others alchemy remained a legitimate undertaking, and Walther's interest in the topic is not surprising at all, nor is the fact that other musicians such as Bokemeyer could have shared and encouraged such pursuits. Indeed, in 1723, the year that Bach took up his post at the Thomasschule, Joachim Boeldicke published his *Gründliche Anweisung zur Hermetischen Wissenschaft und Bereitung der Philosophischen Tinctur* in Leipzig, an unlikely attempt at a clear exposition of alchemical teachings.[58]

There is a good deal of evidence for Bach's own interest in precious metals and coins. His estate included an assortment of silver and gold coins and medals, and he added marks of emphasis in his Calov Bible to a description of precious stones listed in Exodus (28:20); in the margins of a later passage in Exodus concerned with the weights and values of metals used to construct objects in the Tabernacle, Bach wrote: "The sum of the freewill offering amounts to almost eight tons of gold."[59] He based this calculation on the conversions found in a volume in his library, Heinrich Bünting's *De monetis et mensuris sacrae scripturae*, first published in 1582 but reprinted as late as 1718. The book provided the equivalent contemporary values for biblical units of weight, measure, and money, and in the preface Bünting claimed that this information would be of particular interest to alchemists, among others, since they could then use them to derive the proper proportions of materials when referring to scripture.[60] Bach must, of course, have known something of the practice of alchemy, though one can hardly imagine him having had much time to spend exploring its principles. But given his interest in coins, precious metals, weights and measures, it would be surprising if he had not known and appreciated something of the alchemical arts. Whether Bach ever encountered the Weimar *Kunst-Kämmerer* himself or the alchemists and numismatists employed by Prince Anton Günther II during his employment in Arnstadt will probably never be known. Whatever the merits of speculating on Bach's propensity for alchemical thinking, my concern is less to establish his hermetic credentials than to examine the ways in which his canons, and strict counterpoint more generally, may have been viewed by contemporary musicians receptive to occultist thought. If Buttstett, Walther, and Bokemeyer – all of them prolific composers and devotees of learned counterpoint, who published

---

[57] Lorenz Mizler, *Neu eröffnete musikalische Bibliothek*, 4 vols. (Leipzig, 1739–54), I, part 4, 45; part 5, 77.

[58] Johann Boeldicke, *Gründliche Anweisung zur Hermetischen Wissenschaft und Bereitung der Philosophischen Tinctur* (Dresden and Leipzig, 1723).

[59] Leaver, *J. S. Bach and Scripture* (St. Louis, 1985), 75, 79.

[60] Bünting, *Itinerarium sacrae scripturae...mit einem Büchlein de monetis et mensuris*, 3rd edn. (Magdeburg, 1589), preface.

The alchemy of Bach's canons

on music theory and who harbored more than a passing interest in occult science – can be taken to represent a substantial segment of the music profession, then their views might help us consider anew some of the possible meanings Bach and his colleagues might have attached to strict counterpoint.

Henrich Bokemeyer, in his writings on music, often described canon and its companion, double counterpoint, using hermetic concepts and language. In 1722, probably the same year in which he wrote his first letter to Johann Mattheson in defense of canon, Bokemeyer added a title page and short preface to his personal copy of a treatise entitled *Gründlicher Unterricht von den gedoppelten Contrapuncten* by Johann Theile, the greatest counterpoint pedagogue of the generation before Bach and a musician who will figure prominently in my investigation into the connections between alchemy and canon. In his title page to Theile's treatise, Bokemeyer describes the hoarding of contrapuntal knowledge deplored by Mattheson and Heinichen:

This treatise (*Aufsatz*) on double counterpoint is to be treasured as more precious than a great deal of gold (*kostbarer als viel Gold zu schätzen*). Therefore one must not throw such things before swine so that the secrets of music become common and consequently a thing of disdain. But worthy enthusiasts are strengthened inexpensively, even free of charge (*ohne Entgeld*), thus satisfying their great curiosity to learn (*ihre große Lernbegierde*), and allowing them to strive for the peak of noble music.[61]

Bokemeyer's seemingly extravagant claim that these contrapuntal teachings should be more highly prized than precious metal, parallels and is informed by his desire as an alchemist to fabricate something more valuable than ordinary gold. Bokemeyer's preface reads like a gloss on a paradigmatic passage from the widely disseminated alchemy treatise *Splendor Solis*, surely known to Bokemeyer; the book was first published in 1598 and reappeared in a beautifully engraved Hamburg edition of 1708: "Hence it is clearly to be understood that the Gold of the Philosophers is something other than the common gold."[62]

Members of the contrapuntal fraternity boasted, of course, that they were not motivated by the prospect of financial success. Heinrich Buttstett described with some bitterness the tension between the intellectual demands of counterpoint and the monetary rewards of more popular and accessible music such as that championed by Mattheson: "Which

---

[61] Heinrich Bokemeyer, preface to Johann Theile, *Gründlicher Unterricht von den gedoppelten Contrapuncten*, Staatsbibliothek zu Berlin, Mus. ms. theor. 917, part I.
[62] [Salomon Trisomsin], "Splendor Solis," in *Aureum vellus oder Guldin Schatz und Kunstkammer*, 163–213, esp. 210; trans. Joscelyn Godwin, in *Magnum Opus Hermetic Sourceworks* 8 (Grand Rapids, 1981), 74.

musician devotes himself to double counterpoint...? Very few. Why? It is too difficult and does not pay. Therefore it happens that instead of the true essence (*Wesen*), one manages only with trinkets (*Galanterien*)."[63] In Bokemeyer's view the "secrets" of counterpoint, like the coveted precepts of alchemy, must be guarded by their committed practitioners seeking not financial gain, but the "philosophical," spiritual rewards more lasting than earthly riches. Nevertheless, Buttstett's actions were less high-minded than his public pronouncements; he had been one of Walther's teachers, and in one of his letters to Bokemeyer Walther described how Buttstett had forced him as a student to pay a total of twelve thalers – six up front – to see a particular treatise, none other than Johann Theile's *Unterricht von einigen gedoppelten Contrapuncten*. Lamenting the fact that no contract had been drawn up for this transaction, Walther recounts how Buttstett would stand over him and permit him to copy only a few lines of the book at a time. Frustrated by this arrangement, Walther eventually bribed Buttstett's son, who sneaked him the treatise, which Walther copied in its entirety in a single night.[64] Johann Valentin Meder – the Danzig Kapellmeister, one-time student of learned music, and dedicatee of a canon by Dieterich Buxtehude, also complained that contrapuntal study "doesn't put food on the table" (bringt kein Brodt), citing this as one of his reasons for having given up the discipline.[65] Beer used the same metaphor in arguing that brilliance in counterpoint would not bring financial gain to a composer since it rarely pleased the ear.[66]

In the same letter to Bokemeyer in which he detailed Buttstett's exploitative pedagogical methods, Walther noted that the extraordinary substances used to effect alchemical transformations could not be bought, and could only be fabricated by those with the requisite moral fortitude and expert knowledge; the "true philosophical material" (die wahre *materia philosophica*), like a work of double counterpoint, "is nowhere to be bought, but must first be prepared through artifice."[67] This "true philosophical material," the compound contrived by the alchemist and added to quantities of imperfect metals in order to transform them into gold, was the philosopher's stone. It was not a readily available physical substance that could be bought and sold, nor was its

---

[63] Buttstett, *Ut, mi, sol, re, fa, la tota musica et harmonia aeterna*, 9. "True essence" is also a stock alchemical phrase. For a typical passage that uses this language, see the well-known anonymous poem *De prima materia lapidis philosophorum* (On the Prime Matter of the Philosopher's Stone), in *Eröffnete Geheimnisse Des Steins der Weisen Oder Schatz-Kammer Der Alchymie* (Hamburg, 1718; reprint, Graz, 1976), 360–70, esp. 363.

[64] Walther to Bokemeyer October 3, 1729, in *Walther Briefe*, 65–83, esp. 68–69. See Schünemann, "J. Walther and H. Bokemeyer," 90.

[65] Mattheson, *Grundlage einer Ehren-Pforte* (Hamburg, 1740; reprint, Berlin, 1910), 219.

[66] Beer, *Musikalische Diskurse*, 96.

[67] Walther to Bokemeyer, October 3, 1729, in *Walther Briefe*, 77.

analogue, learned counterpoint, a common musical material that should be freely disseminated. While he was probably appalled at Buttstett's opportunistic dealings with the young Walther, Bokemeyer's concern for the close protection of contrapuntal secrets articulates a moral viewpoint found throughout the alchemical literature, here summarized by Carl Jung: "On the one hand the alchemist declares that he is concealing the truth intentionally, so as to prevent wicked or stupid people from gaining possession of the gold and thus precipitating a catastrophe. But, on the other hand, the same author will assure us that the gold he is seeking is not – as the stupid suppose – the ordinary gold, it is the philosophical gold."[68] Counterpoint, too, was powerful stuff and to be handled with care.

Many of Bokemeyer's arguments and analogies in "Die canonische Anatomie" have a thinly veiled hermetic subtext, and throughout the article Bokemeyer's interest in hermetic science comes clearly into relief, as when he describes the labors of the contrapuntist as he would an alchemist working in his laboratory. Referring to a metaphorical workshop of learned counterpoint, Bokemeyer writes that those who "have the luck to fabricate in this secret laboratory (*geheimes Kunst-Zimmer*) of *Minerva* [i.e. invention]" will, through the elaboration of canons, necessarily discover all the possible inversions allowed by these pieces and therefore gain a solid grounding in double counterpoint.[69] Fabrication (zimmern), *Kunst-Zimmer*, indeed a *"secret* laboratory," are taken directly from the alchemist's lexicon. Bokemeyer calls learned counterpoint "a secret art" (eine heimliche Kunst) – a pervasive reference to alchemy –[70] and refers to the contrapuntist as an *artifex*, the Latin word for alchemist; this is not just an "artist" but an artificer, one who works in the laboratory trying to fabricate gold.[71] His description of the untiring contrapuntist laboring in his isolated laboratory brings to mind an image from Heinrich Khunrath's *Amphitheatrum sapientiae* ... printed in 1604 (Figure 2.4). The task of alchemist and contrapuntist was a solitary one that required unfailing dedication; both disciplines demanded "unrelenting toil and diligence" on the part of the *artifex*.[72] Both arts relied on secrecy and required a profound technical knowledge of complex procedures in the search not only for physical results but also for spiritual advance.

These clear references to alchemy parallel more fundamental influences found throughout Bokemeyer's discussion, since his arguments

---

[68] C. G. Jung, *Psychology and Alchemy*, trans. R. F. C. Hull (London, 1953), 232.
[69] "Die canonische Anatomie," 351.
[70] Ibid., 316. For an example of references to alchemy as a secret art see "Liber secretorum Ioannis de Padua" in *Eröffnete Geheimnisse*, 376–447, at p. 409.
[71] Ibid., 301. For the use of the term *artifex*, see Jung, *Psychology and Alchemy*, 261.
[72] Johann Theile, *Musicalisches Kunstbuch*, Staatsbibliothek zu Berlin, Mus. ms. theor. 913, fol. 1r. "Vorrede," Valentinus, *Chymische Schriften*, unpaginated.

Figure 2.4 Alchemist in his laboratory with musical instruments, Heinrich Khunrath, *Amphitheatrum sapientiae aeternae solius verae, Christiano-kabalisticum, divino-magicum . . . tertriunum* (1609)

for canon derive from the hermetic view of art and *artifex*. According to Bokemeyer, the goal of the *artifex* was to master the most demanding and complex procedure – canon in the case of the contrapuntist and fabrication of the philosopher's stone in the case of alchemy. Bokemeyer asserted that fugue, imitation, and even modern concerted vocal music all derived ultimately from canon, and that without a knowledge of learned counterpoint one could not succeed in the more common, and practically important, genres of modern music; therefore "canons, from which these [other genres] flow, have the greatest use in music."[73] (Never mind that Bokemeyer had already established himself as a composer

---

[73] "Die canonische Anatomie," 240–241.

The alchemy of Bach's canons

before even embarking on the study of canon in his mid-twenties.) Here Bokemeyer was in agreement with the hermetic enthusiast Buttstett, who used alchemical language to describe learned counterpoint, finding in it the "true essence" of all other musical forms.

One of the most celebrated alchemical texts was the short exposition of principles known as the "Emerald Table" or *Tabula Smaragdina*, a list reprinted frequently in treatises, and known to all alchemists including Walther and Bokemeyer.[74] The second sentence of the table intimated, in the mystifying language of many hermetic texts, that all the forms of matter originated from one source: "As all things were by the contemplation of one, so all things arose from this one thing by a single act of adaptation."[75] This concept of interrelatedness, derived from the Aristotelian theory of matter, was the basis for the entire enterprise of alchemy. Aristotle argued that the most basic substance of the universe was the *prima materia*, which gained a real, material existence when it was "formed." This *prima materia* yielded the four Aristotelian elements of fire, air, water, and earth. Since all substances were composed of differing quantities of these four elements, the trick of alchemy was simply to change the proportions of a lower metal, for example lead, to accord with those of gold, thereby transforming the common into the precious. This was not simply a chemical reaction, but was possible because matter was itself alive, and given the proper impetus, could combine with itself, transmuting one substance into another. This transformation was effected by the philosopher's stone, which could be added to the base metals (the amount of metal that could be so changed varied in different accounts) in order to create gold.[76] Attending this theory of matter was the alchemical metaphor of the spring, which encapsulated the notion that all substances were born from a single, living source, and were thus united by their origins. In the treatise "Vom grossen Stein der uhralten Weisen" (On the Great Stone of the Ancient Philosophers) by the well-known author Basilius Valentinus, it is the spirit mercury whose penetrating power provides the active ingredient in alchemical transformations: "from the spirit of mercury all art flows and has its beginning."[77] In Bokemeyer's hierarchical view of music, all genres and techniques, from imitation and fugue to concertos, had the same

---

[74] Walther to Bokemeyer, October 3, 1729, in *Walther Briefe*, 77.
[75] *Eröffnete Geheimnisse*, 336. Translated in Eric Holmyard, *Alchemy* (Harmondsworth, 1957), 95.
[76] See Holmyard, *Alchemy*, 19–22. This theory of matter is articulated mainly in Aristotle's *De generatione et corruptione* and *Meteorologica*, Book 4. In many alchemical tracts the *materia prima* is equated with the philosopher's stone, as in the poem *de prima materia lapidis philosophorum* in *Eröffnete Geheimnisse*, 360–370. See also Jung, *Psychology and Alchemy*, 222, 273.
[77] Basilius Valentinus, "Vom grossen Stein der uhralten Weisen," in *Chymische Schrifften* (Hamburg, 1700), 243. Walther owned a copy of the work. See *Walther Briefe*, 77.

ultimate origin: "canons are the original source from which all these kinds of artistic work (*artificia*) flow."[78]

According to Bokemeyer even the most perfect melodies (the focus of Mattheson's aesthetic of naturalness) derived from this one true essence, and late in his dispute with Mattheson he introduced a new category, the *canon naturalis* which "flows directly from melody."[79] Bokemeyer argued that

> Natural canons have their primordial beauty (*ursprüngliche Schönheit*), and artificial canons flow immediately from this, as from their source... Indeed, simple, natural melody is the norm, for otherwise its beauty would have no basis.[80]

By deriving the *canon artificialis* from the *canon naturalis*, Bokemeyer attempted to link the most complex contrapuntal procedure with the most pleasing natural melody. And he went even further: "Thus no melody is to be valued as perfectly artful (*künstlich*), but that one which can yield an artificial canon."[81] In this curiously circular argument Bokemeyer asserted that the best canons derive from the most natural melodies, and the best melodies are those that can be molded into finely wrought canons. Just as alchemy required untainted raw materials, so too, in Bokemeyer's view, the fact that a melody could yield a canon proved its original purity. One could well hear in the sweet melodiousness of Bach's *Concordia discors* an evocation of the *canon naturalis*.

For Bokemeyer it was the *artifex*, mediator between the natural and the artificial, who could "find" the *canon naturalis* and from it produce the highest prize of musical erudition, the *canon artificialis*. The *artifex* uses his skill and knowledge of "the secret art" (die heimliche Kunst) of learned counterpoint to mold beautiful compositions from raw, undisturbed nature.[82] One of the basic tenets of alchemy was the notion that nature alone could not achieve perfection, that base metals could not be transformed into gold without the intervention of the alchemist, that "art is a helper (*gehilffin*) of nature."[83] The task of the *artifex* was to encourage nature in this path towards perfection; typical is the promise made by one hermetic treatise to show "how, through the help of art, nature is to be brought to perfection."[84] Without the skillful intervention of the *Künstler*, in music as in alchemy, nature remains an undifferentiated mass; following his alchemical model, Bokemeyer argued that "The perfection of nature would not be recognized were it not brought

---

[78] "Die canonische Anatomie," 329.
[79] Ibid., 290. Later in the article Mattheson dismisses the *canon naturalis* as a nonentity. Ibid., 336.
[80] Ibid., 315.   [81] Ibid., 337.   [82] Ibid., 316–317.
[83] *Eröffnete Geheimnisse*, 591.   [84] Ibid., 501.

to light by the investigations of art."[85] Incidentally, this view of art, artist, and nature was also held by Bach, in so far as the words of his defender J. A. Birnbaum can be taken as a reliable indication of them:

> Many things are delivered to us by nature in the most misshapen states, which however, acquire the most beautiful appearance when they have been formed by art. Thus art lends nature a beauty it lacks, and increases the beauty it possesses. Now, the greater the art is – that is, the more industriously and painstakingly it works at the improvement of nature – the more brilliantly shines the beauty thus brought into being.[86]

Likewise for Bokemeyer, the *Künstler* molds nature but he must remain true to it,[87] a view that informed much contemporary alchemical literature: "Art is and shall be a follower of nature, for no art is valid that does not have nature before it."[88]

Throughout "Die canonische Anatomie" Bokemeyer's account of the role of the artificer is virtually identical with that of the alchemist:

> so through the investigation of art, one discovers, by virtue of the accompanying understanding of the artist, the traces of Nature whereupon, she [Nature] rushes – by step not by leap – towards perfection.[89]

This is an apt description of one of the plates from *Atalanta fugiens* (1618), a collection of fifty musical canons on alchemical texts by the early seventeenth-century alchemist and composer Michael Maier (Figure 2.5).[90] The book appeared in a German edition entitled *Chymisches Cabinet*, published in Frankfurt in 1678, and may well have been owned by Bokemeyer. The engraving depicts Nature walking, not leaping, towards perfection, with the alchemist following behind carrying a lantern which shines with the metaphorical light of his understanding. The first part of Maier's motto echoes Bokemeyer's description of the contrapuntist (bottom of page 176): "Nature be your guide; whom you must follow from afar / Willingly, otherwise you err, where she does not lead you / Reason be your staff." The laws of nature applied equally to alchemy and counterpoint, and the role of the *artifex* in both secret disciplines was essentially homologous. Bokemeyer practiced learned counterpoint with the same set of assumptions he brought to his hermetic investigations, ever seeking the path towards perfection.

---

[85] "Die canonische Anatomie," 331. [86] *NBR*, 345.
[87] "Die canonische Anatomie," 332.
[88] *Eröffnete Geheimnisse*, 590.
[89] "Die canonische Anatomie," 331. See also Valentinus, *Chymische Schrifften*, part 2, 69.
[90] Michael Maier, *Atalanta fugiens* (Oppenheim, 1618); English edition translated and edited by Joscelyn Godwin in *Magnum Opus Hermetic Sourceworks* 22 (Grand Rapids, 1989). See also Christoph Meinel, "Alchemie und Musik," in *Die Alchemie in der europäischen Kultur- und Wissenschaftsgeschichte*, ed. Meinel (Wiesbaden, 1986), 201–227.

Figure 2.5　The *artifex* following Nature, Michael Maier, *Atalanta fugiens* (1618)

When Mattheson engaged Bokemeyer in "Die canonische Anatomie," the Hamburg critic would easily have guessed that his opponent's defense of canon was built on an elaborate, if concealed, web of occult ideas. Mattheson had been fighting against such beliefs for at least a decade. After Bokemeyer had conceded defeat, Mattheson demanded, in the final pages of the article, that all contrapuntists provide explanations for the metaphors of unity (canon as the peak, the source, and the fundament) which could withstand "the obvious truth" (die Sonnenklare Wahrheit) that the prevailing forms of musical expression were concerned more with melody than harmonic complexity. How is it, he demands to know, that canon can claim a "special influence" (Special-Influenz) or be considered the "quintessence" (Quint-Essenz) of composition? These can be read not only as direct references to Bokemeyer's arguments, but as questions concerning the hidden powers of complex music, powers which were elucidated in hermetic sources.

The network of beliefs that informed the alchemical and contrapuntal views articulated by Bokemeyer and were cherished by many of his contemporaries may well have been in Mattheson's mind when he chose for the article the title "Die canonische Anatomie." For readers of "Die canonische Anatomie" such as Bokemeyer, Buttstett, and other devotees of hermeticism, Mattheson's choice of the anatomical metaphor was significant; many of these men not only must have continued to believe in the magical, healing powers of music, but would have been familiar with hermetic medicine's strictures against dissection of the human body.[91] Furthermore, to imply, as the title "Die canonische Anatomie" seemed to do, that dissection could answer all the questions about the inner workings of music was to discount the relevance of the hidden effects of the stars, and, by inference, to challenge the notion that man was a microcosm of the universe. Another crucial effect of such an enterprise of demystification would be to disentangle the practice of counterpoint from the great web of resemblances which, as Bokemeyer wrote in "Die canonische Anatomie," allowed the infinite canon to serve as a metaphor for "the eternal harmony" of the cosmos.[92]

Bokemeyer's followers would have sensed that Mattheson's polemic was meant to be a kind of rational dissection of canon, a careful, well-lighted examination that would expose learned counterpoint's metaphysical underpinnings as a dangerous illusion. The Enlightened scientist would draw back the shroud of secrecy and cut into the corpse of canon, demystifying the strange creature once and for all. For the followers of the Paracelsian tradition dissection threatened to exclude the spiritual element from any viable investigation into the phenomenal world. Eighteenth-century devotees of hermetic science would have known that for "anatomists" such as Mattheson, occult explanations were inimical to truth; to embrace anatomy was to assume that no causes were hidden, and that the body, and by extension the universe, could be understood on a purely physical level, without the aid of magical insight.

By 1725 Bokemeyer had publicly renounced his claims for canon, though he continued to cultivate it along with its parallel discipline, alchemy, and was especially interested in one of the manuscripts in Walther's possession, Johann Theile's *Musicalisches Kunstbuch*. Born in 1646, Theile was one of the leading musicians of his day: a founding member and first Kapellmeister of the Hamburg opera, friend of Dieterich Buxtehude and Johann Adam Reincken, praised by Christoph

---

[91] Lois N. Magner, *A History of Medicine* (New York, 1992), 168. See also Walter Pagel, *Paracelsus* (Basel, 1958), 49. For Walther's citations of works by Paracelsus in letters to Bokemeyer see *Walther Briefe*, 77, 143.
[92] "Die canonische Anatomie," 342–343.

Bernhard, and for three generations the most famous German teacher of counterpoint, he was hailed as "the father of contrapuntists."[93] Walther's connection to Theile is almost one of apostolic succession, since, as he informed Bokemeyer in 1740, he owned Theile's copy of that bible of counterpoint, Zarlino's *Istitutioni harmoniche*. It is also possible that his copy of the *Kunstbuch* had come directly from Theile as well.[94]

Walther first mentioned his ownership of Theile's *Kunstbuch* to Bokemeyer in a letter of August 1731, which, incidentally, includes an extended discussion of alchemy.[95] Walther made a copy of the *Kunstbuch* and sent it to Bokemeyer in installments between 1735 and 1738, a period in which Bokemeyer was still troubled by his defeat in the pages of "Die canonische Anatomie." In 1737 Bokemeyer even added an annotation to the introduction to his personal copy (see above, p. 65) of Theile's *Gründlicher Unterricht von den gedoppelten Contrapuncten* renouncing his former views: "I proffered this altogether too severe view fifteen years ago, when I was prejudiced in favor of the harmonic art (*harmonische Kunst*)."[96] But despite this uncertainty tinged with shame, Bokemeyer was eager to augment his already substantial collection of counterpoint manuscripts. The same was apparently true of alchemy. Not long after Bokemeyer received the final installment of the *Kunstbuch*, Walther took a great deal of trouble making a copy of a nearly illegible hermetic manuscript, and then sent it to Bokemeyer because he believed it confirmed some of his friend's views on certain aspects of alchemical practice.[97]

When he received the *Kunstbuch* Bokemeyer had already made copies of three of Theile's other counterpoint treatises for his collection, and he had received two other manuscripts by Theile from his teacher Georg Österreich.[98] Österreich had studied with both Theile and Johann Philipp Förtsch, another leading contrapuntist and student of Theile, in Hamburg in the 1680s. In 1689 Österreich succeeded Förtsch as Kapellmeister in Gottorf and later took up Theile's former post in Wolfenbüttel. It was Österreich who gave Bokemeyer his first lessons in learned counterpoint in 1706; Bokemeyer was then twenty-seven, about the same age that Bach was when he seems to have begun his cultivation of canon in Weimar. (This represented a much later start in contrapuntal study than that of Mattheson, who began this work at

---

[93] Jakob Adlung, *Anleitung zu der musikalischen Gelahrtheit* (Erfurt, 1758; reprint, Kassel, 1953), 184. Mattheson, *Critica musica* II, 82–83.
[94] Walther to Bokemeyer, August 6, 1740, in *Walther Briefe*, 229.
[95] Walter to Bokemeyer, August 3, 1731, in *Walther Briefe*, 138–148.
[96] Heinrich Bokemeyer, introduction to Johann Theile, *Gründlicher Unterricht...*, title-page.
[97] Walther to Bokemeyer, August 6, 1740, in *Walther Briefe*, 229.
[98] Kümmerling, *Katalog der Sammlung Bokemeyer*, 11–12.

the age of ten.) After 1720, Bokemeyer and Österreich were colleagues in Wolfenbüttel where the younger man bought his teacher's extensive collection of theoretical works and concerted music. Bokemeyer would have been delighted to receive from Walther two precious works he had not inherited through the more direct teacher–student lineage that led directly back to Theile. In 1723, the year of "Die canonische Anatomie," Mattheson noted that "many of his [Theile's] teachings are also circulating in manuscript,"[99] and copies of his treatises continued to be made through the middle of the eighteenth century.[100] Theile's fame as a master of counterpoint spread across Germany: far to the east, the Königsberg Kapellmeister Johann Valentin Meder, who had probably met Theile when on a trip to Lübeck to visit Buxtehude in 1674, praised the great contrapuntist in a letter of 1708;[101] Theile also sent his music as far south as Vienna for the edification of Emperor Leopold I, himself an enthusiast of learned music.[102]

Although it has been compared with Bach's *Musical Offering* and the *Art of Fugue*,[103] Theile's *Musicalisches Kunstbuch* is not a unified set of pieces but rather consists of miscellaneous compositions probably dating from the 1670s and 80s.[104] The collection is made up of fifteen pieces of varying lengths and styles, including short canons, several pieces entitled aria (without words), dance suites, mass movements in vocal polyphony, and three sonatas unified only by their use of double counterpoint. The *Kunstbuch* stands as Theile's greatest effort in composing pieces based on the secret precepts of learned counterpoint.

With its very title, Theile explicitly linked the collection to alchemy. A *Kunstbuch* was often defined specifically as a book of hermetic knowledge or magic: "Diocletian burned all magic books (*Kunstbücher*) he found in Egypt so the Egyptians could not make gold."[105] A Leipzig dictionary of 1711 defines *Kunstbuch* as a book of magic, a *livre de*

---

[99] "Die canonische Anatomie," 353.
[100] At least one copy of Theile's *Musicalisches Kunstbuch* (Staatsbibliothek zu Berlin, Am.B. 451) was made in the middle of the eighteenth century.
[101] Mattheson, *Grundlage einer Ehren-Pforte*, 220.
[102] Mattheson, *Critica musica* II, 57.
[103] Carl Dahlhaus, "Einleitung," to Johann Theile, *Musicalisches Kunstbuch*, Denkmäler norddeutscher Musik 1 (Kassel, 1965), vii.
[104] The mass movements, for example, were probably taken from a printed collection of contrapuntal pieces, the now-lost *Noviter inventum Opus musicalis Compositionis 4 & 5 vocum* (1686). This work is listed in J. G. Walther, *Musicalisches Lexicon* (Leipzig, 1732; reprint, Kassel, 1953), 603. See also Dahlhaus, "Einleitung," to Theile, *Musicalisches Kunstbuch*, viii.
[105] Georg Rollenhagen, *Froschmeuseler: Der Frosch und Meuse wunderbahre Hoffhaltunge* (Magdeburg, 1618), [nij]. The book was reprinted numerous times in the seventeenth century. See also Jacob and Wilhelm Grimm, *Deutsches Wörterbuch*, 33 vols. (Leipzig, 1854–1971; reprint, Munich, 1984), V, col. 2687. For an eighteenth-century reference to the *Kunstbücher* of the Egyptians see [Christian Liebezeit], "Vorrede," *Aureum vellus, oder Guldin Schatz und Kunstkammer*; reprinted in *Eröffnete Geheimnisse*, 588.

secrets.¹⁰⁶ So too, Theile's title-page introduces a book of precious and powerful knowledge: "Musical *Kunstbuch*, in which fifteen *Kunst* pieces and secrets, which spring from double counterpoint, are to be met."¹⁰⁷ The language and imagery are common to alchemy: in the book the contrapuntal *artifex* learns of the secrets that can be used to contrive strange and wonderful artifacts. In the copy of the *Kunstbuch* that he sent to Bokemeyer, Walther referred to double counterpoint as "the highest art and ornament of composition" (die höchste Kunst und Zierlichkeit der Composition), a paraphrase of Zarlino, but, as we have seen, not without alchemical resonance when used by Bokemeyer and Walther.¹⁰⁸ On opening the *Musicalisches Kunstbuch* the contrapuntal *artifex* entered a secret, magical world.

Theile provides each of the pieces in the *Kunstbuch* with a rhyming motto that has the character of a magical incantation. Many alchemical tracts were written in verse, and the combination of emblems (graphic depictions of allegorical figures and processes) and rhyming mottoes is found throughout the hermetic literature; as is the case in these treatises, each piece in Theile's *Kunstbuch* provides a "musical emblem" demonstrating a particular "secret" of the discipline, and Theile's rhymes provide epigrammatic commentary on them. In *Atalanta fugiens*, a work Theile could also have known, particularly in its 1678 German translation, Maier provided rhyming mottoes that comment on the allegorical depictions of alchemy, both visual (the engravings) and musical (the canons).

Theile's mottoes also appropriate hermetic language. Alchemy was concerned with the "transformation of metals" (Verwandelung der Metallen);¹⁰⁹ *verwandeln* (to transform) was the most common verb used to refer to the alchemical change in German treatises. *Verwandeln* is used twice in the *Kunstbuch* to describe the process of rearranging the voices of a piece, following the precepts of invertible counterpoint, in order to produce another composition.¹¹⁰ In the tenth piece, for example, a suite of four movements, Theile writes that only the clever *artifex* can discover a second piece hidden within:

---

¹⁰⁶ Johann Rädlein, *Europäischer Sprach-Schatz...oder Wörter-Buch* (Leipzig, 1711; 2nd edn., 1719), 572. The same dictionary bears out the link between *Kunst* and alchemy: "artifice can transform (*verwandeln*) lead into gold."
¹⁰⁷ Johann Theile, *Musicalisches Kunstbuch*, fol. 1r. See also Dahlhaus, "Kritischer Bericht," 131. In other treatises as well, Theile encouraged the notion that the contrapuntist's art depended on secret, magical concepts; in the introduction to his *Curieuser Unterricht von denen doppelten Contrapuncten* (Staatsbibliothek zu Berlin, Mus. ms. theor. 916), Theile describes the contents as the "never before known secrets of the art (*niemals bekanten Kunstgriffe*)."
¹⁰⁸ Theile, *Musicalisches Kunstbuch*, fol. 1r.
¹⁰⁹ "Vorrede" to Valentinus, *Chymische Schrifften*, unpaginated.
¹¹⁰ Theile, *Musicalisches Kunstbuch*, ed. Dahlhaus, 76, 104.

Diese alle lassen sich noch einmal verwandeln, man muss aber auch dabei klüglich damit handeln.	All of these can be transformed once more, but one must also proceed very cleverly with them.

No one has yet found the solution to this particular puzzle.[111]

The riddle for the fourth piece of the collection, a suite consisting of a praeludium and five dances in which the staff for the bass line is empty, outlines a similar process of discovery. Only a sufficiently intelligent student, equipped with the requisite knowledge of the secrets of learned counterpoint will be able to find the solution:

Der Baß hat sich hierinnen wo verstecket, ein Kluger aber solchen bald entdecket.[112]	The bass has hidden himself somewhere within, But a clever person will soon enough discover it.

In his copy of the piece (Figure 2.6), Walther did not fill in the bass part. But the enterprising *artifex* will, after some study, recognize that the soprano line of Theile's *Praeludium* divides into two eleven-bar units which are, in fact, harmonically invertible with each other at the twelfth: the soprano from mm. 11 to 22 is taken down two octaves and becomes the bass line for the first half of the piece; transposed down an octave-and-a-half, the soprano line from mm. 1 to 11 provides the bass for the second half of the piece (Example 2.5). (To conclude the piece Theile appends a plagal cadence, which is non-invertible and therefore outside the parameters of the puzzle.)

Like the alchemist, the contrapuntal *artifex* hunts for properties intrinsic to the raw materials at hand, as in the rhyme to the ninth piece:

Ob ich gleich steh' nur einmal hier, so komm ich doch zweimal herfür. Wer finden kann, was steckt in mir?[113]	Although there is but one of me here, I appear two times. Who can find what is hidden in me?

The musical content of the seventh piece, a five-bar double counterpoint, perhaps bears the most striking similarities to alchemy. Once the alchemist had fabricated the philosopher's stone, he could add this to much larger quantities of base metals and convert them into gold. In the rubric to no. 7 Theile alludes to the magical properties of double counterpoint; with sufficient diligence the *artifex* can fabricate a single counterpoint which can then be expanded into endless riches: "This completely simple song / yields of itself many a tone and sound."[114]

---

[111] Dahlhaus, "Kritischer Bericht," 134. [112] Ibid., 25.

[113] Ibid., 75. Like no. 10 from the *Kunstbuch*, the contrapuntal problem of no. 9 remains unclear.

[114] "Dieser ganz einfältige Gesang / gibt von sich vielen Ton und Klang." Theile, *Musicalisches Kunstbuch*, ed. Dahlhaus, 35.

Figure 2.6   Johann Theile, *Musicalisches Kunstbuch*, no. 4 (copy by J. G. Walther)

Theile constructed the piece so that it could be inverted at the octave and tenth, and allow for melodic inversion, retrograde, and retrograde inversion (Example 2.6). Thus, the initial counterpoint yields innumerable transformations. Once the *artifex* successfully contrives a pure contrapuntal nugget such as this it brings forth, almost magically, prodigious quantities of valuable material. Walther's copy of the *Kunstbuch* includes a great many of the possible permutations of the five-measure double counterpoint, including thirty-two of the possible two-voice melodic inversions and retrogrades. Through the addition of one or two voices in parallel thirds above and below both voices, a procedure described by Bernhard in the *Tractatus compositionis augmentatus*,[115] the two-part counterpoint can be expanded into numerous *Tricinia* and *Quatricinia* which also work in retrograde and are subjected to the same procedures of melodic and harmonic inversion that Theile had applied

[115] Müller-Blattau, *Die Kompositionslehre Heinrich Schützens*, 123.

Example 2.5 Johann Theile, *Musicalisches Kunstbuch*, no. 4, solution

to the original two-part piece. Walther also wrote out no fewer than sixty-eight *Tricinia* and fifty-six *Quatricinia* derived from Theile's short piece of counterpoint (Example 2.7);[116] the permutations from this single five-measure exercise along with their inversions take up a quarter of the manuscript, and their inclusion represents the kind of extended enumeration of combinatorial possibilities taken to an even greater extreme by Graupner in his canonic research. In both the Theile and Graupner counterpoints, the original two-part piece is a sort of "philosopher's

[116] Ibid., 35–38.

Example 2.5 (cont.)

counterpoint" that can be transformed and added to other elements to produce seemingly endless quantities of new contrapuntal material.

At the close of the *Kunstbuch* Theile demonstrated that the different inversions of a contrapuntal matrix of three or more voices – expanded versions of the pure "contrapuntal stone" of no. 7 – could be linked together to form lengthy, independent compositions such as the three fugal sonatas (nos. 13 through 15) that conclude the collection.[117] This orderly succession of contrapuntal combinations is called a permutation

---

[117] Theile's own regard for these pieces is suggested by the fact that he sent the final sonata – and perhaps no. 14 as well – to Johann Mattheson in 1718. Theile to Mattheson, January 1718, printed in Mattheson, *Critica musica* II, 282–283.

The alchemy of Bach's canons

Example 2.6 Johann Theile, *Musicalisches Kunstbuch*, no. 7, selections

fugue, a technique which Theile apparently invented.[118] Just as the controlling assumption of alchemy was that it was possible to bring about the transmutation of substances, particularly lead into gold, so too the

---

[118] Paul Walker, *Theories of Fugue from the Age of Josquin to the Age of Bach* (Rochester, 2000), 234. See also Carl Dahlhaus, "Zur Geschichte der Permutationsfuge," *Bach-Jahrbuch* 46 (1959): 95–110.

Example 2.7   Johann Theile, *Musicalisches Kunstbuch*, no. 7, first *Tricinium* and first *Quatricinium*

Example 2.8   J. S. Bach, *Canon a 2*, BWV 1075

fundamental property of double counterpoint was its transformative power; even the simplest of pieces could yield a seemingly endless number of permutations.

In his *Canon a 2 perpetuus*, BWV 1075 (Example 2.8), Bach demonstrates, though far less expansively, the same ingenious transformation of small units into larger ones. Like the five-bar *Kunstbuch* counterpoint,

Example 2.9 BWV 1075 "theme" and "counterpoint"

Bach's canon spins itself out almost magically, though it is a magic made possible by a deep understanding of the principles of contrapuntal combination. The most plausible dedicatee is Johann Gottfried Walther junior, Bach's godchild; the autograph is dated January 1734, that is, just before Walther sent the first solution of the Hudemann canon to Bokemeyer. On looking at and singing through BWV 1075 one can see and hear that the second half of the little piece (the last four measures) repeats the first four measures, but in melodic inversion. How would one go about discovering an ingenious configuration that allows a single line to circle back on its own inversion so perfectly? The procedure is quite simple, though the fact that the melody is so charmingly tuneful in both *rectus* and *inversus* forms speaks to the skill with which Bach has applied these rules, and perhaps also illustrates the natural purity of the melody – or so Bokemeyer might have claimed. The canon can be thought of – and was surely fabricated by Bach – as a single two-measure counterpoint whose two parts I will arbitrarily designate as the subject and its counterpoint (Example 2.9). What this scheme illustrates of course is that the original form is, like Theile's four-measure counterpoint, devoid of dissonance, the prime condition (though by no means the only one) which must be met if the subject is to be combined with the counterpoint in its *rectus* and *inversus* forms, and likewise, if the counterpoint is to be combined with the subject in the same manner. The eight-measure canon is simply a horizontal stringing together of the four permutations inherent in the basic two-bar unit, which when properly fashioned, brings forth a seamless entity that elegantly entwines around itself. The basic material yields the larger infinite canon – yet another example of the *canon naturalis*. A small unit distilled from nature expands towards perfection.

Two of the five surviving copies of the *Musicalisches Kunstbuch*, both of which date from the middle part of the eighteenth century,[119] open with Theile's ten-part canon entitled the *Harmonischer Baum*, a piece which suggests further links with alchemy. The canon is presented in the form

[119] Staatsbibliothek zu Berlin, Am. B. 511/1 and 452.

of a tree with ten branches; the music on the trunk and roots make up a separate canon (Figure 2.7).[120] Theile's tree is similar to representations of the *arbor philosophica*, the symbol of hermetic philosophy (Figure 2.8).[121] Uses of this arboreal metaphor abound in the alchemical literature, as in the passage from an English edition of Paracelsus' *Of the Nature of Things*:

> It is possible also that Gold, through industry and skill of an expert Alchymist, may bee so far exalted, that it may grow in a glass like a tree, with many wonderful boughs, and leaves, which is indeed pleasant to behold, and most wonderfull.[122]

Like the pieces in the *Kunstbuch* – and those in Maier's *Atalanta fugiens* – Theile provides his *Harmonischer Baum* with a rhyme, which is written just below the ten-part canon: "Love you most beloved pair / so that as many children encircle you / as there are branches on the tree" (Liebet so ihr liebstern Beyde / daß ihr einst mit tausend Freude / Kinder sehet um euch gehen / so viel Zweig um Baume stehen). Marriage is a central metaphor in the discourse of alchemy, and the joining of husband and wife commonly represented the joining of elements in alchemical reactions. The product of this fruitful union is a child, and the married couple remain "in the marriage bed of warmth until the perfect birth" (im Ehebett der Wärme bis zu der vollkommenen Geburt) of the philosopher's stone.[123] Erich Schenk, who produced the first solution for the canon, suggested that the *Harmonischer Baum* was a commemorative piece for a wedding.[124] Even if Theile intended only the literal meaning of the text, it is hard to imagine that musician / alchemists such as Bokemeyer and Walther would not have seen the *Harmonischer Baum* as a musical and graphic allegory of alchemy, especially when such a symbolic canon opened a collection provided with the title *Musicalisches Kunstbuch*, Book of Musical Alchemy. It seems completely plausible that this is how Bach would have understood the title if he studied the book in Weimar, discovering for the first time many of the peculiar forms

---

[120] The piece is discussed, and its solution printed, in Erich Schenk, "Johann Theiles 'Harmonischer Baum'" in *Musik und Bild*, ed. Heinrich Besseler (Kassel, 1938), 95–100. Schenk was able to find a four-part solution of the base of the tree, but not one of six parts. Neither Walther's copy of the *Kunstbuch* nor the one he sent to Bokemeyer contains the *Harmonischer Baum*. The other sources of the *Kunstbuch* are listed in Dahlhaus, "Kritischer Bericht," to Theile, *Musicalisches Kunstbuch*, 132.

[121] For other representations of the *arbor philosophica* see Jung, *Psychology and Alchemy*, 229, 338, 390.

[122] Paracelsus, *Of the Nature of Things* (London, 1650), quoted in C. A. Burland, *The Arts of the Alchemists* (New York, 1968), 183.

[123] Valentinus, "Vom grossen Stein der uhralten Weisen," *Chymische Schrifften*, part 1, 73.

[124] Schenk, "Johann Theiles 'Harmonischer Baum.'"

The alchemy of Bach's canons

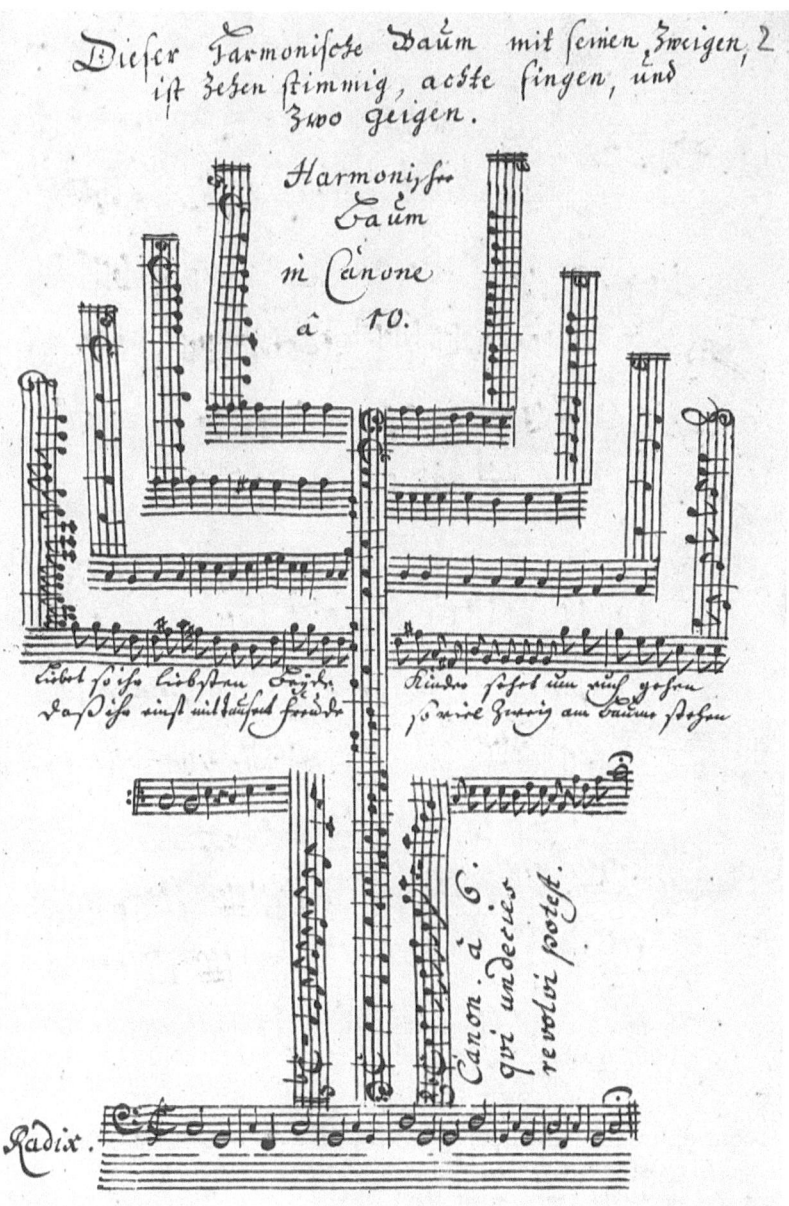

Figure 2.7   Johann Theile, *Harmonischer Baum*

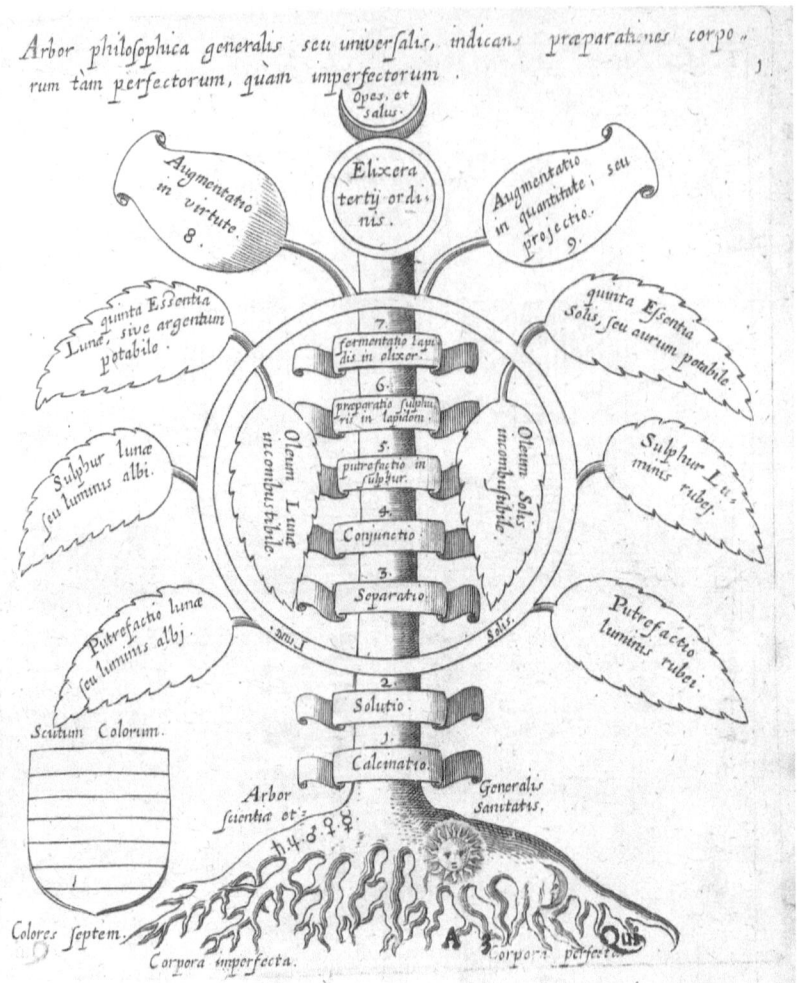

Figure 2.8 *Arbor philosophica*, Samuel Norton, *Mercurius redivivus* (1630); reprinted in Vigilantius, *Dreyfaches Hermetisches Kleeblatt* (1667)

of contrapuntal magic contained within. Bach would have known that in Theile's most famous collection, the "father of contrapuntists" presents himself as musical alchemist.

It comes as no surprise, in light of his contempt for antiquated modes of thought, that Mattheson did not deign to give Bokemeyer a place among the biographical sketches of great German musicians published in his *Grundlage einer Ehren-Pforte*, only noting, under another man's entry, that Bokemeyer "still lives in Wolfenbüttel, where he capably discharges his functions as cantor."[125] However, a year after Walther sent him the Hudemann canon's solution, Bokemeyer was to be honored for his musical erudition and contrapuntal knowledge, becoming the fourth member of Lorenz Mizler's "Corresponding Society of the Musical Sciences" (Correspondirende Societät der Musikalischen Wissenschaften). Eight years later the group would be joined by Mizler's teacher, J. S. Bach. For his election into the society Bach submitted the *Canonic Variations* on *Vom Himmel hoch da komm ich her* (BWV 769), and distributed to the other members an off-print of the six-part canon he is seen holding in the famous 1746 portrait by Elias Gottlob Haußmann.

As a member of the Society Bokemeyer would have been in a good position to become acquainted with Bach's *Canonic Variations*, and he would surely have been delighted that the collection could be seen – and heard, for this was crucial in answering aspersions that counterpoint was merely "Augenmusik"– to exemplify his assertion that even the most *galant* of idioms derived from, or at least could be based on, canon. The flowing canons of the first two variations might also be heard to evoke Bokemeyer's *canonis naturalis*, while the third variation,[126] whose modishly ornamented *cantabile* line sings above a foundation of canonic voices, brings to mind Bokemeyer's belief that the most expressive and natural melodies are guided by canon (Example 2.10). A quarter century after "Die canonische Anatomie," Bokemeyer might still have seen Bach's *Canonic Variations* as a demonstration that canon was the starting point in a chain of resemblance connecting all genres.[127]

Whether or not Bokemeyer actually saw Bach's *Canonic Variations*, he would certainly have received the six-part canon (BWV 1076) in the circulating packet that Mizler sent around to members at the time of Bach's induction into the Society, and he would have had the chance to inspect the piece at leisure, now afforded the opportunity to indulge his interest in the intricacies of learned counterpoint with the approval of a learned group of musicians. In fact, the six-part canon (BWV 1076) comes from a larger set of fourteen canons which Bach appended to his personal exemplar of the Goldberg Variations (BWV 1087). That two of the fourteen (including BWV 1076) were known previously in individual copies (the other one, BWV 1077, was dedicated to J. G. Fulde) again illustrates Bach's practice of drawing on his collected canons for

---

[125] Mattheson, *Grundlage einer Ehren-Pforte*, 168.
[126] This numbering of the individual variations follows that of the printed version, BWV 769, rather than that of the autograph, BWV 769a. I discuss the *Canonic Variations* at greater length in Chapter 3.
[127] F. W. Marpurg, *Abhandlung von der Fuge*, 2 vols. (Berlin, 1753–54; reprint, Hildesheim, 1970), II, 30–31.

Example 2.10 J. S. Bach, *Canonic Variations*, BWV 1079, movement 3, mm. 1–4

various occasions, as tributes to friends and colleagues. Based on the first eight notes of the Goldberg Variations bass line, the fourteen personal canons progress from the simple configurations of the opening number to the staggering complexity of the last, a quadruple augmentation canon (Example 2.11). This series of investigations into the prosaic eight-note figure, a soggetto dating back at least to the early seventeenth century, draws out an astounding array of combinatorial possibilities which are, of course, inherent in the material itself. The scholarly research into these possibilities demonstrates again that the most basic melody can yield tremendous contrapuntal riches when it is labored over by an *artifex* of Bach's skill and moral rectitude. Progressing from simple combination to tremendous intricacy, Bach demonstrates by increment the underlying interrelatedness of all these contrapuntal elaborations, and the fundamental role of the *artifex* in leading nature – the raw material that is the eight-note bass line – towards perfection. That Bach wrote "etc." at the conclusion of the fourteenth canon implies his belief in the limitless potential of even the most common of musical materials, materials whose richness was to be unlocked though never depleted through

Example 2.11   J. S. Bach, "Goldberg" canons, BWV 1087/1 and 1087/14

untiring labor.[128] As the Hudemann canon also demonstrated with such sublime reticence, the seemingly simple, but in fact highly skilled act of arranging the building blocks of music in the proper proportion and configuration could result in a kind of magical expansion of the natural material. By activating musical substances in this way canon came to life.

It is on this basic level that the principles of alchemy might be brought to bear on Bach's contrapuntal music. Leibniz and Newton had turned

---

[128] Christoph Wolff, *J. S. Bach: Essays on his Life and Works* (Cambridge, Mass., 1991), 176.

to Renaissance occultism and undertaken their alchemical investigations in part as a response to the mechanical philosophy of Descartes, which threatened to endorse atheism in that it removed God's continuing agency from the physical world, and therefore his control over the forms and interactions of matter. If successful alchemical transmutations could be achieved, however, they would demonstrate that matter itself was imbued with what Newton called a "vegetable [i.e., living] spirit." Only the talented and righteous contrapuntal artificer could fabricate a powerful and active subject – the analogy to the philosopher's stone again presents itself – which could be used to create vast musical treasures: the greatest composers were those most adept at fashioning musical material that revealed God's agency in the world. Magically, the simple D minor subject of the *Art of Fugue* could yield innumerable fugues and canons in a multitude of genres, and could mingle with numerous countersubjects; for alchemist/contrapuntists such as Bokemeyer, these miraculous combinations could be proof that God's living spirit was present at the most basic level of musical creation.

In 1722, when Bokemeyer was writing his letter in defense of canon, the scientific periodical *Parnassus Boicus* began publication in Munich. In its empirical approach, with an emphasis on verifiability, the journal is an important early document of scientific methods in Germany.[129] A year after Bokemeyer's defeat in "Die canonische Anatomie" an article appeared in *Parnassus Boicus* claiming to give "Fundamental proof, that it is impossible to make gold" (Gründlicher Beweiß / daß es unmöglich seye / Gold zu machen).[130] Alchemy continued to enjoy wide acceptance, however, through the remainder of the first half of the eighteenth century; both the 1732 and 1744 editions of the preeminent German scientific compendium, Zedler's *Universallexikon aller Wissenschaften und Künste*, sanctioned the validity of the hermetic project;[131] and as we have seen hermetic tracts were still appearing in Leipzig during Bach's lifetime. But the articles in *Parnassus Boicus* marked the beginning of the end for alchemy as an accepted practice, calling as they did for a rigorous, scientific examination of hermetic principles. Such investigations would expose the quasi-secret, cherished principles of alchemy as fraudulent, robbing the discipline of its mystique.

Likewise Matthenson and Heinichen called for the rational codification of principles of counterpoint in order to demystify its closely guarded precepts. The mid eighteenth-century advocate of counterpoint

---

[129] Herwig Buntz, "Alchemie und Aufklärung: Die Diskussion in der Zeitschrift Parnassus Boicus (1722–1740)," in *Die Alchemie in der europäischen Kultur- und Wissenschaftsgeschichte*, ed. Christoph Meinel (Wiesbaden, 1986), 327–338.
[130] *Parnassus Boicus, oder: Neu-eröffneter Mosen-Berg* 3 (Munich, 1725), 149–158, 221–225.
[131] Buntz, "Alchemie und Aufklärung," 337.

and fervent Bach supporter F. W. Marpurg answered their call, codifying the procedures of learned counterpoint in his *Abhandlung von der Fuge* (1753–54). In his treatise Marpurg looks back on the cult of counterpoint like a scientist regarding the irrational ways of a strange mystical group of musicians, through generations sworn to a conspiracy of silence. Of a contrapuntal composition which could be inverted in each of the three types of double counterpoint (at the octave, tenth, twelfth), but could also be performed in contrary motion, in retrograde, and in retrograde contrary motion, Marpurg writes:

> One reads not only in Mr. Capellmeister Heinichen that the musicians of old must have considered this kind of piece the greatest secret in music, but one can also come to this conclusion because the topic was only passed on through oral tradition, and was without doubt thought of as being as valuable as gold. No one trusted himself to write a word of it, until it gradually disappeared completely.[132]

The piece he is describing is, of course, very much like the five-measure counterpoint from Theile's *Kunstbuch* (Example 2.6),[133] a collection Marpurg knew. Because the knowledge of how to create such a piece had, according to Marpurg, vanished with the secret "cult" itself, Marpurg brings the skills of the rational investigator to bear on this lost art; he describes and explains the peculiarities of this contrapuntal tour-de-force and provides his own example, rescuing the secret and telling it to the world.

The program to debunk counterpoint urged on by Mattheson and Heinichen and executed by Marpurg and others had started from the premise that the nature of music, even learned counterpoint, was ultimately knowable and explicable, that obscure mysticism and secret practices should be exposed to the unforgiving light of rational investigation for the general enlightenment of what they called the musical republic. But contrapuntists in the tradition that extended from Theile to Bokemeyer saw counterpoint as possessed of magical properties that would always remain unknowable and would attract musicians in an atmosphere of awe and fascination. As Theile's student and colleague Johann Philipp Förtsch put it in his *Musicalischer Compositions Tractat*, a treatise later owned by Bokemeyer: "The unfathomable nature (*Unergründlichkeit*) of music is certainly to be perceived in [canon and double counterpoint] more than in other pieces of music."[134]

---

[132] Marpurg, *Abhandlung von der Fuge* II, 45–46. Heinichen mentions this procedure in *Der General-Bass in der Composition*, 936.

[133] The only requirement Theile's piece does not satisfy is that it is not invertible at the twelfth.

[134] Johann Philipp Förtsch, *Musicalischer Compositions Tractat*, Staatsbibliothek zu Berlin, Mus. ms. theor. 300, fol. 33r.

Encyclopedists of double counterpoint and canon, such as Marpurg, could codify the precepts of a once secret art, but they could never explain its mysterious magical properties. Bach's position in and influence on this transformation is complex, conflicted, and perhaps contradictory. While I have tried to suggest some possible ways in which his music might have been interpreted and understood according to hermetic principles, I would not want to minimize the rationalistic impulses evident in so much of his work. Rather, it seems more likely that like Walther, Bokemeyer, and others, scientific, theological, and occult tendencies all influenced his conception of learned counterpoint's significance. By contrast, the later eighteenth-century devotees of learned music, all of them followers of Bach, dealt largely with mechanics and rules rather than with the associated meanings and mysteries which had been an intrinsic part of the discipline for preceding generations fascinated by this "highest and most beautiful art." In the aftermath of this important shift, Bach's contrapuntal work has been seen primarily as a rationalistic project concerned with comprehensiveness and categorization – fugues in all keys, canons of a multitude of types. But this view of Bach's learned music perhaps reveals more about subsequent ideologies of scientific progress than about the many layers of meaning that surrounded the contrapuntal arts during his lifetime and which gave them their unknowable allure.

3

Bach's taste for pork or canary

"What would music be without other literature?" Johann Mattheson once asked. His response to this rhetorical question grandly claimed for music a place at the center of humanistic study: "Exactly what the other branches of learning would be without music."[1] Here, from a man whose enviable education had included not only music but modern and ancient languages, history, literature, drawing, fencing, riding, and dancing, was a manifesto for a broad and integrated approach to musical practice, aesthetics, and criticism. But however liberating this expansive conception of musical thought may have been for some, to others it was deeply threatening, for one of the most important consequences of this inclusive formulation was a challenge to the traditional autonomy of professional musicians: they would now have to know about more than their craft alone. No longer would musical competence, not to mention excellence, be measured purely by one's command of the requisite musical tools. The musician would now have to be a discerning thinker as well.

Along with the enlightened impulse underlying Mattheson's claim came a distrust of arcane knowledge such as mathematical speculation, Neoplatonic interpretation of musical phenomena, and intricate contrapuntal procedures – topics which were understood primarily by experts. The new musical knowledge would have to be useful and the music written according to its precepts should be understandable and engaging, just as the new discourse of music criticism should be opinionated, discriminating, and intellectually accessible. Mattheson's first book on music, *Das neu-eröffnete Orchestre*, had not only attacked occult

---

[1] Johann Mattheson, *Behauptung der himmlischen Musik* (Hamburg, 1747), introduction, unpaginated.

and obscurantist thinking; the volume's instructive purpose had been far more broad, intended as it was to explain "How a gentleman (*galant homme*) may acquire a perfect understanding of the loftiness and dignity of noble music, form his taste accordingly, and understand the terminology, and argue skillfully about this excellent science."[2] After completing the course of study provided by Mattheson's book, the *galant homme* would be capable of informed judgments, and, in emulation of the author, be more than willing to offer them, though never in a rude or boring manner. This was a listener – to be sure an opera-goer but also someone whose critical faculties were ready to be engaged while listening to music in the church and in the chamber – who could discuss and criticize intelligently, who would challenge where necessary but rarely offend. (Never mind that this last ethical standard was one that Mattheson himself breached constantly.) The educated tastes of the amateur, the main buyer for collections of music and books of music criticism such as those Mattheson wrote and from which he profited handsomely, were as legitimate as the learned pronouncements of the professional.

Like Mattheson, Bach's friend J. D. Heinichen placed special emphasis on the intelligibility of music to the general public: "[the essence] of a good composer of taste," he wrote in *Der General-Bass in der Composition* of 1728, "consists once and for all in the art of making his music, as a matter of course, popular and pleasing to the reasonable world."[3] Mattheson gave this listener-based aesthetic a memorable exposition in "Die canonische Anatomie":

> It is true, and I have previously experienced it myself, that quick progress with... artistic pieces (*Kunst-Stücke*) [i.e., canons and the like] can engross a sensible composer so that he can sincerely and secretly delight in his own work. But through this self-love we are unwittingly led gradually away from the true purpose of music, until we hardly think of others at all, although it is our goal to delight them. Really we should follow not our own inclinations, but those of the listener. I have often composed something that seemed to me trifling, but unexpectedly attained great favor. I made a mental note of this, and wrote more of the same, although it had little merit when judged according to its artistry.[4]

The changing conception of the composer, whose value was now to be measured not just against and by his peers but according to the tastes and opinions of an increasingly bourgeois audience, plays a crucial part in the controversy between Bach – represented in print by the musical amateur and teacher of rhetoric at Leipzig University Johann

---

[2] Johann Mattheson, *Das neu-eröffnete Orchestre* (Hamburg, 1713; reprint, Hildesheim, 1993), title-page.

[3] Heinichen, *Der General-Bass in der Composition* (Dresden, 1728; reprint, Hildesheim, 1969), 23.

[4] Johann Mattheson, *Critica musica*, 2 vols. (Hamburg, 1722–25), I, 346.

Abraham Birnbaum – and Bach's former student Johann Adolph Scheibe, for this was a dispute that went far beyond stylistic questions concerning the complexity of Bach's music. In March of 1738, in the second of his polemics against Bach, Scheibe explained the inadequacies of Bach's music in no uncertain terms as the result of the Thomascantor's ignorance of aesthetic issues, attacking Bach for his lack of broad-based philosophical knowledge and his deficient critical skills. Bach's works were full of "not inconsiderable errors" (nicht geringe Fehler), which stemmed from the fact that:

> This great man has not sufficiently studied the sciences/humanities (*Wissenschaften*) which actually are required of a learned composer (*gelehrter Componist*). How can a man who has not studied philosophy and is incapable of investigating and recognizing the forces of nature and reason be without fault in his musical work? How can he attain all the advantages which are necessary for the cultivation of good taste when he has hardly troubled himself with critical observations, investigations, and with the rules which are as necessary to music as they are to rhetoric and poetics (*Redekunst und Dichtkunst*). Without them it is impossible to compose movingly and expressively.[5]

In the midst of his exchange with Birnbaum, Scheibe sent a letter to Mattheson in which he both complimented the soon-to-appear *Vollkommener Capellmeister* and condemned Bach for his aesthetic failings. In the letter, which Mattheson printed in a 1738 advertisement for his book, Scheibe praised the author's privileging of *natürlich* melody over *künstlich* harmony [i.e., counterpoint], citing Bach as an example of a composer unwilling to accept these new aesthetic precepts.[6]

Scheibe had argued along the same lines in his initial satire of Bach, claiming that "Turgidity (*Die Schwulstigkeit*) has led [Bach] ... from the natural to the artificial, and from the lofty to the somber ... one admires the onerous labor and uncommon effort – which, however, are vainly employed, since they conflict with Reason"; Bach eschewed pleasing music, "darkening its beauty through an excess of art."[7] Scheibe had treated canon and double counterpoint cursorily – and somewhat sarcastically – in his unpublished composition treatise *Compendium musices* written around 1736,[8] and strict counterpoint appears throughout his

---

[5] Johann Adolph Scheibe, "Rechtfertigung der Gegen Bach Erhobenen Vorwürfe" (Hamburg, 1738); reprinted in *BD* II, 312–320, esp. 316.

[6] Scheibe, in Johann Mattheson, *Gültige Zeugnisse über die jüngste Matthesonisch-Musicalische Kern-Schrifft* (Hamburg, 1738), pp. 10–11. Scheibe's letter is dated January 1738, the same month that Birnbaum printed his reply to Scheibe's earlier attack.

[7] Johann Adolph Scheibe, *Critischer Musikus*, rev. edn. (Leipzig, 1745), 62; trans. *NBR*, 338.

[8] Johann Adolph Scheibe, *Compendium musices* (1736), ed. in Peter Benary, *Die deutsche Kompositionslehre des 18. Jahrhunderts* (Leipzig, 1961), appendix. In his instruction on canon Scheibe refers the reader to "Die canonische Anatomie," Mattheson's critique of learned counterpoint.

public writings as an emblem of the antiquated style, "nothing other than the fruits of a disheartened diligence (*niederschlagener Fleiß*), of worthless toil (*faule Mühe*), and of a pedantic spirit (*pedantischer Geist*)."[9] In language similar, at times almost identical, to Mattheson's, Scheibe denigrated strict counterpoint's "forced and unnatural essence (*Wesen*)" characterizing its procedures as "Artificialities (*Künsteleyen*) which serve only those dispositions which are unable to think freely and in an orderly fashion, and to whom a vile fascination with toil is more agreeable than lively and sublime fire (*lebhaftes und erhabenes Feuer*)."[10] Scheibe was no enemy of pleasing fugue and natural imitation, but he saw learned counterpoint as a stultifying discipline which diverted composers and listeners from more valuable musical considerations; contrapuntal enthusiasts were victims of their own slavish adherence to accepted practices, and their reliance on arbitrary rules belied an inherent laziness and an inability to think critically and independently. In a later pamphlet of March 1738 published in Hamburg, Scheibe reiterated the same themes, stating his strong support for "the so-called fashionable taste (*neumodischer Geschmack*)," and against the "old-fashioned taste (*altfränkischer Geschmack*)" which "prefers constraint (*Zwang*) to nature," concluding that Bach failed to take nature into account in his compositions.[11]

The years 1737 and 1738 were difficult for Bach, with ugly strife at his place of employment and unkind words about him being published by his former student, the one-eyed gadfly Scheibe. Bach's apparent diffidence in the controversy with Scheibe had less to do with writing ability than with ideology: he was competent enough in the flourishes of bureaucratic prose when asserting his traditional rights as a cantor, but unprepared to engage in the argumentative, interdisciplinary style of the new music criticism. In his parting shot Scheibe was mercilessly clear, and extremely unkind, in describing the humanistic breadth he considered to be a prerequisite for modern, Enlightened musicians. Writing satirically from Bach's perspective, Scheibe lampoons the narrowness of the traditional musician: "I [Bach] have always been of the opinion that a *Musikant* had enough to do with his art itself, without concerning himself with the writing of extensive books, or with learned and philosophical investigations, and wasting his time in such fashion."[12] For Scheibe, Bach's failure to defend himself in Enlightened prose and his retreat behind the concerns of the music profession reflected an uncritical, regressive viewpoint. Scheibe clearly hoped to imply that while such a narrow attitude was to be expected from an uneducated fiddler – that

---

[9] Scheibe, *Critischer Musikus*, rev. edn., 98. [10] Ibid.
[11] Scheibe, "Rechtfertigung," in *BD* II, 317. [12] *NBR*, 351–352.

is, a *Musikant* – it was unacceptable in the person of Leipzig's Director of Music and Saxon Court Composer.

But Bach's reluctance to enter the debate in no way meant that its outcome was unimportant to him, or that he was insensitive to, or unconcerned with, the issues at stake. Indeed, the degree to which Bach provided his surrogate with the raw materials for his argument is evident throughout Birnbaum's so-called "Unpartheyische Anmerkungen" (Impartial Comments) – and nowhere more so than when Birnbaum defends Bach's written-out ornaments by citing the example of the French organists Nicolas de Grigny and Pierre DuMage, whose *Livres d'Orgue* had been published almost forty years earlier.[13] This was obscure music to say the least, and although Bach had been making copies of it in the mid 1730s – about the time that Scheibe published his inflammatory letter – a musical amateur such as Birnbaum could not have known anything about this repertoire without Bach's help. The idea of adducing it as a rationalization for Bach's florid ornamentation must have come from the composer himself. (The appearance of the names prompted a mordant footnote from Scheibe when he reprinted the entire controversy in the second edition of *Der critische Musikus* in 1745.)[14] It is likely that the substantive philosophical arguments – those concerning the role of the artist in shaping nature, the value of complexity, the merits of the antique as well as the modern style, the importance of upholding higher standards than those found in what the "Unpartheyische Anmerkungen" described as "insipid little *galant* pieces" (läppische *galant*erie Stückgen) – were formulated, or at least refined, by Birnbaum.[15] The points of rebuttal were to be given forensic power by this teacher of rhetoric, but Bach was clearly supplying most of the musical details of the "impartial" arguments himself.

Bach was certainly not unaware of the changing character of music criticism. Leipzig was a leading center for the German book industry and every year during the three annual trade fairs new ideas on music flooded into the city. The theorist and composer Martin Fuhrmann attended the fair in 1729 and noted that musicians were perusing the latest publications of Mattheson (*Der musicalische Patriot*) and Heinichen (*Der General-Bass in der Composition*). Furhmann may have been referring to Bach when he quoted a great musician who described these two treatises as "somewhat heavy reading... but quite accurate nevertheless... Whoever fails to learn from Mattheson's and

---

[13] Johann Abraham Birnbaum, "Unpartheyische Anmerkungen..." (January, 1738) in *BD* II, 296–306, esp. 303; trans. *NBR*, 338–348, esp. 346. See also Christoph Wolff, *Bach: Essays on His Life and Music* (Cambridge, Mass., 1991), 393.
[14] Scheibe, *Critischer Musikus*, rev. edn., 854.
[15] Birnbaum, "Unpartheyische Anmerckungen," in *BD* II, 302.

Heinichen's writings is a blockhead."[16] In his 1730 memorandum to the Leipzig town council, Bach had himself borrowed from the lexicon of *galant* criticism, perhaps even directly from a passage in Heinichen's *Der General-Bass in der Composition*, when he noted that "taste (*gusto*) has changed astonishingly, and accordingly the former style of music no longer seems to please our ears."[17] Leipzig also encouraged a vibrant culture of musical criticism; its two leading figures were Scheibe and another Bach student, Lorenz Christoph Mizler, both of whom produced widely circulating music periodicals. Scheibe's *Critischer Musikus*, which began to appear bi-weekly in 1737, and Mizler's *Neu eröffnete musikalische Bibliothek*, published from 1739 to 1754, considered important aesthetic and theoretical concerns of the day, discussed the works of leading theorists, including Mattheson, and contained numerous polemical battles. Public debates such as Birnbaum's exchange with Scheibe were followed by professionals and amateurs, and just as the success of a piece of music was to be based not on the verdict of musicians alone but, more importantly, on the response of the *galant homme*, the retreat to the safety of professional elitism was no longer possible. Whether he liked it or not Bach's music was now entangled in the aesthetic debates of the day.

Scheibe's attack yielded a great many pages of aesthetic colloquy, personal attack, and irrelevant asides; pamphlets were printed and then reprinted, collected and footnoted, rejoinders rebutted and rebuttals rejoined. Like most polemics it went on too long, yet throughout it all Bach had remained on the sidelines, signing his name to nothing, preferring to let his defenders speak on his behalf. His first public pronouncement in the immediate aftermath of the controversy was not literary but musical – the *Clavierübung III* of 1739. Mizler for one described it as a resounding response to Scheibe: "This work is a powerful refutation to those who have dared to criticize the composition of the Honorable Court Composer."[18] Even if Bach did not intend the *Clavierübung* as a response to his critics it was being received as such by some. Although it is likely that some of the work had already been composed before the beginning of the exchange with Scheibe, the issues involved in the ensuing debate would certainly have had a bearing on Bach's conception of the music and the reception it could anticipate in the wake of the controversy. It is hard to imagine that Bach did not foresee responses to the *Clavierübung III* like that given by Mizler, or intend in part for

---

[16] Martin Fuhrmann, *Die an der Kirchen Gottes gebauete Satans-Capelle* (Berlin, 1729), 32. See also George Stauffer, "Johann Mattheson and J. S. Bach: The Hamburg Connection," in *New Mattheson Studies*, ed. George J. Buelow and Hans Joachim Marx (Cambridge, 1983), 353–368, esp. 362.

[17] Heinichen, *Der General-Bass in der Composition*, 10.   [18] *NBR*, 333; *BD* II, 386–387.

the work to have this effect. Indeed, the themes of the Scheibe/Bach controversy are everywhere to be heard in this monumental collection, a sprawling amalgam of the pleasing and the ungainly, the modern and the retrospective, the complex and the accessible.

Nowhere is the sense of refutation more palpable than in the bizarre Duetto in F major, BWV 803, from the *Clavierübung III*. Bach could surely not have issued such a work to the musical public without suspecting that critical musicians would hear in its collision between the artificial and the natural something of the composer's own aesthetic convictions. Without the four Duettos, *Clavierübung III* would be an extended collection of chorale preludes bracketed by the Prelude and Fugue in E♭, BWV 552: thus the four Duettos, whose genre and instrument (harpsichord or organ or both) have often puzzled commentators, are something of an oddity in this context. They were probably composed during the summer of 1739 and inserted into the collection towards the end of the protracted engraving process.[19] Their inclusion in the volume was therefore decided upon relatively soon after the Scheibe controversy. I mention this not to promote the idea that Bach appended the duets to an already well-stocked collection exclusively in order to answer his critics musically; Bach's reasons for adding the set were undoubtedly complex and the result of a number of factors: revisiting and expanding a genre of central importance to Bach's pedagogical approach, last explored in the 1722 two-part Inventions, is perhaps one of these. But if, as I will argue, the F major Duetto is a provocative piece, whom was it trying to provoke? Certainly someone with sufficient grounding in aesthetics, someone familiar with the suppositions of contemporary music criticism.

Bach's use of the term *Duetto*, unique among his keyboard works, is suggestive in itself, for the Duetto or duet was a genre of considerable importance for eighteenth-century theorists: in vocal music it denoted two voices singing above a bass line (three parts in total); in instrumental music it generally referred to a two-voice texture. Mattheson signalled the importance he accorded the genre by claiming in *Critica musica* that "a composer's true masterpiece" can be found "in an artful, fugued duet, more than in a many-voiced counterpoint or allabreve."[20] Here and elsewhere Mattheson opposes the freedom and skill found in a good fugal duet with the constraining artificiality of stricter forms of counterpoint, in particular canon. In an earlier section of *Critica musica*, Mattheson presents a didactic dialogue in which a would-be composer (Melophile) questions his master (Mattheson). Eager to impress, the fictional

---

[19] Gregory Butler, *Bach's Clavier-Übung III: The Making of a Print, with a Companion Study of the Canonic Variations on "Vom Himmel Hoch," BWV 769* (Durham, 1990), 85.

[20] Mattheson, *Critica musica*, I, 131.

young composer says he would like to introduce a canon into a piece; Mattheson responds that "if one wants to be severe (*arg*), one can do so,"[21] but he does not believe it is worth the trouble, taking a cautious view as to the cognitive powers – not to say overall attentiveness – of his audience: "Among 2,000 listeners there will be barely one who notices this subtlety (*Finesse*), and he would have been warned beforehand."[22] This is a common theme in Mattheson's work, as it was later to be in Scheibe's: working out a piece of music too fully not only detracted from its rhetorical power but was usually a waste of effort. Visible exertion undermined *galant* affectation. Nonetheless, says Mattheson, a duet was not to be without some contrapuntal nuance; in "Die canonische Anatomie" Mattheson cited the duet as a genre which typically featured imitation at the unison or octave.

Imitation was held to be so vital apparently because the term itself (imitatio) connotes mimesis, in this case, the imitation of nature. Because of this curious linguistic parallelism nothing could be more natural than imitation, though it requires some skill to be able to manipulate a subject effectively; imitation might involve some canonic relationships, but these must not become too lengthy or intricate. In *Der vollkommene Capellmeister* Mattheson wrote that one "cannot possibly do without imitations if he wants to express something pleasant," and he again contrasted the freedom of imitation with the restrictive demands of extended canon.[23] For his part, Scheibe referred to the duet only once when discussing the stylistic features appropriate to mass composition; he makes it clear that in composing such pieces one must be particularly attentive to the "harmonic work" (harmonische Arbeit), that is, the proper handling of the counterpoint.[24] The pair of voices should work through a striking melody (ein besonderer Hauptsatz), which is pleasant and moving (annehmlich u. rührend). For both Scheibe and Mattheson the duet provides a prime opportunity to mix the natural with the appropriate amount of art.

While Mattheson is primarily concerned with text-setting in his treatment of the duet in *Critica musica*, the genre appears to have been particularly popular towards the middle of the century. Mattheson had anticipated his own theoretical interest in the duet with his first publication, a collection of twelve sonatas for recorders without bass;[25] six were duets and included considerable contrapuntal activity, mostly imitative writing and double counterpoint but also two canonic

---

[21] Mattheson, *Critica musica*, II, 28.   [22] Ibid., 29.
[23] Johann Mattheson, *Der vollkommene Capellmeister* (Hamburg, 1739; reprint, Kassel, 1954), 338, 332; translation based on Johann Mattheson, *Der vollkommene Capellmeister*, trans. Ernest C. Harriss (Ann Arbor, 1981), 647, 638.
[24] Scheibe, *Critischer Musikus*, 173.
[25] Johann Mattheson, *XII Sonates à Deux & Trois Flutes sans Basse* (Amsterdam, 1708).

movements – those elements he would later elucidate for the would-be composer in *Critica musica*. The genre received renewed attention just prior to the publication of Bach's *Clavierübung III*. In 1738 Telemann brought out his *Canons mélodieux*, canonic duets for a pair of flutes – engaging and *galant*, they were largely intended for the instruction and recreation of amateurs and, of course, students. The genre remained popular after Bach's death. In 1759 J. J. Quantz published a collection of six duets, providing the volume with a characteristically illuminating preface. According to Quantz such pieces should aim higher than simple flattery of the ear, and should therefore include double counterpoint and fugal imitation, so that the musicians who play them can learn how musical ideas should be developed and articulated, and can also engage in the kind of conversational give-and-take so prized in *galant* musical interaction. There should be art and elegance. While Quantz's title-page calls for two flutes, he expands the appeal of the volume by encouraging a variety of instrumental combinations. A great admirer of the then late J. S. Bach's organ music, Quantz goes so far as to recommend performance of his pieces on the organ, perhaps with Bach's *Clavierübung* duets in mind. For instruction in performance and composition the duet, though seemingly inconsequential to many, is in Quantz's view a genre of vital importance for the practice and appreciation of music. (W. F. Bach and C. P. E. Bach would both contribute to the genre with charming pieces that incorporate much contrapuntal artifice.) Quantz had heard Bach play in the 1730s in Dresden and would meet and hear him again in Berlin in 1747. In light of the widespread appreciation of the duet by leading theorists and practical musicians, from Mattheson to Quantz, Bach's decision to include such pieces in his *Clavierübung* series might well represent an attempt to fill a significant lacuna in his survey of keyboard practice, which would, with the publication of the Goldberg Variations, run to four volumes.

The opening section of Bach's F major Duetto (Example 3.1) corresponds to Mattheson's ideal of the "fugued" duet, and it presents all the important elements of the genre as outlined by Quantz: dialogue between the parts, timely appearances of the subject (*Hauptsatz*), harmonic viability without the addition of a third voice. A reference to the vocal duet can be seen in the piece's *da capo* (ABA) form, ubiquitous in vocal works but relatively rare in Bach's keyboard music. The A section of the piece is perhaps closest in style to that of Bach's Inventions and Sinfonias of 1722–3, the title-page of which states that the collection "[will show a clear way to] those eager to learn ... not only of having good inventions but also of developing these ... and, above all, of arriving at a *cantabile* style of playing."[26] The exposition of the F major Duetto

[26] *NBR*, 97–98; *BD* I, 220–221.

Example 3.1 J. S. Bach, Duetto in F major, BWV 803

DUETTO II.

(Example 3.1, mm. 1–37) exemplifies this pleasing, *cantabile* style so central to the progressive music criticism of the day. The subject is diatonic, comprised of a triad and scale, and the whole section is harmonically unadventurous. It follows the generally accepted precepts, later articulated by Mattheson in *Der vollkommene Capellmeister*, that the melody be intelligible and naturally charming.[27] The counterpoint is beautifully

---

[27] Mattheson, *Der vollkommene Capellmeister*, 22–23; trans. Harriss, 57.

Example 3.1 (cont.)

constructed, but only reinforces the sense of freedom. The A section contains two passages of short imitations (mm. 10–13, 22–25), which were for Mattheson "the most beautiful thing in harmony,"[28] and the closest "harmonic" music could come to the original beauty of nature in all its simplicity.[29] Here is one kind of answer to Scheibe's criticism that Bach's music is too dissonant: there is not a single dissonance in the A section, unless one points to the second eighth of m. 7 (an accented fourth, whose effect is ameliorated by a trill). Even passing notes are rare.

[28] Mattheson, *Critica musica*, I, 245.   [29] Ibid.

Example 3.1 (cont.)

All is calm and sweet, appealing and not intellectually intrusive. The piece so far is a model of decorum, clarity, and naturalness – so much so that one suspects Bach of a certain disingenuousness in his unhesitating embrace of these Enlightened values.

The B section quickly confirms such suspicions. After the affirmative cadence to the tonic at m. 37 the listener is jarred by a new subject. A less *cantabile* theme could scarcely be imagined: to be sure it is a striking melody (besonderer Hauptsatz) – to borrow from Quantz – but perhaps too striking. In contrast to the triadic, diatonic subject of the A section, the opening figure of the B section baldly traverses an almost exotic

Example 3.1   (*cont.*)

augmented second and concludes with a descending diminished seventh (mm. 38–41). Not only is the melodic writing tortured, totally unnatural as Scheibe and Mattheson would have it, but it is subjected to intense and long-running canonic imitation and contrapuntal manipulation, which result in disjointed and jarring cross-relations. It is not that Bach's sense of *cantabile* necessarily means diatonic: the serpentine chromaticism of the Sinfonia in F minor – part of a collection described by Bach as "cantabile" – is just one of many examples of this. But the bracing juxtaposition of compositional styles in the F major Duetto undoubtedly increases the apparent awkwardness of the subject of the B section.

Measured against the aesthetic ideals exemplified in the opening section of the F major Duetto, the melodic and harmonic content of the B section verges on the unintelligible. In contrast to the gently contrapuntal texture of the opening, with its ample four-measure spacing between the *dux* and *comes* and the lengthy interludes between the two

Example 3.2   BWV 803, m. 38, cross-relations

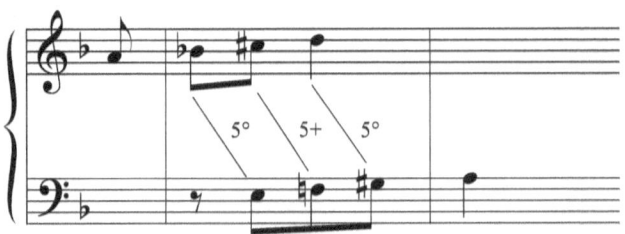

other appearances of the subject, the canonic imitation of the B section is severely compressed, coming at the uncomfortably close spacing of a quarter note. As a result the counterpoint is thick with jarring cross-relations; the B subject is layered onto itself so that in the first contrapuntal complex (fourth mm. 38–51), the canonic writing produces a tritone, an augmented fifth, and another tritone in the first full measure (m. 38) of the B section alone (Example 3.2). This jagged opening to the B section provides a good idea of what is to come; both the melodic and harmonic treatment will be unforgiving throughout.

When the opening subject reappears at m. 46 (refer again to Example 3.1 for the remainder of my discussion of the F major Duetto) the close stretto – the voices are still canonic, separated temporally by only a quarter note – punctures the sense of *cantabile* attached to it in the graceful A section. The unmediated juxtaposition (mm. 46 and 47) of the minor triad form of the head motif against the major version distorts the once elegant theme until it is almost unrecognizable. No concession is made towards a tonal answer like that of the amply spaced *dux/comes* pair of the opening; the real answer required by canonic exactitude in this case runs counter to the precepts of good fugal writing of the kind sanctioned by Mattheson in his account of such duets. Bach has shackled himself with a canon and he will ignore the demands of tonal clarity and melodic gentility. Harmony – that is, contrapuntal treatment – vitiates melody: reason has superseded sense, flaunting the accepted balance required by Enlightened judgment between *sensus* and *ratio*, hearing and the intellect. As for Mattheson's advice to his hypothetical student to avoid canons because they will go unnoticed by most who play and hear them, Bach's canon is so starkly presented that it forces the listener to confront the artifice. There is nothing tasteful or demure in this canon, and coupled with the untuneful melody, these contrapuntal contortions unsettle, almost violently, the naturalness that had prevailed in the A section.

In mm. 51 and 52 the canon momentarily abates, apparently to make way for a logical cadence to the relative minor. But before this cadential gesture can be completed, the B subject intrudes in the lower voice on the last eighth note of m. 52; there will be no respite from the relentless contrapuntal machinations in this section of the piece, as even the clarifying, or at least orienting, effect of a cadence is brusquely set aside. Although this cadential elision propels the piece forward, there is a curious circularity in the chromatic subject's reappearance: the left hand is given the identical material with which it began the B section. This voice has made no progress at all, and the piece threatens to spiral in on itself, purposefully solipsistic, if not downright anti-teleological. It is true, of course, that this left-hand material is re-contextualized: beginning in m. 53 Bach will show that the B section's opening canonic complex is invertible at the octave, which means that the left hand will now become the *dux*, and the right hand will follow at the upper fifth. The B section so far is essentially one canon played twice in a different harmonic configuration.

After rehearsing the harmonic inversion of his contrapuntal framework, Bach unexpectedly offers a glimpse in measure 69 of the ingratiating diatonic imitations heard in the A section, which leads quickly to the tonic and the introduction of the subject in F major, initially harmonized (in m. 70) without dissonance. But this calming recollection of the opening is shortlived, and the contrapuntal assault is renewed in the very next measure where Bach overlays the remainder of the subject with a chromatic counter-subject (mm. 69–71) traversing the better part of an octave from f^2 to a^1. Who could have recognized that this pleasant subject would have admitted such a counter-subject, and who would have had the audacity and bad taste to introduce it? Only Bach. It is a remarkable and virtuosic demonstration that even the simplest and most natural of themes can be subjected to the most artificial of procedures.

Two more consonant measures follow (mm. 72–73) – another glance back at the now distant opening section. But then the "natural" subject, which had been given a complete statement in the lower voice in mm. 69–73, confronts its dark, mirror image: mm. 74–78 are an exact melodic and harmonic inversion of the previous four measures, but the major mode of the opening and of the preceding statement of the subject is now negated, a negation all the more arresting as it comes in the minor tonic itself. The importance of this bizarre recontextualization of the opening material so representative of an "ideal" Duetto is evident in its placement. The A section is 37 measures long (74 with repeat); the B section is 75. The two halves are therefore of almost exactly the same weight, artifice and nature given equal space to make their claims. The total length of the Duetto (with da capo) is 149 measures, thus the inverted minor form of the subject stands at the center of the piece, with the entire edifice balanced around it. Indeed, each individual compositional

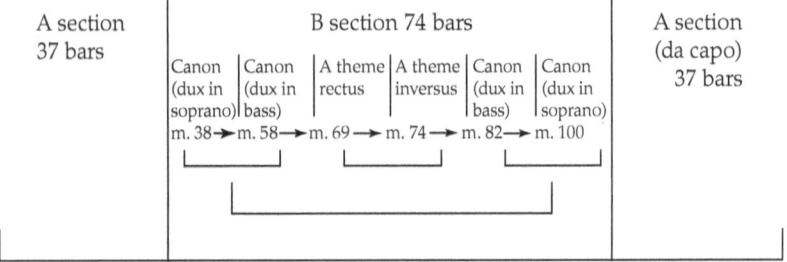

Figure 3.1 J. S. Bach, Duetto in F major (BWV 803), symmetrical layout

segment is mirrored around this axis. It is, literally, the pivotal moment of the piece.

What follows, after a short transition comprised of busy scales in contrary motion, is a replay of the first contrapuntal complex of the B section but in a different key and with the order of the voices reversed: the left hand begins as the *dux* with the pick-up to m. 82. Then, following the pattern established in the first half of the B section, the right hand takes the *dux* when this segment is presented again in invertible counterpoint at m. 100. Thus the two halves of the B section are not only symmetrical with each other across the central divide formed by the recall of the opening theme in the tonic and minor tonic, but they deliver the same canon twice, so that we hear this material a total of four times in the B section (Figure 3.1). The constantly shifting counterpoint of the B section belies a broader stasis: apart from crucial combination of the chromatic countersubject with the tonic subject in mm. 70–77, the section is composed of the same contrapuntal framework repeated four times. As against the loose and engaging style of the opening, we have less dialogue than clinical examination of contrapuntal material: erudite recitation supplants the logical succession of rhetorically persuasive ideas. It was no doubt this compulsive contrapuntalizing that Spitta was commenting on when he claimed that "the strong scholastic character" of the middle section "[left behind] an impression that the enormous wealth of harmony, the severity of the ideas and the length of the working out, are not quite proportionate to the poverty of the material which represents them."[30] But what Spitta did not touch on is the context of this severity, both in the piece itself and in the aesthetic climate of 1739. Indeed, the B section aggressively questions almost every precept of progressive theory: it is a puzzle of canonic writing in invertible counterpoint using "unpleasant" melodies – a glaring transgression of Scheibe's *galant* "middle style" (mittelmässiger Schreibart) to which the first section can

---

[30] Philipp Spitta, *Johann Sebastian Bach*, trans. Clara Bell and J. A. Fuller Maitland, 3 vols. (London, 1889), III, 168.

be heard to appeal, and a willful and tasteless incursion of the turgid into the natural. But it is a provocation that cannot be ignored; it is too challenging, too argumentative, too unrelenting.

As we have already seen with the abrupt announcement of the chromatic second subject (in m. 38) after the final cadence of the A section, the points of contact between the natural and artificial in the F major Duetto are fraught with tension. So when the *da capo* form leaves behind the harrowing contrapuntal territory of the B section to return to the bucolic landscape of the opening, the transition is similarly severe. In terms of coherent key relations, the preparation for this return is fatally weakened by the cadence, which comes not on the dominant but on the minor dominant. Indeed, only eight measures earlier the opening subject had been treated for the last time in close stretto, a C minor triad followed quickly by a G major triad – thus firmly establishing the dominant minor against the F major of the opening. The cadence to the unison Cs at m. 113 strongly confirms C minor; the next sixteenth note is an A♮ which descends, instead of ascending towards the tonic as it should in C minor and as it has just done in m. 111. Rather than introduce any sort of viable harmonic transition, however, Bach has the descending F major scale abruptly depart C minor; it is the sparest of efforts towards uniting the two key areas, less a bridge than a brazen confirmation of the piece's manifest contradictions.

With the *da capo* and the return to the opening section, the subject can no longer be heard as it was before. Its confrontation with chromatic counterpoint and astringent canonic artifice has made this impossible. The listener is forced to be critical. The singing, pastoral mode has been so thoroughly compromised that on its return there is a palpable torpor in the perpetual consonance, a shallowness in the lively conversational idiom, a predictability in the clear projection of key and affect. The piece's sprightliness now seems coy, its pleasantness more like mockingly undemanding pleasantries. It might be going too far to claim that Bach was being ironic in crafting this section so elegantly; but in problematizing the naturalness of the opening section and showing that such raw materials can be deeply and meaningfully investigated by the artist, he has presented an infinitely more varied account of musical style and invention than that offered by Scheibe.

The A section of the F major Duetto is everything Scheibe could have asked for – and that is not enough for Bach, who moves here far beyond the clarity and unity of the F major Invention. Without the B section the Duetto is the perfect work of 1739, completely in and of its time. In its entirety, however, the piece is a perfect blasphemy – a powerful refutation indeed of the progressive shibboleths of naturalness and transparency. The potential superficiality of respectable amenity (Scheibe's *Annehmlichkeit*) is brought into stark relief against the turgid and difficult interior of the work. Laid out with striking formal symmetry around a central revelatory synthesis (mm. 77–78), the Duetto's two parts, which represent the poles of Enlightened music criticism, demonstrate the composer's complete mastery of both the natural and its dark mirror image. Rather than allowing these two apparently irreconcilable forces to remain in comfortable isolation, as the arbiters of *galant* style demanded, Bach brings them into a dynamic confrontation that transforms the merely provocative into the profound. Yet the richness Bach achieves in the F major Duetto comes at some cost. Ease and simplicity have their virtues, their place, their appeal. The odd, eccentric, and flamboyantly brilliant – in a word, the baroque – are not for all tastes and not for all occasions. Bach, too, would certainly have known this, as he resolutely transgressed the bounds of Enlightenment decorum. The internal dialogue of the piece is, therefore, much more than a mere display of ingenuity or an unhinged aesthetic diatribe: it is critical music *par excellence*.

In June of 1747, nearly ten years after Scheibe's initial attacks on the artificiality of his music, Bach became the fourteenth member of Mizler's "Corresponding Society of the Musical Sciences" (Correspondirende Societät der Musicalischen Wissenschaften), and for his induction submitted the *Canonic Variations* on *Vom Himmel hoch da komm ich her* (BWV 769). The engraving of the work, like that of *Clavierübung III*, was a drawn-out process, probably extending from the spring of 1746 to mid-1747.[31] Scheibe, by then in the service of the Danish court in Copenhagen, published the second edition of his *Critischer Musikus* in Leipzig in 1745, probably at the same time that Bach was composing the first three canons on *Vom Himmel hoch*. Rather than simply reprinting the various earlier essays by himself and Birnbaum, Scheibe took the opportunity to add more than 150 of his own footnotes to Birnbaum's arguments. In this often sardonic commentary – a tribute to how well he had learned the art of the polemical footnote from Mattheson – Scheibe argued again that the Thomascantor remained committed to antiquated ideals and that his music exemplified "altogether too much art" rather than, as Birnbaum had asserted, the "greatest art," and trotted out the old arguments advocating a balance between naturalness and artifice, a balance that would maximize expression.[32] This equilibrium was necessarily upset by the introduction of learned counterpoint into a piece: complete

---

[31] Butler, *Bach's Clavier-Übung III*, 91–116, at p. 110. For a final demolition of the idea that either the print or the autograph constitutes a definitive version representing Bach's final intentions see Butler, "J. S. Bachs Kanonische Veränderungen über 'Vom Himmel hoch' (BWV 769): Ein Schlußstrich unter die Debatte um die Frage der 'Fassung letzter Hand,'" *Bach-Jahrbuch* 86 (2000): 9–34.

[32] Scheibe, *Critischer Musikus*, 851–852.

coddling of the ear was to be avoided, but undue artistic intrusion – especially learned counterpoint – obscured the true goals of music.[33] It seems highly unlikely, given Bach's interest in Scheibe's original attack on him, that he would have remained oblivious to its continuation. The *Canonic Variations* would, like the *Clavierübung III*, have been interpreted by some as another response, if not directly to Scheibe, then to the larger aesthetic debate which played such an important part in the reception of Bach's music, particularly his contrapuntal works.

Bach had, of course, published many canons in the years after the first phase of the Scheibe controversy, in the third (1739) and fourth (1741) volumes of the *Clavierübung* series. But whereas the canons in these two collections were presented in fully realized form, those in the first three of the *Canonic Variations* employed enigmatic notation. Earlier in the second edition of *Critischer Musikus*, Scheibe had heaped scorn on this type of puzzle notation, claiming that "these follies (*Thorheiten*) have justifiably been discarded."[34] Such conventions were as important to the self-consciously progressive critics of the eighteenth century as they have been to twentieth-century scholars concerned with issues of printing, layout, and chronology. Indeed, there is a curious congruence between these two viewpoints, representing diametrically opposed opinions of Bach's counterpoint, for both place great importance on notation, on the appearance of the music on the page. That is, both locate much of the meaning of the work in the score itself, which is then said to reflect Bach's speculative inclinations.[35]

Ironically, the modern focus on notation unwittingly endorses Scheibe's vision of an isolated Bach, unwilling to confront aesthetic issues. Yet even a cursory look at the first three of the *Canonic Variations* reveals a disquieting disjunction between the style of the music and the putatively old-fashioned, "speculative" way in which it is notated. Rigorously contrapuntal, these pieces are anything but abstract and severe, and in this collection Bach seems self-consciously to appeal to *galant* idioms; while involving himself further in the aesthetic debate concerning nature and art, he creates here the most modern "beautiful" music on the most artificial of foundations. Indeed, the direction "à 2 Clav. et Pedal" which appears at the top of the first variation points at the outset beyond the abstract to "real" performance. The trills near the beginning of the first variation and the trills and slurs in the second, are by definition decorative, that is, to be performed, and are not deeply structural, or in any way abstract. Decisively, the third variation is provided with the marking *Cantabile*, prompting the question, How can "singing" be abstract?

---

[33] Ibid., 856–857.   [34] Scheibe, *Critischer Musikus*, 98.
[35] See Butler, *Bach's Clavier-Übung III*, 105.

111

Example 3.3 J. S. Bach, *Canonic Variations*, BWV 769, variation 1, mm. 1–2

From their first measures the *Canonic Variations* seem to embrace *galant* values: beauty, apparent simplicity, grace. The descending scale that begins the opening variation in flowing 12/8 immediately suggests something of the natural and pleasing modern style. Nothing dissonant or difficult intrudes to disrupt the idyll; the canonic artifice is not heavy-handed or intrusive as it was in the F major Duetto. The "natural" scale and the detailed irregularity of what follows it is characteristic of the nuanced modern style (Example 3.3). The diatonic make-up of the chorale melody and the demands of canonic writing in the accompanying parts might seem to restrict the harmonic possibilities of the setting, although Bach had already demonstrated his ability to write chromatically adventurous canons above a placid *cantus firmus* – as in the Fulde canon (BWV 1077) on the Goldberg bass-line, which is similar, after all, to the opening line of *Vom Himmel hoch*. In the *Canonic Variations*, however, Bach avoids harmonic extremes, projecting instead an affect of "beauty" and "naturalness."

The second of Bach's variations on *Vom Himmel hoch*, a canon at the fifth, is also a predominantly consonant piece with a pair of pleasing canonic voices, and the slurred figures of its opening measure once again demonstrating Bach's concern with surface detail, and not just the intrinsic, "abstract" contrapuntal features of the work (Example 3.4). Played without the *cantus firmus*, both of the first two variations could almost pass for one of Telemann's *Canons mélodieux*, praised by Quantz, emulated by W. F. Bach, and presumably known to J. S. Bach. Telemann's duets share with the *Canonic Variations* many quintessentially *galant* features: paired slurs, Lombardic rhythms, regular phrases, "feminine" endings, and performance directions such as *Cantabile* and *Soave* (Example 3.5).[36] Even the last of Quantz's flute duets of 1759, headed *Canone infinito*, has much in common with the style of the *Canonic Variations* (Example 3.6).

[36] Georg Philipp Telemann, *XIIX Canons mélodieux, ou VI Sonates en duo* (Paris, 1738).

Example 3.4 J. S. *Canonic Variations*, BWV 769, variation 2, mm. 1–3

Example 3.5 G. P. Telemann, *Canons mélodieux* (1738), Sonata no. 4, second movement, mm. 1–2

Example 3.6 J. J. Quantz, *Sei duetti* (1759), no. 6, third movement

Example 3.7 Ornamented paired slurs: J. S. Bach, BWV 769, fourth movement; C. P. E. Bach, *Versuch* (1753–62), Table V

Much more contrapuntally complex than the first two variations, the fourth, which features an augmentation canon between soprano and tenor voices, is also heavily decorated with *galant* touches, such as the paired slurs with trills; this figure is also to be found among the distinctly modern ornaments of C. P. E. Bach's *Versuch*, a valuable resource for contemporary performers and students hoping to acquire such refinements (Example 3.7). Bach is concerned here not just to maintain contrapuntal rigor but with expression as well: the canonic soprano voice includes trills, slurs, and appoggiaturas that do not appear in the tenor and therefore violate the contrapuntal dictates of the work, demonstrating Bach's concern with the elegant elaboration of the

Example 3.8 (a) J. S. Bach, *Canonic Variations*, BWV 769, variation 5, mm. 1–6; (b) J. G. Kauffmann, Chorale prelude on *Vom Himmel hoch* from *Harmonische Seelenlust* (1733–6), bars 5–11

basic contrapuntal framework. The final variation, which explores the canonic possibilities of the theme and its melodic inversions, also transcends its manifest contrapuntal parameters. Here Bach adopts a style not unlike a setting of the same chorale, *Vom Himmel hoch*, from a collection entitled *Harmonische Seelenlust* (Leipzig, 1733–35), by the late G. F. Kauffmann, former organist in nearby Merseburg.[37] In the preface to the volume, Kauffmann, using the *galant* language of contemporary music criticism, describes his chorale preludes as having been "elaborated with particular invention and good grace" (nach besondern *Genie* und guter *Grace* elaborirte).[38] Both Kauffmann's setting of *Vom Himmel hoch* and Bach's have an active walking bass line below a vigorously ornamented chorale melody, although Bach's is a canon in contrary motion at the sixth, while Kauffmann's soprano provides a free accompaniment (Example 3.8). The fifth variation of Bach's *Vom Himmel hoch* is clearly far beyond the scope of Kauffmann's pleasing chorale, but although Bach's setting is much more intricate and impressive it hardly disregards

---

[37] For a discussion of the parallels between the two pieces see John Butt, "J. S. Bach and G. F. Kauffmann: Reflections on Bach's Later Style," in *Bach Studies* 2, ed. Daniel R. Melamed (Cambridge, 1995), 56–57.

[38] G. F. Kauffmann, "Vorrede" to *Harmonische Seelenlust*, reprinted in part in modern edn., ed. Pierre Pidoux, 2 vols. (Kassel, 1951), I, 2. Likewise in his now-lost composition treatise, advertised in 1725 in Mattheson's *Critica musica* (II, 31–32), Kauffmann promised to offer an inclusive approach to old and new styles of composition; double counterpoint was a vital component of the program as well.

fashion. Indeed, modern tastes were just as receptive to the exuberance of such music, as they were to the kind of elegance heard in the opening movements of the *Canonic Variations*. The magnificent closing stretto of the print's last variation, which combines all lines of the chorale and in which Bach even manages to sign his own name, ignites into "sublime fire" (Scheibe's phrase). This increased contrapuntal density generates an expansion of the texture and with the accompanying dynamic boost the piece bursts the shackles of counterpoint, erupting into expressive grandeur and brilliance – the ultimate rhetorical summation. Even Scheibe could hardly have been disappointed or chagrined at such an apotheosis.

But it is the third variation, the central movement in the print, that is the most modern of the set. Here the two lower voices form a canon at the seventh made up predominantly of flowing eighth notes; in the print the pleasing *Cantabile* melody stands directly above the canon, which is written on a single line in puzzle notation – the modern and archaic juxtaposed on the page. The marking *Cantabile*, with its allusion to the music of the human voice, associates the piece with the ideal of the natural aesthetic espoused by Mattheson and Scheibe, the same ideal referred to by Bach in the title-page of the Inventions and Sinfonias. Mattheson, Scheibe, and Heinichen all agreed that effective music must have a "pervasive Cantabile" which was "the outstanding part of an exceptionally good taste."[39]

In the the third movement of the *Canonic Variations* (refer to Example 2.10) the direction *Cantabile* applies to the alto part, heard in the right hand – to be played on a second manual – above which the chorale melody sounds, and below which in the left hand and pedal flow the canonic voices, for the most part a succession of sixths and thirds. Scheibe stressed the importance of ornamentation in imbuing melody with a sense of *Cantabile*;[40] the spontaneous and unpredictable ornamentation of the *Cantabile* line of Bach's variation is full of the kinds of figures also treated by Quantz in his *Versuch einer Anweisung die Flöte traversiere zu spielen* (1752), a lexicon of *galant* figuration. Like Scheibe, Quantz viewed such decoration as indispensable:

Without *Vorschläge* a melody would often sound very meagre and plain. If it is to have a *galant* air, it must contain more consonances than dissonances; but if many of the former occur in succession... the ear may easily be wearied by them. Hence dissonances must be used from time to time to rouse the ear. And in this connection *Vorschläge* can be of considerable assistance.[41]

---

[39] Heinichen, *Der General-Bass in der Composition*, 23; Mattheson, *Critica musica*, I, 329.
[40] Scheibe, *Critischer Musikus*, II, 397.
[41] J. J. Quantz, *Versuch einer Anweisung die Flöte traversiere zu spielen* (Berlin, 1752; reprint, Kassel, 1953); trans. Edward R. Reilly as *On Playing the Flute* (London and Boston,

Example 3.9 Galant ornamentation of basic melody line: (a) J. S. Bach *Canonic Variations*, BWV 769, variation 3, with melodic skeleton; (b) J. J. Quantz, ornamented Adagio, from *Versuch* (1752)

When stripped of its *galant* graces the alto line of the third variation reveals a skeleton of simple consonant melodic notes; Bach introduces dissonance through grace notes, accented passing tones, slides – all of which are mentioned by Quantz. *Galant* conceits like these appear frequently in the music of mid-century, as for example in the ornamented Adagio from Quantz's *Versuch*. Bach's variation, like Quantz's paradigmatic Adagio, is embroidered with shifting rhythmic patterns (Example 3.9), moving effortlessly between duple groupings and triplets; this irregularity is emphasized in the later autograph version with its elegant reading of measure 6, where Bach transforms

---

1985), 91. C. P. E. Bach also praised this ornament: "Appoggiaturas are among the most essential embellishments." C. P. E. Bach, *Essay on the True Art of Playing Keyboard Instruments*, trans. and ed. William J. Mitchell (New York, 1949), 87.

Example 3.10 Comparison of BWV 769, variation 3, and BWV 769a, variation 4 (slightly different versions of same piece), m. 6

Example 3.11 Leaping appoggiaturas with turns: J. S. Bach, *Canonic Variations*, BWV 769, variation 3; C. P. E. Bach, *Versuch*, Table V

the figure into suave triplets, followed by a thirty-second-note figure (Example 3.10). Also very expressive in Bach's variation are the turns that become leaping appoggiaturas, a highly gestural figure, which, like so many of the decorations in the *Canonic Variations*, is similar to examples found in C. P. E. Bach's *Versuch* (Example 3.11). The thirty-second-note slides, on the first beat of mm. 2 and 3, are among the modern figures Scheibe refers to with the term *Galanterie*, useful, he writes, in "delicate things" (*delicate* Sachen).[42] The third variation

---

[42] Scheibe, *Compendium Musices*, in Benary, *Die deutsche Kompositionslehre des 18. Jahrhunderts*, appendix, 38.

Example 3.12   J. S. Bach, *Canonic Variations*, BWV 769, variation 3, mm. 26–27

concludes with a long rising chain of appoggiaturas to the lowered seventh degree with the obligatory final appoggiatura marking the apogee of this natural elegance (Example 3.12).

Bach's mastery of just this kind of ornamentation had been highly praised by Scheibe himself in an article in *Critischer Musikus* published in 1739, as the hostilities with Bach and his defenders were dying down – an article that may represent an attempt at rapprochement. The third of the *Canonic Variations* is one of the finest examples of what Scheibe called "lavish ornamentation" in Bach's keyboard music, and demonstrates an unmatched command of contemporary musical idioms. These nuances of ornamentation and rhythm suggest that Bach concentrated not purely on canonic artifice – on the "abstract" – but on the immediate and engaging elements of style as well. Bach appeals to an ideal of pleasantness even though the basis of the piece is utterly "artificial." Not only the "singing" melody, but the canonic parts as well, sound utterly free and flowing. Contrary to Scheibe's assertion, Bach does not prefer artifice to nature, at least not in the *Canonic Variations*; instead, he presents an argument for their integration.

It was just as a later eighteenth-century commentator, who was most likely C. P. E. Bach, put it: the Bachian art of organ playing "happily and inimitably united the old, dark burrowings with the brighter taste and more beautiful expression of our newer music."[43] Birnbaum too, in his second defense of Bach, had uncharacteristically adopted a *galant* literary manner in asserting that Bach had the ability "to move most tenderly the hearts of his listeners through playing

---

[43] *NBR*, 407.

that is at once pleasing and artistic."[44] The terms of modern music criticism continued to be used by Bach's proponents in defense of his music. In the preface to the 1752 edition of the *Art of Fugue* Friedrich Wilhelm Marpurg stressed, as he would again a year later in the dedication to the second volume of *Abhandlung von der Fuge*, that while Bach's music was profoundly intellectual and highly crafted, it also appealed to current aesthetic values: it was Bach who had kept to the golden mean, and who had taught those who would learn from him "how to combine an agreeable and flowing melody with the richest harmonies [i.e., counterpoint]."[45] In a similar vein Marpurg had praised Telemann's *Canons mélodieux*: "The masterpieces from your pen have long disproven the false opinion that the so-called *galant* style (*die sogenannte galante Schreibart*) cannot be joined with the traits taken from counterpoint."[46] In the *Canonic Variations* Bach embraced the modern style and elevated it with intricate counterpoint. The reverse is also true: that modish stylistic conceits and their elegant performance enliven and enlighten the dark burrowings of counterpoint. In the F major Duetto Bach's music displays a contrary attitude towards the categories of Enlightenment criticism and its strictures regarding the clear projection of genre and the purity of style – high, middle, and low all dutifully kept within their appropriate borders;[47] in the *Canonic Variations*, however, Bach presents a constructive approach to genre, producing a varied collection of chorales both *galant* and highly complex, enigmatic and yet unambiguously clear in their expressive intentions.

There were compelling reasons for arguing on behalf of art in the *Canonic Variations*, for the listener-based aesthetic championed by Mattheson and flirted with by Scheibe threatened a perilous relativism. As we have seen, one of Mattheson's preoccupations was the listener's ability, or lack thereof, to perceive musical complexity. In "Die canonische Anatomie" he treated this problem with a picturesque translation of musical taste back to its culinary origins:

Most musical listeners are uninformed people with respect to art. What a great deed I have done when I know how to disguise an art-piece (*Kunst-Stück*) from

---

[44] Birnbaum, "Verteidigung Bachs gegen Scheibes Angriffe" (March, 1739) in Scheibe, *Critischer Musikus*, rev. edn., 900–1031, at p. 980; reprinted in part in *BD* II, 340–360; quote at p. 347.
[45] Marpurg, *Abhandlung von der Fuge*, 2 vols. (Berlin, 1753–54), II, dedication [to C. P. E. and W. F. Bach]; trans. *NBR*, pp. 360–361. F. W. Marpurg, "Vorwort" to *Die Kunst der Fuge*, 2nd edn.; reprinted in *BD* III, 14–16; trans. *NBR*, 375–377.
[46] Marpurg, *Abhandlung von der Fuge*, I, preface.
[47] See Laurence Dreyfus, *Bach and the Patterns of Invention* (Cambridge, Mass., 1996), 33–58.

their ears, so that when they hear it they don't notice it at all. What a miracle! Just as when a farmer unknowingly swallows along with his sauerkraut a roasted canary that cost six thaler, and after he has done this, he would rather have stuffed himself with roast pork.[48]

Progressive critics had frequently equated undue artifice on the behalf of the composer with self-indulgence, a contempt for the audience, and, above all, a fundamental lack of taste. However extreme this position sometimes appeared, it was not an absolute. Even Heinichen, at his most polemical, acknowledged that "it is true, as good practical musicians now and then prove, that it is possible to combine counterpoint with good taste (*mit dem* Gout)."[49] If nothing else, the *Canonic Variations* demonstrated that artifice need not conflict with nature, that music could be full of contrapuntal complexities and still be tasteful and appealing. Bach's music epitomized the artistic manipulation of nature, but, as his champions were quick to claim, it did not disregard in any way the sentiments of his audience. Lorenz Mizler, in a brief note on Bach's behalf in the exchange with Scheibe, argued that while Bach's music was often more carefully worked out than that of other composers, when so inclined his teacher could compose "in accordance with the latest taste" (nach dem neuesten Geschmack) and, with a nod to prevailing views on the proper relationship between audience and composer, that Bach knew how "to suit himself to his listeners" (sich nach seinen Zuhörern zu richten).[50] With the exception of the augmentation canon, a piece which exceeds the cognitive skills of even the most learned and perspicacious listener, the rest of the *Canonic Variations* are hardly covert or obscure. Bach's third variation appeals both to Mattheson's amateur and to the learned professionals of Mizler's society; rather than descend to the level of the musical farmer, Bach refuses to abandon artifice simply because it might be underappreciated, and even if the fundamental ingredients are not recognized, the work as a whole still pleases, and thereby satisfies. The entire collection, and especially the third variation, can be seen to reflect this same aesthetic goal: the refinement of taste through counterpoint.

It was not only progressive critics who drew on the culinary origins of the metaphor of musical taste: Bach did so himself most famously in the last of the thirty Goldberg Variations, BWV 988. Instead of a culminating canon, which was called for if Bach had followed the pattern he had set up over the course of the variations, he concocts a Quodlibet, an incongruous contrapuntal stew using two folk melodies (Example 3.13).

---

[48] Mattheson, *Critica musica*, I, 347.
[49] Heinichen, *Der General-Bass in der Composition*, 9, fn. b.
[50] Lorenz Christoph Mizler, *Neu eröffnete musikalische Bibliothek*, 4 vols. (Leipzig, 1739–54), I, part 6, 43; trans. *NBR*, 350.

Example 3.13   Folk tunes in *Quodlibet*, BWV 988/30

Example 3.14   J. S. Bach, Quodlibet, Goldberg Variations, BWV 988, mm. 1–4

One is the earthy "Kraut und Rüben" (Cabbage and Beets), whose tune is derived from the widely circulated *Bergamasca* (known to Bach as the concluding piece of Frescobaldi's *Fiori musicali* and as the basis for Buxtehude's variation set entitled *La Capricciosa*),[51] and whose text runs as follows: "Cabbage and beets / have driven me away; / had my mother cooked meat / I might have longer stayed." Bach combines "Kraut und Rüben" with another tune, "Ich bin so lang nicht bei dir g'west" (I have been so long away from you) in artful counterpoint (Example 3.14). The point is not to disguise the tune's humble origins, but to tout them. The humor, of course, comes from having the ingenious elaboration of lowly melodies stand in for the refined and exacting canons that have come before. The possible meanings are deliciously open-ended, but no less suggestive. I see the Quodlibet as a sublime anti-climax, a wonderfully self-ironizing gesture in which Bach archly implies that had the menu been more succulent and less austerely canonic he might even have treated his audience to another thirty variations, and thereby matched Handel's sixty-two variations on the chaconne bass (HWV 442) that may itself have been an inspiration for the Goldberg Variations.[52] That Bach in no way believes that his series of canons is austere and unappetizing – the

---

[51] David Schulenberg, *The Keyboard Music of J. S. Bach* (New York, 1992), 336–337.
[52] Christoph Wolff, *Johann Sebastian Bach: The Learned Musician* (New York, 2000), 377–378.

Example 3.15   Handel, Prelude and Chaconne in G major, HWV 442, variation 62

fifteenth variation with its *galant* touches is evidence of this – makes the joke even funnier, imbuing the false modesty with a bravura that is itself reflected in the contrapuntal ingenuity of this concluding variation. The Quodlibet might also be seen as a mischievous response to the concluding variation of Handel's expansive chaconne, a simple, even simplistic, two-part canon at the octave with none of the contrapuntal panache of those in the Goldberg set (Example 3.15). Considered in these terms, the entire canonic enterprise of the Goldberg Variations becomes a surpassing continuation of the tentative canonic elaboration of the bass-line with which Handel closes his chaconne. The crucial canonic aspect of Bach's Goldberg project would then be an attempt to eclipse its Handelian inspiration. Finally, the Quodlibet might be taken as a response to Domenico Scarlatti's preface to the *Essercizi* of 1739, whose thirty sonatas may have been another of the widely circulating keyboard collections that Bach hoped the Goldberg Variations would be measured against. In his preface Scarlatti disclaimed any attempt to demonstrate profound learning, describing himself as having pursued "an ingenious jesting with art." An afterword rather than a preface, Bach's Quodlibet acknowledges that there has been much profound learning in the preceding variations, but that the jesting has been not so much with art as through it.

In the introduction to *Der General-Bass in der Composition*, Heinichen had colorfully compared composers laboring over counterpoint in a piece of music to "farmers when they shovel manure onto the wagon."[53] Heinichen's rustic language marks counterpoint as anti-*galant*, for what could be further from the world of the *galant homme* than shoveling

[53] Heinichen, *Der General-Bass in der Composition*, 8.

Example 3.16 C. P. E. Bach, *Bauerntanz* Canon, solution by J. P. Kirnberger printed in *Die Kunst des reinen Satzes* (1776–79)

manure? The Goldberg Variations Quodlibet is just one example of the ironic removal of elaborate counterpoint from the music room to the farmyard. Like the Quodlibet, the intricate canon in the form of a *Bauerntanz* that C. P. E. Bach sent to his father's student J. P. Kirnberger is another piece of rusticated counterpoint (Example 3.16); in C. P. E. Bach's canon, however, one of the most complex of contrapuntal procedures – augmentation – is made to dance the farmer's dance. Here the humor derives from the use of learned procedures for outlandish purposes: loading up a *Bauerntanz* with shovelfuls of artifice is inherently funny, for a more stylistically inappropriate application of contrapuntal technique could scarcely be imagined. But this is hardly peasant music; rather it is the aestheticized experience of connoisseurs admiring the compositional technique as well as the incongruity of introducing it to the lowliest of genres. The joke, which certainly would have been lost on Mattheson's hungry farmer though not on Mattheson himself, turned on the wastefulness of abstruse counterpoint as the accompaniment for a country stomp. (Is it a coincidence that C. P. E. Bach's canon appears in Kirnberger's treatise soon after a reference to Heinichen's polemical introduction to *Der General-Bass in der Composition*, in which Kirnberger claims that the author expressed a harsher view of learned counterpoint than he actually subscribed to himself?) Thus the ironic humor in C. P. E. Bach's canon fills the gap between form and content; the abominable mixture of high and low becomes the stuff of comedy.

Example 3.17 G. P. Telemann, Sonatina no. 1 in A major, first movement, mm. 1–6

Bach and his sons were not the only composers in the middle of the eighteenth century with a penchant for expanding the complexity of a genre, and for seeing great contrapuntal potential in unlikely places. A curious item in Telemann's *Getreuer Music-Meister* suggests how, for accomplished composers and their amateur and professional audiences, the lightest of musical inventions might encourage learned elaboration. In the third issue of Telemann's serial there appeared *Etliche contrapunctische Veränderungen über die telemannische Sonatina*, a title which, coincidentally, shows a certain similarity to that of Bach's *Canonic Variations* (*Einige canonische Veränderungen über das Weyhnacht-Lied: Vom Himmel hoch da komm ich her*). As the title suggests, the main theme of Telemann's *Veränderungen* comes from the first movement of a sonatina published a decade earlier in 1718 (Example 3.17). However charming the sonatina may be, it is utterly vacuous. The piece contains not the slightest hint of artifice; there is nothing bold or even interesting in its harmonic language or formal construction. Yet in *Der getreue Music-Meister* Telemann adds to the sonatina's theme a countersubject which he shows to be not only invertible at the octave, but which also allows the theme to be melodically inverted against it (without this countersubject itself being inverted). Still more impressive is Telemann's demonstration to his readers that the original theme will work against itself in retrograde (Example 3.18). What are we to make of these seemingly erudite contrapuntal variations on material taken from a banal sonatina? Perhaps Telemann's contrapuntal suggestions imply that admonitions against confusing the natural style with contrapuntal artifice – the critical position staked out most stridently by Scheibe – are overstated; perhaps Telemann is also saying that the complex can be not only palatable but engaging, an appropriate object of *galant* connoisseurship.

Example 3.18 G. P. Telemann, *Etliche Contrapunctische Veränderungen des ersten Taktes der telemannischen Sonatinen* [A few contrapuntal variations on the first measure of the Telemann sonatina], in *Der getreue Music-Meister* (1728)

At the very least Telemann's *Etliche contrapunctische Veränderungen* show that Bach was not the only one who, when contemplating a theme, could assess the contrapuntal operations which could be performed on it: as C. P. E. Bach told Forkel, J. S. Bach could predict the contrapuntal ramifications of a subject, and would nudge his son knowingly when "his expectations had been fulfilled."[54] Although no match for Bach's erudite genius, Telemann was plainly not averse to exploring the latent contrapuntal possibilities to be discovered in even the most anodyne piece of *galant* music: his *Etliche contrapunctische Veränderungen* certainly show how an artful double fugue, concluding, perhaps, with a good deal of complex canonic interplay, could be generated from the theme of a garrulous sonatina, transforming an "insipid *galant* piece" – as Birnbaum put it – into a grander oration. It is true that in *Der getreue Music-Meister* these contrapuntal variations are relegated to the sideline, an interesting teaser (without any commentary) in a popular publication. The sonatina itself is not in fact transformed; it is not altered into a richer art piece that would flout the generally agreed limits of a genre which, according to the dictates of Enlightened theory, should avoid dense contrapuntal work. But in so far as Telemann's contrapuntal suggestions lay out a plan for lifting a trifling *galant* piece towards loftier goals it shares the elevating spirit of Bach's *Canonic Variations*. Clearly, the genre of the chorale prelude, already treated

[54] *NBR*, 397.

with considerable canonic artifice by Bach in his Weimar *Orgelbüchlein*, would also admit such learned treatment. The role played by counterpoint in effecting the mocking attitude towards genre that gives life to C. P. E. Bach's canonic *Bauerntanz*, a charmingly disrespectful mode that Bach senior often adopted, is not the role played by counterpoint in the *Canonic Variations*. The refined style of the *Canonic Variations* is a long way from the barnyard, and evinces not incongruousness but integration. While Bach shows a penchant for exploding generic conventions, as in the F major Duetto, he is also capable of commenting on the status of genre gently, even politely, as if demonstrating an awareness that manners, even in music, were the standard by which the *galant homme* was ultimately to be judged.

In a letter to Mattheson published at the close of "Die canonische Anatomie," Telemann had claimed that canons could "fall agreeably on the ear and delight the judgment of the understanding."[55] Telemann followed Mattheson in criticizing unnatural and excessive artifice, but described a metaphorical house of music in which "canons make up a room, if you will, but do not provide the foundation itself."[56] Whether Bach agreed completely with his friend's assessment of the state of canonic artifice in contemporary musical practice is a matter of speculation, but clearly there was a place for counterpoint in the world of modern music. While Bach could certainly become obsessive in his use of counterpoint, he could also be tasteful in the sense that Heinichen, Mattheson, and others would have understood it. And although he could gleefully dismantle genres (as in the F major Duetto), his use of contrapuntal artifice could also be positively constructive of genre while commenting insightfully on Enlightened aesthetic categories. Like Telemann and several other contemporaries, Bach could integrate supposedly antiquated methods into the contemporary realities of musical practice – lightening the dark burrowings with modern touches, taking from the old in pursuit of the new. That the complexity of Bach's *Canonic Variations* went far beyond the scope of any contemporary work does not mean that when Bach wrote canons he was necessarily assuming the pose of an aesthetic maverick, or that he was indifferent to or scornful of the issues of naturalness and complexity constantly being argued over in the critical literature. Instead of marking a withdrawal, strict counterpoint was one of the most trenchant means by which Bach's music engaged with the theoretical concerns of his day.

While Bach's early admirers – Mizler, Marpurg, Kirnberger, and his own sons among others – asserted that his music participated in

---

[55] Mattheson, *Critica musica*, I, 360.
[56] Telemann's letter is printed in *Critica musica* I, 358–360. Heinichen's derogatory letter is printed in *Critica musica*, I, 357–358.

contemporary critical discourse on many levels, subsequent hagiographers more often suggested the opposite. The extreme statement of this position comes not unexpectedly from Forkel's 1802 biography: "in his compositions for the organ [Bach] kept himself infinitely more distant from [everything common]; so that here, it seems to me, he does not appear like a man, but as a true disembodied spirit, who soars above everything mortal."[57] The residue of this conception of Bach music persists in the modern musicological literature: Bach is an archaist, a perfectionist, a progressive (but *not* when his writing involved counterpoint), or even a trans-historical force at odds with his Age. But instead of reflecting abstract tendencies or metaphysical transcendence, most of Bach's late works place him firmly on the ground among his contemporaries, engaging them rather than retreating from them; contrapuntal complexity is not a marker of sublime abstruseness and self-absorption. The very fact that the vast majority of Bach's most learned contrapuntal works were published and were intended, or so the title-pages claimed, for the refreshment of amateurs, makes isolation and ignorance an unlikely intellectual environment for their composition in the first place. Indeed, it is precisely Bach's keen understanding of contemporary aesthetics that frames the diverse arguments of the F major Duetto and the *Canonic Variations*, as well as much of his late music. Although he produced neither a theoretical treatise nor a written defense of his musical beliefs – a glaring demerit as far as Scheibe was concerned – Bach actively entered the aesthetic debates of his time through his music, demonstrating that, contrary to Scheibe's aspersions, he was indeed a "critical composer."

[57] *NBR*, 438.

4

The autocratic regimes of *A Musical Offering*

When J. S. Bach was ushered into the music room at Potsdam city palace on Sunday May 7, 1747, he not only encountered for the first time the most powerful and famous German ruler of the day, Frederick the Great, but he was also about to be on display before a gathering of the era's most celebrated musicians: Bach's two eldest sons, Wilhelm Friedemann and Carl Philipp Emanuel, as well as Johann Joachim Quantz, Franz Benda, Johann Gottlieb Graun, and the Prussian Kapellmeister Karl Heinrich Graun. Even Frederick's valet, Michael Gabriel Fredersdorf (the monarch's flute partner and the man to whom Bach dedicated his flute sonata in E major, BWV 1035), was ready to judge the illustrious visitor's performance with discerning ears. In addition to this distinguished collection of musical figures, one of the most demanding fugue subjects in the history of the genre lay in wait.

All the members of this august audience, with the exception of Friedemann, were employed by Frederick. Friedemann was then working in Halle, not far from Leipzig, and had accompanied his aged father on the coach ride from Leipzig; it was his version of the encounter which found its way into Forkel's 1802 Bach biography. In this account the flute-playing king had been about to begin the private concert that he held every night, and in which he was the featured performer, when he was shown a list of arriving visitors. Forkel writes that Frederick "immediately turned to the assembled musicians and said, with a kind of agitation: 'Gentlemen, old Bach is come.' The flute was now laid aside, and old Bach... was immediately summoned." As Forkel goes on:

I must say that I still think with pleasure on the manner in which Friedemann related [the story to me]. At that time it was the fashion to make rather effusive compliments. The first appearance of J. S. Bach before so great a King, who did not even give him time to change his traveling dress... must necessarily be attended with many apologies. I will not here dwell on these apologies, but merely observe that in Friedemann's mouth they made a formal dialogue between the King and the apologist.

With this awkward choreography of submission concluded, the evening was given over to the elder Bach's improvisations on the king's new Silbermann fortepianos, a performance highlighted by Bach's execution of a learned fugue on the subject Frederick had prepared for him. It was this "royal" theme that would form the basis for *A Musical Offering* (BWV 1079), whose trio sonata, two ricercars, and ten diverse canons were completed within just two months of Bach's Berlin journey, printed as a set by September of that year and duly dedicated to the Prussian king.

Even more unsettling than Friedemann's acting out for Forkel of his obsequious father's self-abasement before the king is the urgency with which Bach's devotees have attemped to explain away this story. Where Forkel may have found Friedemann's mimicry quite amusing, subsequent historians, beginning with Philipp Spitta, have been fearful that the famous product of this encounter, *A Musical Offering*, might be tarnished by the servile tone of Bach's first exchange with Frederick; these historians have done their best to discredit the prime witness (Friedemann) and restore to Bach his self-respect in the face of absolute power.[1] The problem is exacerbated by Bach's subsequent dedication of the work to Frederick in a formulaic style which is nonetheless overladen with manifest submissiveness.

Most Gracious King,
   In deepest humility I herewith dedicate to Your Majesty a Musical Offering, the noblest part of which derives from Your Majesty's own august hand. With reverence and pleasure I still remember the very special Royal grace when, some time ago, during my visit in Potsdam Your Majesty's Self deigned to play to me a fugue theme on the keyboard, and at the same time charged me most graciously to carry it out in Your Majesty's most august presence. To obey Your Majesty's command was my most humble duty.[2]

Bach goes on to claim that in preparing the collection he had "no other intent than to glorify, if only in a small way, the fame of a monarch whose greatness and power, as in all the sciences of war and peace, so especially in music, everyone must admire and revere."

---

[1] Philipp Spitta, *Johann Sebastian Bach*, trans. Clara Bell and J. A. Fuller Maitland, 3 vols. (London, 1889; reprint, New York, 1979), III, 231. Christoph Wolff also doubts the reliability of some elements of Friedemann's account, though he finds J. S. Bach's servile excuse-making believable. See Wolff, *Kanons, Musicalisches Opfer: Kritischer Bericht* (Kassel, 1976), 103.

[2] For the dedication in the German original see *BD* I, 241–242.

Albert Schweitzer, for one, strained to assert that in spite of the genuflections of Bach's prose, the composer addresses the king frankly as an "equal."[3] Others have chosen to interpret *A Musical Offering* not as a glorification of Frederick the Great but rather as a critique of his, and by extension all, worldly dominion; in this view *A Musical Offering* is a tribute not to an earthly king but to the heavenly one instead. So thickly armored with his belief is this Bach that one scholar finds it "unlikely that [he] would have shied away from making bold statements before a king."[4] The effect of this hermeneutic mode is to protect the integrity of the artist, and in place of Friedemann's groveling *Musikant* of an age gone by, Hegel's "grand, truly Protestant, robust and, so to speak, erudite genius" emerges unsullied.[5]

The overlap between the religious view of Bach and the Romantic conception of him is readily apparent, for in both the great composer must resist the interferences of the world. Vigorously at odds with his times, this Bach is also a man without politics, and the main concern his music shows with configurations of power is to demonstrate their futility. Two hundred and fifty years after his death Bach is still almost universally seen as a stubbornly independent musician, whose work was untarnished by political or otherwise opportunistic impulses. The strict contrapuntal writing that dominates *A Musical Offering* has been read as tending towards abstraction, since there is no finer, more artfully worked out product of Bach's intellect, no more cerebral a succession of seemingly autonomous musical perfections. Although many would like to divorce these famous canons from the vivid scenario of a deferential musical functionary bowing before a great musical sovereign, such wishes ignore the historical circumstances that attended the creation of *A Musical Offering* and the political views held by its creator. These readings of Bach's tribute to Frederick also misrepresent the critical standing of canon in the middle of the eighteenth century in order to portray Bach as the last unflinching defender of the contrapuntal arts, a man fighting tenaciously against the dominant musical fashions and the decline in standards represented most egregiously by the Prussian court. Bach remains an anachronism. But Bach the fiercely autonomous artist is incompatible with the Bach who appeared before Frederick the Great in the spring of 1747, and who sent him an impressive collection of contrapuntal music four months later. What I want to suggest here is that *A Musical Offering* is indeed profoundly shaped by the composer's politics.

---

[3] Albert Schweitzer, *Johann Sebastian Bach*, trans. Ernest Newman, 2 vols. (Leipzig, 1911), I, 153.

[4] Michael Marissen, "The Theological Character of J. S. Bach's *Musical Offering*," in *Bach Studies 2*, ed. Daniel R. Melamed (Cambridge, 1995), 85–106, esp. 105–106.

[5] G. W. F. Hegel, *Aesthetics: Lectures on Fine Art*, trans. T. M. Knox, 2 vols. (Oxford, 1975), II, 950.

Political life during Bach's tenure in Leipzig was dominated by the overriding conflict, played out across Europe, between the Estates – comprising mostly the nobility and the cities – and the absolutist aims of the monarchy.[6] In terms of efficiency and completeness, the continued consolidation of the Hohenzollern regime under Frederick the Great far outstripped the centralized power accrued by his Saxon neighbors to the south. Nonetheless, both houses had involved themselves in similar contests between monarchic ambition and the prerogatives of the Estates, conflicts which strongly shaped Bach's professional experience in Saxon Leipzig. The Leipzig town council which selected Bach in 1723, and with which he was to have so much trouble, was made up of competing factions with allegiances to the monarch (the Saxon elector) and to the city respectively. The absolutist party had sought a Kapellmeister, while the city faction wanted a good old-fashioned cantor more concerned with education at the Thomasschule than the production of ambitious, quasi-operatic vocal music for the church. Eventually, after the council's failure to entice other more desirable candidates, the machinations of the competing factions resulted in the unlikely selection of Bach as the city's director of music.

Bach had been a candidate, albeit not the preferred one, of the absolutist camp, and his allegiances were ultimately to the Saxon elector and his proxies rather than to those on the council committed to ideals of municipal self-government. As Bach's 1730 letter to his old friend Georg Erdmann seems to make clear, Bach wanted to see himself as a Kapellmeister,[7] a more prestigious image in his view, and one that accorded with the absolutist conception of the post and the monarchic affiliations of the council party that had supported his selection. In his imbroglios with the town administration, Bach appealed directly to Saxon judicial authority, a course of action which was only possible because of a vacuum in the municipal legal system created by the incursions of monarchic power.[8] And despite the focus of Bach's personal Bible studies, in which he sometimes highlighted passages critical of social hierarchies,[9] he was virtually obsessed with improving his situation by securing titles and royal favors which would shore up his prestige and help him prevail in his tediously protracted struggles with his Leipzig superiors.

---

[6] The following outline of Leipzig politics is taken from Ulrich Siegele's essay, "Bach and the Domestic Politics of Electoral Saxony," in *The Cambridge Companion to Bach*, ed. John Butt (Cambridge, 1997), 17–34.

[7] *NBR*, 150.

[8] Walter Bruford, *Germany in the Eighteenth Century: The Social Background of the Literary Revival* (Cambridge, 1971), 183.

[9] Michael Marissen, *The Social and Religious Designs of J. S. Bach's Brandenburg Concertos* (Princeton, 1995), 111–119.

These political matters had musical consequences: after 1732 Bach composed no more pieces in honor of the council, whereas he continued to produce cantatas glorifying the elector and members of the absolutist camp, such as Count Joachim Friedrich von Flemming, one of the most powerful politicians in Saxony, whom he had first met in 1717.[10] (Flemming's residence was the venue for Bach's aborted contest with the visiting French organist Louis Marchand.) Throughout his Leipzig years and probably before, Bach was firmly in the absolutist camp, and he consistently attempted to draw on these allegiances, most notably by appealing directly to the absolutist judicial apparatus or, indeed, the elector himself.[11]

Given Bach's political affiliations it is hard to miss the absolutist message projected by the dedication of *A Musical Offering*. Bach's curiously archaic prose with its use of the words "weyhen" (to consecrate) and, indeed, "Opfer" (Offering) is colored by sublimated religious overtones, and this was not in itself unusual: the dedication of J. J. Quantz's seminal *Versuch einer Anweisung die Flöte traversiere zu spielen*, published just five years after *A Musical Offering* and likewise dedicated to Frederick the Great, concludes with the "most humble request" for the "preservation" of Frederick's "Sacred Person" (Geheiligter Person). Princely power was entrusted to eighteenth-century rulers by God, even in the case of Frederick, a man notably lacking in commitment to Christianity. Although Frederick was not a believer, a fact which would certainly have been known to his music master, Quantz, he would not have been offended by language which elevated him towards god-like status; nor is it likely that Frederick would have been irritated by Bach's religiously tinged dedication. Such language only increases the collection's absolutist connotations.

Bach's language has more often been glossed in the musicological literature as reflecting the stilted humility found in so many eighteenth-century tributes to kings and lesser rulers. *A Musical Offering*'s dedication does not depart significantly from this standard,[12] nor, for that matter, does the first set of keyboard sonatas by Bach's second son, Carl Philipp Emanuel, published in 1742.[13] Emanuel's dedication, written in modish Italian rather than the French favored at the Prussian court,

---

[10] See, for example, cantatas BWV 215, BWV 210a performed in honor of the elector, Friedrich August II, and Flemming respectively.
[11] See Erich Reimer's trenchant interpretation of the *Jagdkantate* (BWV 208), composed in 1713, as a reflection of the power structures supporting the Duke of Saxe-Weissenfels. Reimer, "Bachs Jagdkantate als profanes Ritual: zur politischen Funktion absolutischer Hofmusik," *Musik und Bildung* 12 (1980): 674–683.
[12] Spitta, *Bach*, III, 234.
[13] It is likely that J. S. Bach, who sold keyboard music as well as books on music from his home, would have served as the Leipzig representative for his son's "Prussian" sonatas.

employs generic blandishments regarding Frederick's singular genius and discerning taste, while downplaying the composer's own modest abilities.[14] But cursorily to dismiss dedications such as these as generic is to miss a much wider range of meanings in these curious documents. Compare Bach's prose with the work of more confident literary types like Johann Mattheson. Mattheson's 1749 book entitled *Mithridat wider den Gift einer welschen Satyr* was also dedicated to Frederick and presents an unmistakable contrast to the obsequious tone adopted by Bach.[15] The longtime secretary to the English ambassador to Hamburg, Mattheson was not only confident in diplomatic and aristocratic discourses, he was also wealthy, and had no need to appease monarchs in order to increase his prospects. This independence coupled with the extremely high opinion Mattheson had of himself goes a long way towards explaining the self-assurance of the dedication to the *Mithridat*. A full translation (printed alongside the original Italian) and refutation of the seventeenth-century painter Salvator Rosa's attack on the immorality of theatrical music, the *Mithridat* was particularly appropriate to Frederick, who had committed so much of his financial and musical resources to the establishment of the Berlin opera. Though some of the usual rhetorical tropes of flattery are to be found in the introduction they are kept to a minimum; Frederick is lauded not only as a most gracious patron but as a "particularly fine connoisseur" (besonders feiner Kenner), a reference to his fame as a flute soloist and his accomplishments as an amateur composer. But rather than minimizing his own talents Mattheson deems it perfectly logical that this latest opus in his voluminous oeuvre – he immodestly enumerates the treatise as his "sixty-fourth publication" – should be dedicated to this "most magnanimous monarch" (Höchstedelmüthiger Kronenträger). One hardly has to read between the lines, as Schweitzer did with the dedication to *A Musical Offering*, to find Mattheson addressing the king with an assurance that verges on the impudent, a threshold which he confidently oversteps in the body of the text. If Bach's is an assured address to the sovereign, as Schweitzer and Spitta would have us believe, it is an infinitely less confident one than Mattheson's.

While the sedulous cultivation of monarchic favor was nothing extraordinary in the eighteenth century, Bach's efforts occurred at a time when members of a new caste of wide-ranging humanistic critics were

---

[14] C. P. E. Bach, *Sei sonate* (Berlin, 1742; reprint, New York, 1986). Marissen also makes much of the fact that the elder Bach's dedication was written not in French, the language of the Prussian court, but in German, which Frederick did not speak much and wrote only rarely. I find this unconvincing; C. P. E. Bach's dedication is in Italian, while Mattheson, who wrote fluently in several languages, including French, chose to address the king in German (as we will see below). See Michael Marissen, "The Theological Character of J. S. Bach's *Musical Offering*," in *Bach Studies 2*, ed. Daniel R. Melamed (Cambridge, 1995), 85–106, at pp. 101–102.

[15] Johann Mattheson, *Mithridat wider den Gift einer welschen Satyr* (Hamburg, 1749).

keen to differentiate between the pronouncements of powerful figures and the more meaningful judgments of the community of *virtuosi*, of learned and moral musicians trained in both the theory and practice of music. In the introduction to his 1720 collection of solo flute sonatas, the flamboyantly independent Mattheson criticized those musicians who pegged their reputations to the costly gifts and inflated honorifics bestowed on them by "emperors, kings, electors, and lords." Mattheson implicitly impugned the musical opinions of monarchs by likening the all-too-frequent success of a second-rate musician at court "to a blind hen who occasionally finds a barleycorn."[16] Mattheson favored educated taste as the most reliable measure of musical value – and it did not always accord with royal judgment.

With the rising prominence of university-educated composers and critics, the validity of princely taste became increasingly suspect, and writers persistently sought to supplant these rulers as the ultimate arbiters of musical worth. The conflict between the idea that aesthetic value was a matter to be appraised by one's peers, and the alternative view that the most meaningful forms of recognition were to be granted by social and political elites lies at the center of the Scheibe–Birnbaum controversy. Scheibe's provocative use of the word *Musikant* was especially insulting for someone like Bach who had worked hard for his titles and certainly deserved them. It can hardly be a coincidence that Scheibe began referring to Bach with this tauntingly disrespectful term in the same year (indeed, only three months after) Bach received his most prestigious title, that of Court Composer at Dresden. Bach was making no secret of his new-found prestige and the royal protection it signified. Indeed, soon after being granted the honorific in November of 1736 Bach set about brandishing his credentials, drafting a letter to the Leipzig Town Council demanding that his prerogatives as Thomascantor be respected, and signing himself "Composer of the Court Capelle of His Royal Majesty in Poland, and Dir. Chori Musici in this Place."[17] In a letter to his own employers, many of whom wanted a locally oriented cantor not a Saxon superstar, the relegation of his Leipzig position to secondary status was telling. Scheibe apparently also knew of Bach's new title quickly, and his polemic was at least partly an attempt to puncture Bach's ballooning pomposity with his sharpest quill.

In his response to Birnbaum – a response which obstreperously refers to Bach as the Herr Capellmeister and which uses "Court Composer" only when recapitulating Birnbaum's arguments and in an otherwise sarcastic tone – Scheibe mocks Bach's disavowal of the modest but

---

[16] Johann Mattheson, *Der brauchbare Virtuoso* (Hamburg, 1720; reprint, Florence, 1997), 9.
[17] *NBR*, 191; *BD* I, 96. "*Johann* Sebastian Bach, *Compositeur* von Königlicher Maj. in Pohlen Hoff-Capelle, u. *Dir; Chori Musici* allhier."

(claims Scheibe) respectable term *Musikant*, and states brusquely that "titles elevate no one,"[18] accusing the Bach camp of a "zealousness regarding official positions" (Amtseyfer) which presumably was also a way of saying that Bach was guilty of the same sin.[19] Scheibe's attack was just as much about pretentiousness as about music, as much social comment as aesthetic critique. It was not just from Scheibe that the title-proud Bach came in for criticism. Following the Scheibe–Birnbaum controversy bemusedly from Hamburg, Mattheson sided with his companion in iconoclasm Scheibe, admitting that the term *Musikant* was often repudiated by professional musicians, but condemning the arrogance of those – i.e., Bach – who would feel insulted by it.[20] Yet in spite of such sentiments, Birnbaum's clinching argument in his initial response to Scheibe unequivocally locates the most enduring form of artistic approval at the top of the social hierarchy: "The great Augustus [Elector of Saxony] bestows his favor upon [Bach] and rewards his deserts; this [alone] suffices for his praise. Whoever is loved by so great and wise a prince must certainly possess true skill."[21] There could be no clearer endorsement of a monarchist aesthetics.

In terms of his ability to judge musical accomplishment, Frederick the Great was a special case, for he was both king and musician. It would be hard to overestimate the extent of his musical and military fame, and these attributes of his persona often seemed to be inseparable. The impressive musical establishment he had built up in Berlin, boasting many of the finest German musicians of the day, was frequently praised in journals such as Scheibe's often cantankerous *Critischer Musikus*, and Mizler's *Musikalische Bibliothek*.[22] As Mattheson's dedication of his *Mithridat* illustrates, the Prussian king was held in the highest esteem by musicians and critics, and no one was more famous for his love of music than Frederick.

An overlooked report in a 1746 issue of Mizler's magazine gives us an idea of the veneration with which Frederick was regarded by musicians across Germany. In December of 1745, the Second Silesian War had concluded with a stunning Prussian victory at the Battle of Kesseldorf.[23] Frederick triumphantly entered the Saxon capital, Dresden, three days later. Mizler presents a glowing account of Frederick's week-long stay in the city, depicting the king's activities as those of a conquering warrior-musician: while busy with peace negotiations during the day, Frederick arranged for a reprise of the opera *Arminio*, composed by the Saxon Kapellmeister Johann Adolph Hasse for the elector's birthday

---

[18] *BD* II, 313. [19] Ibid.
[20] Mattheson, *Grundlage einer Ehren-Pforte* (Hamburg, 1740; reprint, Berlin, 1910), xxxii.
[21] *NBR*, 348.
[22] References to Scheibe, *Critischer Musikus*, rev. edn. (Leipzig, 1945), 36.
[23] See Robert Asprey, *Frederick the Great: The Magnificent Enigma* (New York, 1986), 346.

two months earlier; chamber music concerts with famed soprano Faustina Bordoni and instrumentalists from the court orchestra took place every evening, and Frederick himself performed several solo sonatas he had composed, along with one specially written for him by Hasse, who accompanied the monarch at the harpsichord. Imagine the chagrin of the Saxon Elector Friedrich August II, now decamped to Prague: as if losing the war were not bad enough, he now had to suffer the humiliation not only of having his most prestigious and expensive cultural icons – his opera, Kapellmeister, and orchestra – coopted for the enjoyment of his enemy, but of knowing that the victor himself was the featured performer at these widely publicized festivities.

The irony here is compounded by the fact that Frederick had first become enamored of expensive musical institutions such as these in the course of an extended visit to Dresden in 1728 during the reign of Elector Friedrich August I. It was during this teenage trip that Frederick first experienced the glories of Dresden opera and played together with the great flute virtuosos Gabriel Buffardin and J. J. Quantz, both of whom were members of the court orchestra; Frederick would later lure Quantz away from Dresden to become his own private flute master. After his first Dresden concert Frederick confided glowingly to his brother that, "I have been heard as musician."[24] Seventeen years later he would be heard again as a musician, but a conquering one rather than a browbeaten teenager under the Prussian boot of his martinet of a father, Frederick William I. Anecdote books from the period tried to highlight this extraordinary musical and military reversal still further by claiming spuriously that it was during his first Dresden trip that Frederick had received his first flute.[25]

The *Musikalische Bibliothek* article also praises the king's compositional output – vast for an amateur – and expresses further amazement at Frederick's ability to flaunt his skill as a musician even while dealing with epic matters of war and peace. The tone is adulatory, even awestruck, reporting that Frederick's performances were greeted "with the greatest amazement of the entire orchestra, on account of the great insight his Highness possessed in music and especially in playing adagios." The article concludes with a rapturous flourish: "Who cannot see that his Majesty is great in war, great in peace, great in governance, great in sciences, and also in music. Long live Frederick the Great!"[26]

The parallels between the preface to *A Musical Offering* and Mizler's article detailing Frederick's exploits in Dresden suggest not only that Bach, who became a member of Mizler's Musical Society in June of 1747,

---

[24] Quoted in Asprey, *Frederick the Great*, 36.
[25] Thomas Carlyle, *Frederick the Great*, 10 vols. (London, 1875), VI, 125.
[26] Lorenz Christoph Mizler, *Neu eröffnete musikalische Bibliothek* (Leipzig, 1739–1754), III, 366–368.

just after his return from Potsdam, could have read Mizler's account, but that Mizler might have had a hand in crafting Bach's tribute to Frederick. The penultimate sentence of *A Musical Offering*'s dedicatory text claims that Bach's "only blameless purpose is to glorify a monarch...who everyone must admire for his greatness and power as in all sciences of war and peace, so also especially in music."[27] Mizler had been eager to hear about Bach's journey to see the great musical sovereign and had closely followed the progress in the printing of *A Musical Offering*; having earlier come to Bach's aid in the Scheibe controversy, Mizler would certainly have been eager to provide further help to his teacher.[28]

Even before Frederick's military machine had swung through Saxony, Bach was well aware of the king's manifold greatness and of the flourishing musical scene at the Prussian capital; he appears to have thought highly of the developments taking place there, especially after his previous visit to the city in 1741.[29] And of course, as court harpsichordist, C. P. E. Bach would have kept his father apprised of the goings on in Berlin. As for Frederick's martial prowess, Bach had experienced that first-hand, having been forced to miss the baptism of C. P. E. Bach's eldest son owing to the occupation of Leipzig in December of 1745, while Frederick was passing his triumphant ten days in Dresden.[30]

As the report in the *Musikalische Bibliothek* clearly shows, Frederick had succeeded in surrounding himself with an aura of invincibility: here was a king among kings, a man who had defeated the Saxon elector, Friedrich August II, a monarch from whom Bach had so persistently sought justice in his civic conflicts and in praise of whom he had composed much lavish music. A successful meeting with the even more powerful Frederick could gain favor for Emanuel at the Prussian court, and possibly yield benefits for Bach himself, for he could have read in Mizler's journal that Hasse's meeting with Frederick had netted him a "precious ring" and one thousand thalers, more than Bach's annual salary, and almost the total value of his estate at the time of his death. It is hardly surprising, then, that a keen absolutist like Bach would have so quickly humbled himself when meeting the great musical and military hero in person.

That Frederick apparently did not even acknowledge receipt of *A Musical Offering* has often been adduced as evidence that he was not interested in the collection. Before we accept the monarch's facile dismissal of Bach's efforts, it is worth considering Mattheson's experiences with Frederick. In the handwritten afterward to his personal copy of the *Grundlage einer Ehren-Pforte*, Mattheson noted that royal

---

[27] *BD* I, 241–242. For a full English translation see *NBR*, 226–228.
[28] *NBR*, 228.
[29] C. P. E. Bach to J. N. Forkel, January 13, 1775, in *NBR*, 398–400. "In his last years, [Bach] esteemed highly... everything of esteem in Berlin and Dresden."
[30] *BD* I, 117–118.

musicians Quantz and Fredersdorf had told him that Frederick had accepted Mattheson's book and the dedication to him. Yet when no royal thanks had been forthcoming Mattheson was somewhat philosophical: "the great and unparalleled royal hero has since then become occupied with so many immortal deeds that he has perhaps forgotten about the *Mithridat.*"[31] As a diplomatic secretary, Mattheson had a good sense of the demands of statecraft: Frederick's daily regimen commenced at five in the morning with several hours of letter writing and ended after nine in the evening with his private concerts; the staggering volume of his diplomatic correspondence alone reveals his schedule to have been an extraordinarily taxing one. In light of the statements Mattheson claimed to have received from Fredersdorf and Quantz we can be fairly certain that Frederick saw Mattheson's *Mithridat* or at the very least knew of its existence; it is only because of the comprehensive nature of Mattheson's literary estate that this piece of evidence has survived. It also seems likely that Frederick would have seen *A Musical Offering*, and may well have graciously accepted the dedication, just as he had done for Mattheson's book; that Frederick apparently never took the time to acknowledge either Bach or Mattheson directly cannot be taken as a tacit critique of either man's work.

Whatever Bach's motives in creating *A Musical Offering*, some have argued that Frederick would have regarded the results with displeasure, that he would have been either offended or bored by the contents of the collection had he bothered to examine them. In this scenario Bach reproaches Frederick and his secularized musical establishment with antique compositional techniques long associated with the church, and otherwise parodies the *galant* style, as in the third movement of the trio sonata. Bach in Berlin is a man out of place, unable to cross the impenetrable historical boundaries that separate him from the moderns. This claim is a mainstay of the historiographical tradition which finds Bach's use of counterpoint strenuously opposed to, and by, prevailing musical tastes. Thus, when the "robust Protestant cantor" entered the music room at Potsdam palace he confronted a complex of musical and moral values diametrically opposed to his own.[32] In this view Bach's spontaneous display of contrapuntal ingenuity was enjoyed by his hosts more as a curiosity, a historical re-enactment, rather than as a valued contribution to the musical culture of the Prussian capital.

The above-mentioned conception of Bach's last decade as a retreat into abstraction is built largely on the supposition that by the middle of

---

[31] Mattheson, *Ehren-Pforte*, Anhang, 26. Quoted in Beekman C. Cannon, *Johann Mattheson: Spectator in Music* (New Haven, 1947), 95.

[32] See Marissen, "The Theological Character of J. S. Bach's *Musical Offering*," 89.

Example 4.1   J. S. Bach, Sonata in E major for flute and harpsichord, BWV 1035, second movement, mm. 1–5

Siciliano

the eighteenth century counterpoint had become an antiquarian pursuit that had little commerce with the *galant* style. But this view mistakenly collapses the distinction between compositional technique (in this case, canon) and style.[33] Jeanne Swack's description of Bach's E major Sonata for flute and continuo (BWV 1035; Example 4.1), a piece apparently written for the Prussian court (see p. 128 above), is paradigmatic. Swack allows that elements of the piece are modern, but "for Frederick's *galant* taste... some features, for example the canonic imitation in the Siciliano [2nd movement] must have seemed old-fashioned."[34] But consider the more thoroughly canonic progress of the second slow movement of the Sonata in A major for violin and harpsichord BWV 1015 (Example 4.2). In a 1774 letter to Forkel, C. P. E. Bach described the entire set as "among the best works of my dear departed father," and claimed that they "still sound excellent... although they date back more than fifty years."[35] In particular, he praised the adagios as thoroughly modern, since they "could not be written in a more singable manner today."[36] The flowing canonic writing of the slow movement of BWV 1015 in no way disqualified the piece from being fashionable: it is both "singable" and canonic. As the *Canonic Variations* so authoritatively demonstrated, Bach was the greatest master of the *galant* canon; the Sarabande from the B minor Orchestral Suite, BWV 1067 is a classic presentation of canonic artifice in a modish, courtly genre (Example 4.3). Simply because an old technique is used does not make a piece old-fashioned; several mid-eighteenth-century writers were clear on this point. Marpurg for one observed that a number of respected composers had applied canonic devices and other forms of "*galant* counterpoint" (galanter Contrapunct) to the "most pleasing kind of chamber sonatas."[37] Among fashionable musicians who had contributed to what he called the "galant, canonic

---

[33] For a trenchant discussion of the conflation of style and technique see Laurence Dreyfus, *Bach and the Patterns of Invention* (Cambridge, Mass., 1996), 189–219.
[34] Jeanne Swack, "Flute Sonatas," in *Oxford Composer Companions: J. S. Bach*, ed. Malcolm Boyd (Oxford, 1999), 174–175.
[35] *NBR*, 388.   [36] Ibid.
[37] F. W. Marpurg, *Abhandlung von der Fuge*, 2 vols. (Berlin, 1753–54), II, 94.

Example 4.2 J. S. Bach, "canonic trio," Sonata in A major for violin and harpsichord, BWV 1015, second movement, mm. 1–4

Example 4.3 J. S. Bach, "*galant* canon," Orchestral Suite no. 2 in B minor, BWV 1067, Sarabande, mm. 1–7

style (Schreibart)" were Telemann, Pepusch, Graupner, and J. F. Fasch (Examples 4.4 and 4.5) – three of whom had been candidates for the Leipzig post of Thomascantor eventually offered to Bach.[38] And while Marpurg had lamented the declining interest in counterpoint in the first volume of the *Abhandlung*, in the preface to the second volume, which appeared the following year, he remarked that he had been pleasantly

[38] Ibid.

The autocratic regimes of A Musical Offering

Example 4.4 J. F. Fasch, Canonic Trio in D major, second movement, mm. 1–9

Example 4.5 Christoph Graupner, Canonic Trio in B♭, mm. 1–14

surprised to find so many more devotees of the discipline than he had originally expected.[39]

Although canon continued to be employed in the *stile antico* by Fux, Stölzel and others following in the august tradition of Palestrina, the device migrated comfortably to the modern style with the general, though not total, approval of most musicians. Indeed it is important to note that Bach's first use of canon in a *stile antico* piece comes late in his career, in the Credo from the B minor Mass.[40] By the time of *A Musical Offering* it seems that canon was more likely to be encountered in *galant* instrumental music than in its traditional context of vocal polyphony. Mattheson, who, as we have seen, showed a markedly ambivalent attitude towards the device even though he was himself an adept practitioner, describes this shift quite clearly in *Der vollkommene Capellmeister*: "Canons should [not] be subsumed under the motet style [i.e., *stile antico*] just because canons sometimes appear in motets: for similar devices are also used in chamber as well as theatrical pieces, indeed even more than in church music, without therewith also giving the appearance of being in the slightest motet-like."[41] This transplantation of various types of counterpoint and canons from church to stage is also remarked on by J. P. Kirnberger in the preface to a collection of operatic ensemble numbers by Frederick's first Kapellmeister Karl Heinrich Graun, who was also present at J. S. Bach's Potsdam performance, and who on occasion included such devices in his theatrical music.[42]

In a remarkable passage in an essay entitled "Die Musikalische Geschmacksprobe" (The Test of Musical Taste) Mattheson disparaged the wayward practices of modern musicians, particularly their appalling mixture of genres in which even dance movements such as sarabandes, gigues, and courantes were introduced in sacred, vocal music, "as long as [the word] fugue, canon, double counterpoint and the like is written above it, and, to be sure, in Italian."[43] It is often hard to get a sure handle on Mattheson's sense of irony, but this passage reveals the extent to which strict contrapuntal techniques, or at least their pretensions, were called upon by even the most vacuous composers. In a word, contrapuntal techniques could at times be simply too modern.

[39] Marpurg, *Abhandlung von der Fuge*, II, dedication.
[40] Christoph Wolff, *Der Stile Antico in der Musik Johann Sebastian Bachs* (Wiesbaden, 1968), 101–102.
[41] Mattheson, *Der vollkommene Capellmeister*, trans. Ernest C. Harriss (Ann Arbor, 1981), 199.
[42] Karl Heinrich Graun, *Duetti, Terzetti, Quintetti, Sestetti, ed alcuni Chori*, 4 vols. (Berlin, 1773–74), I, preface, [c]. See also Kirnberger, *Die Kunst des reinen Satzes*, 2 vols. (1776–79; reprint, Hildesheim, 1968), II, part 2, 232. For an example of Graun's use of canon see the duet "Sia propizia a' desir tuoi" from *Ifigenia in Aulide* (1749) published in the *Duetti*, 122–130, esp. 127–129.
[43] Johann Mattheson, *Die neueste Untersuchung der Singspiele nebst beygefügter musikalischen Geschmacksprobe* (Hamburg 1744; reprint, Leipzig, 1975), 128.

The autocratic regimes of A Musical Offering

If musical study was a grand tour then counterpoint was a destination that had to be visited. Quantz's educational itinerary was a model: during his European journeys of 1724–27 he saw many operas and virtuosic displays of instrumental prowess, but he also spent six months studying counterpoint with Gasparini in Rome. When Quantz met J. A. Hasse, another up-and-coming star of the *galant* style, in Naples, the future Kapellmeister in Dresden (and therefore the man who would be Quantz's superior from 1731 until the flute virtuoso left Dresden for Frederick the Great's court in 1735) was himself taking tuition in counterpoint from the aged Alessandro Scarlatti.[44] The title-page of Telemann's music serial *Der getreue Music-Meister* offers a similarly wide-ranging route through the musical geography of the day (Figure 4.1). Our editor promises to tour not only all national styles (Italian, French, English, Polish, etc.), but all styles and genres of both vocal and instrumental music; "fugues, counterpoints, and canons" would also be visited for the refinement and refreshment of his subscribers – bourgeois dilettantes and learned professionals alike. Counterpoint was less a harsh land of barbarians and recluses – or of pedants and bores, as Niedt put it – than an inviting shore.

In terms of genre, the *Musical Offering* canon that most closely approximates the *galant* trio movements of Bach's colleagues is the *fuga canonica* (no. 6) (see p. 165 below, and Example 4.18). As the name implies the *fuga canonica* is a true generic hybrid: both a fugal trio movement and a canon, in which the great temporal distance between the voices (ten measures) and the fact that this is the only non-perpetual canon produces a looser, conservational mode, responding to *galant* values of enjoyment and uplift.[45] Indeed, C. P. E. Bach directed his chief Hamburg scribe, Michel, to make a copy in parts of the *fuga canonica* for a single violin and harpsichord playing one of the solo lines with the right hand and the bass part with the left. This is the same configuration found in those violin sonatas by J. S. Bach praised by Carl Philipp Emanuel. Clearly the piece was performed – most likely in a domestic context – and did not simply languish as an object of study or a forgotten relic of ancient practice.

Also comparable to contemporary *galant* trios by other composers, the *Canon perpetuus* (no. 8) is the only other canonic number from *A Musical Offering* to have been written out completely rather than in puzzle notation, presumably on account of the exact melodic inversion which Bach wanted to safeguard against errant solutions (Example 4.6). Like the *Musical Offering* trio sonata, and unlike any of the other canons,

---

[44] J. J. Quantz, "Lebenslauf," in F. W. Marpurg, *Historisch-kritische Beyträge zur Aufnahme der Music*, 5 vols. (Berlin, 1754–60), I, 197–250, at p. 242.

[45] Wolff, *Kritischer Bericht*, 83.

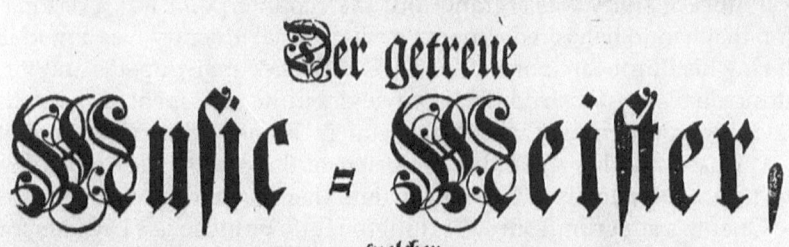

Figure 4.1   Title-page, G. P. Telemann, *Der getreue Music-Meister* (1728)

no. 8 is provided with figured bass; it is a chamber piece, not just a parlor game, and accordingly, is replete with performing indications. There are a number of mid-eighteenth-century copies in performing parts which pair the *Canon perpetuus* and the *Musical Offering* trio sonata; however strange this arrangement – a trio sonata followed by a single

The autocratic regimes of A Musical Offering

Example 4.6 J. S. Bach, *Canon perpetuus* (no. 8), from *A Musical Offering*, BWV 1079

canon for the same instrumentation (flute, violin, and continuo) – might at first seem, it should be viewed as an elevated contribution to the practice of writing canonic trio movements referred to by Marpurg.[46] Although Bach's impressive use of melodic inversion makes the piece far more contrapuntally complex than examples by Telemann, Fasch,

[46] Ibid., 79, 80.

Example 4.6 (cont.)

and Graupner, it does have a coherent and articulated harmonic plan comparable to that of a short sonata movement; by the time of the arrival at the half cadence to V/V at m. 20, a second canonic exposition has been underway for just a single bar (upbeat to m. 19). Thus the thematic content is roughly aligned with this relatively emphatic structural cadence. The overall plan of the movement proceeds from tonic to dominant and, with the (perpetual) repeat, back to the tonic; it is a simple trajectory, but this sense of a larger harmonic design is lacking in all the

The autocratic regimes of A Musical Offering

other canons, save the *fuga canonica*. Up to this point in the collection all the canons (again with the exception of the *fuga canonica*) have treated the royal theme as a *cantus firmus* – without transposition – rather than as thematic material for a canonic trio, and this is yet another aspect of the piece which allies it with the genre of the *galant* canonic trio.

Indeed, with the *Canon perpetuus* Bach has gone out of his way to create a more accessible or at least more rhetorically organized movement: for in fact the piece attains its length by grafting together two different solutions of a single canon – if you will, the initial counterpoint and its *evolutio*. The second canonic complex – beginning with the flute at the last beat of m. 18 – reverses the arrangement of the voices, so that the *dux* now has the *inversus* version of the theme and the *comes* (pickup to m. 20) has the *rectus*. This is simply an alternative solution to the original canon (mm. 1–15) presented in the dominant by way of the insertion of a canonic bridge between mm. 15–18: thus the impressive intricacies of the counterpoint are exposed in the performance of a single piece, rather than solved in separate exercises and presented in enigmatic notation. This method of variation is no different in spirit from that recommended by Mattheson in *Der vollkommene Capellmeister* for integrating the technique into "real" music.[47]

Bach's canon in the mold of a trio is followed directly by the seemingly more speculative *Canon a 2* (no. 9) (Example 4.7). The rubric *Quaerendo invenietis* (Seek and ye shall find) refers to the fact that, unlike the preceding canon (no. 8), this one is presented in puzzle form without clues as to the relationship of the two voices. The chromaticization of the opening C minor triad and the spare two-part texture increase the sense of severity in comparison with the more richly filled-out and harmonically articulated form of the *Canon perpetuus*. However, as Bach certainly knew, the *Canon a 2* also admits a solution in which the inverted form of the subject enters first, and is then followed by the *rectus* version. One of Bach's early admirers (and possibly his former student) Johann Oley, wrote out just such a solution in 1763.[48] Bach could quite easily have created from these two solutions another trio movement through the relatively simple means of adding an energetic continuo line, making a canonic transition to the dominant, and then introducing the second solution before circling back to the beginning. Instead, he left the puzzle unsolved as a challenge, its enigmatic notation devoid of any indications as to the spacing of the voices or their melodic directions. Its seemingly esoteric nature is the result of Bach's choice of presentation and the accompanying impression he sought to achieve; it is not an intrinsic feature of the counterpoint.

---

[47] Mattheson, *Der vollkommene Capellmeister*, trans. Harriss, 744.
[48] Wolff, *Kritischer Bericht*, 75. Another student, J. F. Agricola, presents an alternative *inversus* solution.

Example 4.7 J. S. Bach, *Canon a 2* (no. 9), from *A Musical Offering*, BWV 1079, solution

The *Canon a 2* serves as the unadorned pendant to the *Canon perpetuus*, and the relationship between the two makes it clear that the generic characteristics of these kinds of pieces were determined less by inherent contrapuntal complexity than by style, and that the most arcane devices could be domesticated and given a more "normal" shape and affect.

That counterpoint could appear in vastly different stylistic contexts, from high to low, has already been suggested by the title-page of Telemann's *Getreuer Music-Meister* (Figure 4.1). The music from Telemann's now-lost Hamburg opera *Die verkehrte Welt* (The World Upside-Down), included in one of the installments of the serial, confirms the mutability of these techniques. The comic scene in Example 4.8 ingeniously lampoons several forms of counterpoint: first comes a canon in augmentation in invertible counterpoint with the soprano singing a ponderous melisma on the penultimate syllable of the word "Augmentatione," just before the vocal part takes up the theme at half-speed; this is followed by the three main classes of invertible counterpoint, sung to the words "This is the 12th, the 10th, this the octave"; next a crab canon is announced, and after this creature scurries away, the whole business concludes with a ludicrous succession of tempo changes sung to the words "This [is] Adagio, Presto, etc." Here was a fitting foil to the formidable canons of Zelenka and Bach also printed

The autocratic regimes of A Musical Offering

Example 4.8   G. P. Telemann, "Scene aus der Oper die Verkehrte Welt," printed in *Der getreue Music-Meister* (1728)

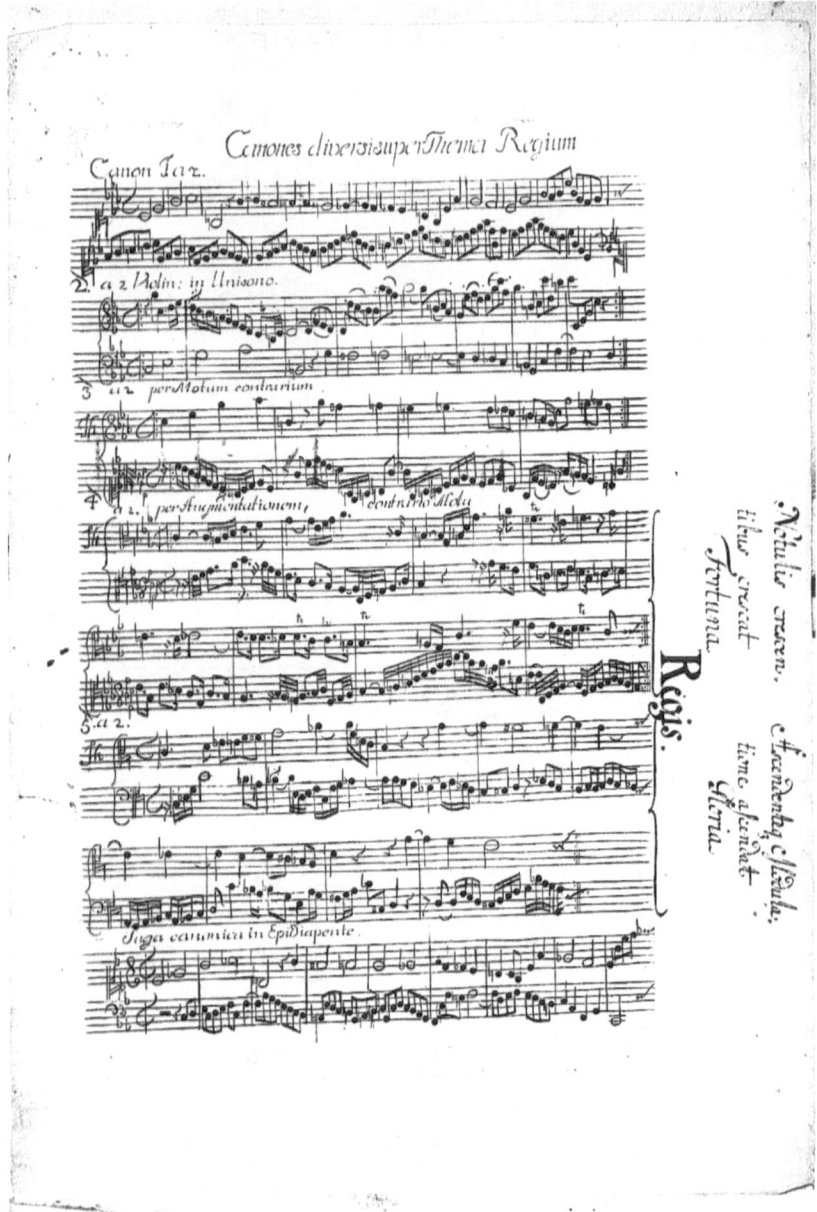

Figure 4.2 J. S. Bach, crab canon (no. 1) from *A Musical Offering*, BWV 1079, original print

The autocratic regimes of A Musical Offering

in *Der getreue Music-Meister*. The entire scene scores its satiric points in part by skewering the overly didactic and artificial qualities that could attend learned music. Of course, for all this to be funny on the stage Telemann's opera audience would have had to know something about the contrapuntal devices being sent up. And indeed, it was Mattheson who had begun the work of educating his bourgeois readers in counterpoint in his first book, *Das neu-eröffnete Orchestre* (1713), in which he had exposed his *galant homme*, that refined and musically informed mainstay of his ideal public, to the curious workings of the genre. If ever a single figure epitomized the *galant homme* it was Frederick the Great.

The scene from Telemann's opera offers an interesting angle from which to view the first canon from *A Musical Offering*. Unlike Telemann, Bach presents his crab canon in puzzle notation, that is, on a single staff with no written clue as to the proper solution (Figure 4.2); however, the reversed clef at the end of the piece signals its proper realization (Example 4.9). Thus Bach begins the canonic explorations of *A Musical Offering* with what appears to be a mysterious and complex construct. The procedure for making a crab canon found in a widely used modern textbook, Kent Kennan's *Counterpoint Based on Eighteenth-Century Practice*, typifies the elevation of the crab canon's artifice to heights of complexity and genius unreachable by most: Kennan directs

Example 4.9   J. S. Bach, crab canon (no. 1), from *A Musical Offering*, BWV 1079*

* Current engraving software is unable to produce reversed clefs and key signatures, a fact that nicely demonstrates the current obscurity of the genre of the crab canon and its semiotics.

151

Example 4.10   G. P. Telemann, crab canon from *Die verkehrte Welt*

(⬅ means retrograde)

Figure 4.3   Scheme for a crab canon

his readers "to compose the first half of the leader (*dux*), then write that part backwards as the last half of the follower (*comes*). Next, *by a process of trial and error*, find a line that will work forward as the last half of the leader, and backward as the first half of the follower [my emphasis]."[49] This dispiriting advice sets out a daunting, not to say impossible task, especially when the textbook's example is Bach's crab canon from *A Musical Offering*. Nor do the arduous experiments of Douglas Hofstadter's "Crab canon dialogue," in his 1979 book *Gödel, Escher, Bach* have much in common with Bach's method for constructing his crab canon.[50] Consider by way of comparison Telemann's satiric four-measure canon. Example 4.10 extracts the crab canon from the rest of the scene, and makes it easier to see that the piece is made up of a single measure repeated four times in various guises. Figure 4.3 gives the permutational scheme for the piece: the letter "T" represents theme (here arbitrarily assigned to the soprano) and "CP" counterpoint (the bass). The arrows indicate retrograde motion. Measure 2 is simply a chiasmus of the first measure, inverting the voices and reproducing them in retrograde; mm. 3 and 4 make an analogous move involving a backwards replay of the first two measures. Thus the piece folds back on itself around the axis of the bar-line dividing mm. 2 and 3. What was Telemann's procedure?

---

[49] Kent Kennan, *Counterpoint Based on Eighteenth-Century Practice*, 4th edn. (Upper Saddle River, New Jersey, 1999), 102–103.
[50] Douglas Hofstadter, *Gödel, Escher, Bach: An Eternal Golden Braid* (New York, 1979), 199–203, 665–668.

The autocratic regimes of A Musical Offering

Example 4.11   Telemann crab canon in enigmatic notation

He simply wrote a single measure of the soprano, then added to it an accompanying voice that was invertible at the octave and avoided dissonances. The viability of the remaining three measures of his crab canon was assured without trial or error; that this snippet is child's play – simply parallel sixths and thirds – is part of its humor.

Infinitely more dissonant and challenging, Bach's crab canon nonetheless follows the same straightforward – not backward – principle, one described with refreshing clarity by F. W. Marpurg in the second volume of his *Abhandlung von der Fuge* (1754): first, write out a two-part counterpoint, avoiding all dissonances except the diminished fifth, minor seventh (on the dominant), diminished seventh, augmented fourth, and augmented second; more common dissonances must not be introduced because when the melodic direction is reversed the resolutions of these dissonances will precede the dissonances themselves and will therefore be ungrammatical. In the case of *A Musical Offering*'s crab canon, then, Bach set out the royal theme on the top staff and provided it with a running eighth-note accompaniment beneath that allowed for invertible counterpoint and that avoided dissonances which required resolution. In order to present the piece in puzzle notation the lower voice is added to the upper voice, but written out in reverse, and equipped with the mirror-clef at its end.[51] Bach's crab canon is much less of an enigma than the enigmatic notation suggests, and even Telemann's frivolous canon can be made to look somewhat more impressive dressed up in this garb (Example 4.11).[52] For musicians aware of the trick, the canon loses much, if not all, of its mystery. And though more interesting than Telemann's tiny crab, Bach's should not be divested of the humorous overtones of his friend's parody. Given their strange look on the page, and their back-tracking course in performance, such pieces are bound

---

[51] Marpurg, *Abhandlung von der Fuge*, II, 38–39. See also Mattheson, *Der vollkommene Capellmeister*, trans. Harriss, 763–764.

[52] Marpurg instructs the student of counterpoint that a complete performance of a crab canon requires one singer (or player) to start at the beginning of his part and continue to the end, then immediately reverse through the same line, i.e., proceed from right to left. The second performer begins at the end and when he comes to the beginning cycles back through his line from left to right. This means that in a complete performance of a crab canon the same music is heard a total of four times. The Bach devotee Johann Oley followed exactly these precepts when he wrote out his solution to the *Musical Offering* crab canon (see Hans T. David, *J. S. Bach's Musical Offering: History, Interpretation and Analysis* [New York, 1945]). Thus, according to eighteenth-century practice the version printed in the NBA is only half the canon. Marpurg, *Abhandlung von der Fuge*, II, 65–66.

Example 4.12 Yearsley, crab canon on Royal Theme

to amuse, perhaps more than any other kind of canon, if only because they are not as difficult as they appear.

Example 4.12 gives my own crab canon on the royal theme, arrived at by approaching the problem following Marpurg's recommendations, that is, in a straightforward, rather than a backward way. Because of the restrictions on dissonance treatment mentioned by Marpurg, most crab canons – i.e., Telemann's and that of Wilhelm Friedemann Bach's included in the *Abhandlung von der Fuge*[53] – are completely without dissonance: deprived of this basic mechanism of tonality, retrograde canons of all types tend to be harmonically inert and rather aimless. Bach's essay in the genre would be no different in this respect without the rhythmic displacement he introduces to the theme; indeed, the piece works perfectly well without these syncopations. This rhythmic shift provides a small but crucial boost to the momentum, pushing things more vigorously than mine while at the same time seeming more static in the uncanny sameness of the aural effect of its two halves – it goes nowhere faster. Thus it is not only a better piece than mine, it's

[53] Marpurg, *Abhandlung von der Fuge*, II, Tab. XIII, no. 4.

The autocratic regimes of A Musical Offering

funnier, too. The piece suggests to me that even the greatest canonist of the day, the composer of the famed Hudemann canon, could treat the canonic enterprise with a certain lightness. Indeed, for the initiate, the crab canon as a genre – witness not only Telemann's satiric canon, but the coy obscurantism evident in Zelenka's contribution to *Der getreue Music-Meister* – was invested with a healthy dose of irony. Bach's crab canon should be viewed not as a piece of dark esoterica,[54] but as an invitation to recreation and amusement. Placed at the entrance to the canonic drawing room that is *A Musical Offering* – to borrow Telemann's pleasant and useful metaphor – this delightfully solipsistic piece allows the connoisseur the chance to give a knowing nod of appreciation, a smile, and perhaps even a laugh, as she glances at this humorous and skillful study in deception, then steps over the threshold to admire the remaining nine contrapuntal tableaux hanging on the walls.

Would Frederick have recognized the peculiar humor of the crab canon? He certainly enjoyed the challenges and possibilities of counterpoint, though this fact is often doubted by Bach scholars, for the historiographical reasons cited above. A well-rounded intellectual who prided himself on his ability to discuss any topic intelligently, Frederick was no stranger to strict compositional techniques. Because this branch of music was in fact afforded a great deal of respect by leading Berlin musicians, it becomes much harder to support the widely held view that Frederick had mostly contempt for counterpoint, a belief that is largely based on his infamous dismissal of a piece from a Berlin opera "because it smells of the church."[55] Frederick had frequently rejected operatic numbers by Graun when they did not accord with his tastes, yet the canonic passages found in Kirnberger's anthology of Graun's duets and trios had obviously passed the royal litmus test. Frederick's nose was clearly not offended by all contrapuntal artifice, since it often occurred not in the church, but at his court and opera. Though counterpoint by no means dominated the musical scene in Berlin, either in Frederick's private music room or on the stage of his opera, it remained in robust health and continued to attract the attentions of theorists, composers, critics, and amateurs.

In light of the more inclusive musical environment at Berlin I have tried to portray here, it is worth reconsidering a sometimes-doubted account of Frederick's interest in counterpoint found in Carl Friedrich Zelter's biography of his friend Karl Friedrich Christian Fasch, founder

---

[54] This is how Douglas Hofstadter reads the crab canon in *Gödel, Escher, Bach* (p. 9).
[55] Burney, *The Present State of Music in Germany, the Netherlands, and United Provinces*, 2 vols. (London, 1775; reprint, New York, 1969), II, 91–92. Fasch for one believed the relevance of this comment to Frederick's views on sacred music and music in general had been vastly overblown. See Karl Friedrich Zelter, *Karl Friedrich Christian Fasch* (Berlin, 1801; reprint, Blankenburg, 1983), 46.

of the Berlin Singakademie. On one memorable evening, says Fasch, he was playing continuo for a flute sonata by Frederick into which the king had introduced a two-part canon (presumably between the bass-line and the flute part); to the king's astonishment, the quick-thinking Fasch extemporaneously introduced a third canonic voice into the texture. Fasch tried to credit Frederick's compositional skill for allowing this artifice, but the king assured his musical servant that he had only thought of the two-voice possibility when composing the piece. Though Frederick acknowledged that he had studied learned counterpoint with Graun, he admitted that his grasp of the subject did not match Fasch's, but registered his appreciation for the refinements of counterpoint: "It always pleases me whenever I find that music concerns itself with the understanding; if a beautiful piece of music sounds learned, it is as pleasing to me as it is to hear pleasant conversation at table."[56]

While some have argued that Bach invested counterpoint with more profundity than did Frederick – the five-part vocal canon that makes up the Christe of the Mass in A major, BWV 234 and the *cantus firmus* canons of the Credo of the B minor Mass, BWV 232, certainly do not bear analogy to light banter – the notion that counterpoint could be comparable to conversation, the ultimate talent of the *galant homme*, would not necessarily have been disagreeable to Bach. Indeed, Fasch's contrapuntal skill while accompanying Frederick sounds quite like the informal Bach's, as told by Forkel, who claimed that when among friends and when he was in "a cheerful mood," Bach would fill out a trio with an additional obbligato part (occasionally even a canonic part?) or make similarly clever extemporaneous additions to another composer's work.[57] These "conversational" modes of music-making were encouraged in the *galant*, domestic space: in a cantor's apartment, a coffee-house, or a royal palace.

Indeed, while Frederick's own surviving instrumental music is certainly *galant* and often amateurish, it not as lacking in artifice as some would make it out to be; take, for example, the modest stretto at the close of the C minor flute sonata, a piece whose theme has marked similarities to that of *A Musical Offering* (Example 4.13).[58] Fasch's canonic exchange with Frederick earned the monarch's respect and admiration as had Bach's Potsdam performance. Is there any reason to doubt that Bach might have reasonably expected a similar reception for the intensely wrought contrapuntal creations he sent to the king in 1747? The notion that Frederick had an interest in counterpoint accords completely with the nature of musical connoisseurship at mid century.

This, then, presents a far different picture of the musical stage which Bach entered in May of 1747. When Friedemann told Forkel that his

---

[56] Zelter, *Karl Friedrich Christian Fasch*, 48.   [57] *NBR*, 435, 460.
[58] Philipp Spitta pointed this out more than a century ago. Frederick II, King of Prussia, *Musikalische Werke* I, ed. Spitta (Leipzig, 1889), viii.

Example 4.13 Frederick the Great, Sonata in C minor for flute and continuo, third movement, closing stretto

father had improvised "to the astonishment of those present" he was referring not to an unknowing group of decadent moderns who treated counterpoint with condescension and near contempt, but rather to appreciative connoisseurs. And while Bach's rigorous contrapuntal standards and knowledge certainly surpassed those of anyone present at his Potsdam display, his reputation for contrapuntal craft was well-established in the ranks of the profession, and among enthusiasts such as Baron von Keyserlingk, who possessed an intimate knowledge of the virtuosic canonic program of the Goldberg Variations and who could have shared his enthusiasms with the Prussian king at court. Indeed, Frederick was clearly eager to witness a demonstration of Bach's skill, and it is easy to imagine these two learned men discussing this collection's fascinating marriage of keyboard practice and contrapuntal virtuosity. The central event in Frederick's encounter with Bach demonstrates the monarch's interest in the topic, for it was he who presented his guest with a fugue subject whose learned profile encouraged extended contrapuntal treatment. Indeed the theme and the meeting it commemorates were indelibly imprinted on the king's memory: nearly thirty years after Bach's performance Frederick sang the royal theme for his visitor, Baron van Swieten. Time had inflated the impressiveness of Bach's skill in Frederick's mind, since he told van Swieten that Bach had improvised fugues in four, five and finally, an impossible eight voices.[59] For the dedicatee of *A Musical Offering*, Bach's contrapuntal heroics had achieved the status of myth.

It is the royal theme which leads us back to the title page of the collection and to the music it prefaces. Bach introduces *A Musical Offering* with a prose version of his initial prostrations before Frederick: "In deepest humility I dedicate herewith to Your Majesty a musical offering, the

[59] NBR, 366–367.

noblest part of which derives from Your Majesty's own august hand."
This is an extraordinary admission, for Bach here states that the central
musical idea of the entire collection is the product not of his imagination
but that of the dedicatee's. This sentence should not be read merely as
a formulaic rhetorical concession to the king, who was wary of undeserved praise and who had written in his *Anti-Machiavel* of 1740 that "an
intelligent man is revulsed by blatant flattery."[60] The opening sentence
of Bach's dedication is certainly submissive, but it need not be taken as
disingenuous, for the formulation of the central idea or melody, which
could be synonymous with "invention," was considered by most writers on music to be the crucial aspect of composition.[61] Although the idea
of the "invention" was not unambiguously restricted to the initial form
of the subject of a piece, the creation of a defining melody according
to Mattheson, and others, "comprise[d] that which is most essential in
music;"[62] likewise, it was with invention "that the beginning of all songs
must be made."[63] A flair for invention was the irreplaceable prerequisite
for becoming a composer in the first place, and it was this innate ability
which Bach attempted to discern in potential students. While *dispositio*
and *elaboratio* were of course vital, the unfathomable creative impulse
of *inventio* was the lifeblood of composition.[64] Because of the privileged
position of invention, it is perhaps not surprising that scholars have often hinted that the *Musical Offering* theme either could not have been of
Frederick's own doing, or that Bach may have made important revisions
when he came to compiling *A Musical Offering*, thus undermining the
"royalness" of the royal theme.[65] However, it seems unlikely that Bach
would have been so bold as to make substantial changes to a theme he
described as "excellent" in the dedication of *A Musical Offering*. Indeed,
in terms of reception, it hardly matters who should be accorded creative
responsibility for the theme; as a public musical gesture, Bach's designation of the subject as the "royal theme" unambiguously presents it as the
work of the Prussian king and thereby allows Frederick's famed gifts for
music – his "fire and spirit," as Mattheson would have it – to pervade the
collection. An extended tribute to Frederick's royal theme and therefore
to his powers of invention, *A Musical Offering* defers to royal prerogative
at the most basic level of eighteenth-century musical thought.

We have already seen how the apparent complexity of the crab canon
(no. 1) is actually a rather straightforward – and not straight backward –
procedure in which the royal theme clearly exerts the controlling

---

[60] Frederick the Great, *Anti-Machiavel*, trans. Paul Sonnino (Athens, Ohio, 1981), 142.
[61] Dreyfus, *Bach and the Patterns of Invention*, 1–32.
[62] Mattheson, *Der vollkommene Capellmeister*, trans. Harriss, 300.
[63] Ibid., 309.   [64] Ibid., 241; trans., 480.
[65] Christoph Wolff, "Überlegungen zum 'Thema Regium,'" *Bach-Jahrbuch* 59 (1973), 33–38. See also Wolff, *Kritischer Bericht*, 103.

The autocratic regimes of A Musical Offering

Example 4.14   J. S. Bach, *Canon a 4*, in enigmatic notation, from *A Musical Offering*, BWV 1079

influence. The same critical approach, taking as a point of departure the "invention-oriented" opening gambit of Bach's dedication, can also be applied to the final musical puzzle in the collection, the heterophonic *Canon a 4* which along with the *Canon a 2* follows the rubric *Quaerendo invenietis* (Seek and ye shall find). To repeat, this epigram alludes to the fact that, unlike the other canons in the collection, neither of these last two is provided with any signs indicating at what point the voices should enter, or whether, for example, they might involve melodic inversion. It is a true puzzle, and, presented in this way, the piece has the look of an extended melodic spinning-out of the royal theme, an almost fantastical succession of ideas composed horizontally one after the other (Example 4.14). But, as Hans David pointed out, this sprawling canon is generated from a four-part harmonization of the royal theme in multiply invertible counterpoint.[66] Needless to say, this is no mean feat, but

[66] David, *J. S. Bach's Musical Offering*, 25.

it does not require the kind of frightening cross-referencing and note-by-note progress through trial and error that the enigmatic notation and dazzling aural effect of the piece might suggest to the uninitiated. The entire canonic "melody" as presented in puzzle notation is really just the royal theme – in decorated form – followed by the three additional counterpoints placed in succession on a single staff. Like the crab canon, this piece is composed as a single contrapuntal matrix, its constituent parts subsequently rearranged horizontally for presentation in enigmatic notation.

Deriving a canon from a piece of invertible counterpoint was a technique well-known in the eighteenth century, and is described succinctly in Marpurg's *Abhandlung*: after fashioning the three- or four-part counterpoint in accordance with the rules for invertibility, one simply staggers the entry of themes to create a canon (Example 4.15).[67] The crucial technique for rendering such a contrapuntal framework convincing is that of elaboration, which, in Marpurg's account, generally comes into play after an unadorned scheme has been devised. Once a progression that passes contrapuntal muster has been created, the separate themes need to be individualized, largely through rhythmic differentiation and melodic profiling with large leaps, rests, figuration, and the like, a process Marpurg characterizes as one of decorating with flowers (Blumen) – a charming metaphor which evokes nothing of the pedantry with which such pieces are generally associated both in the musicological discourse and in eighteenth-century polemics against canon.[68] Example 4.16 gives mm. 22 through 29 of the *Canon a 4*; this represents the first pass through the matrix (plus the first measure, 29, of the next one) with all four voices involved. For heuristic purposes this can be seen as the original block of invertible counterpoint with its *Blumen*; the next step for Bach would have been to string these themes out along a single staff for presentation in enigmatic notation (Example 4.14). The material from m. 8 on in Example 4.14 therefore represents the contrapuntal derivatives of the royal theme, the foundation on which the entire baroque edifice stands; each eight-bar unit simply presents another configuration (*evolutio*) of the initial contrapuntal construct.

Bach steers a course between the safe option of following Marpurg's advice for individualizing the voices and the more dangerous one of creating a texture so unified, "turgid" to use Scheibe's term, that it might unleash a roiling swarm of indecipherable, cognitively overwhelming counterpoint. Where Marpurg recommends a hierarchy of note-values, in Bach's *Canon a 4* eighth-note motion predominates, and the greatest density of sixteenth notes (e.g., the soprano, alto, and tenor at m. 29, Example 4.16) come in a single beat before the entry of the royal theme.

[67] Marpurg, *Abhandlung von der Fuge*, II, 8, 20.   [68] Ibid., 8.

The autocratic regimes of A Musical Offering

Example 4.15 Making a canon from a piece of invertible counterpoint: F. W. Marpurg, *Abhandlung von der Fuge*, vol. II (1754)

The sixteenth-note slide that begins the ascent in the second voice from g^2 to d^3, anticipates by the space of a single eighth note the initial gesture of the royal theme (in the upper voice at m. 28). This imitative move momentarily collapses the spacing of seven measures separating the voices, and the royal theme seems to emerge from the anticipating voices: the sixteenth-note activity of the soprano at m. 22 draws attention to its own ascent while simultaneously preparing the listener for the royal theme to follow, melodically and temporally, close on its heels. It is precisely here that the soprano threatens to escape the contrapuntal orbit of the royal theme, reaching the highest pitch in the entire piece. But no escape is possible, and the ascent to the apex only verifies the impossibility of trying to resist the gravitational force of the controlling contrapuntal paradigm,

Example 4.16 J. S. Bach, *Canon a 4*, BWV 1079, mm. 22–29

and therefore, of the royal theme itself. Like the soprano, two of the other voices mimic the opening gesture of the theme rising from the tonic to the dominant. Thus a majority of the contrapuntally additive voices announce the entry of the theme as well as their own submission to it.

The ubiquitous and controlling presence of the royal theme is intrinsic not only to the canons but also to the other genres found in *A Musical Offering*. Nowhere is this clearer than in the second movement of the trio sonata. The opening subject of the movement has all the markings and generic mixtures of Bachian invention at its finest (Italianate ritornello masquerading as a French bourrée) (Example 4.17a).[69] Not until m. 46, after the first structural cadence to the dominant, is Bach's "subject" (heard in the violin) revealed for what it really is: merely a counterpoint to the royal theme itself (Example 4.17b). It is a stirring moment, with Bach dramatically asserting the royal presence in the basso continuo line. Only after a full exposition of what initially appears to be the first theme, does Bach reveal its true origins as a countersubject. (Perhaps this is one explanation for the fact that the royal theme does not surface in the first

---

[69] Marissen, "The Theological Character of J. S. Bach's *Musical Offering*," 98.

The autocratic regimes of A Musical Offering

Example 4.17   J. S. Bach, *Trio Sonata*, second movement, from *A Musical Offering*, BWV 1079
(a) mm. 1–9
(b) mm. 45–54
(c) mm. 158–167

Example 4.17 (cont.)

movement; its deferral to the following allegro certainly increases its impact when it does finally appear – a forceful answer to the question of whether or not Bach will use the royal theme in the trio sonata.)

Although it is an ingenious turn to present the countersubject first, this disposition ultimately cannot deny the subservient position of the opening ritornello. As many commentators have pointed out, the trio sonata is part of a collection;[70] while individual pieces can certainly be played separately – just as they were copied separately in the eighteenth century – the entire contents should be thought of as a meaningful whole. The most likely ordering of the collection has the trio sonata following the ricercars. Thus we are introduced to the royal theme, the subject of the entire work, before the trio sonata. The lessons in learning the royal theme provided by the ricercars serve to clarify the thematic hierarchies that emerge over the course of the second movement of the trio. When the royal theme appears in the trio sonata for the first time it has already been given the status of a *cantus firmus*, as important as a chorale melody is to a chorale prelude. So when the opening theme of the movement is recapitulated at m. 159 in the tonic (Example 4.17c), Bach arrogates to Frederick's invention its rightful dominion, stating even more powerfully that in the exposition the royal theme, though absent, was nonetheless governing the musical discourse. In its masterly elaboration and disposition Bach's fugal trio augments the importance

[70] Ibid.

The autocratic regimes of A Musical Offering

of the theme, while, of course, demonstrating the artifice of the composer: the perfect, symbiotic relationship between the ruler (Frederick the lawgiver) and Bach, the promulgator of his will.

Finally, let me return to the *fuga canonica*, which, as I pointed out above, seems in many ways the freest of the canons and the closest, in terms of genre, to the canonic trios of Fasch and Graupner. From the outset its contrapuntal sights seem not to be set too high; this is the only canon in *A Musical Offering* which is not infinite, and for this reason is also the most discursive, most spacious, and the most like a "normal" trio. As in the *Canon perpetuus* (no. 8), the bass-line is charged with filling out the texture with free counterpoint, and the overall structure is made up of two contrapuntal complexes whose harmonic position allies it with the sub-genre of the fugal trio movement, though Bach's has a far higher degree of contrapuntal difficulty than similar examples. The opening canonic complex featuring the royal theme has a typical arrangement of *dux* and *comes* in the tonic and dominant respectively, but unlike a fugue, or, more pertinently, unlike the ricercars in the same collection, the answer must be real rather than tonal on account of the requirements of exact imitation (Example 4.18a). The second canonic appearance of the theme in tandem begins on the sub-dominant of f minor which allows for the *comes* to return to the tonic. At this point all seems headed for closure. But through an extraordinary use of contrapuntal elaboration, Bach subjects the final entry of the royal theme in the canonic voices (flute, m. 49) to invertible counterpoint at the twelfth (beginning m. 49; see Example 4.18b); this use of double counterpoint at the twelfth makes it possible for the royal theme to sound forth in the voice (the bass-line) that had seemingly been free from it, and for the *comes* to adhere to its canonic responsibilities, that is, mimicking the material from the *dux* at the upper fifth. (In other words, m. 59 is where the basso continuo and flute begin their *evolutio* of the violin/flute matrix which starts in m. 48.) The final bass entry participates in the canonic writing for nine measures, and brings the king himself to the forefront of the musical discourse in a thrilling and unexpected staging of contrapuntal theatrics. Here Bach not only demonstrates thorough control of the mechanics of counterpoint, but an unmatched brilliance for giving them a resonance both dramatic and allegorical.[71]

By re-evaluating counterpoint's place in the musical culture of the mid-eighteenth century, and trying to show how Bach's work sometimes drew on *galant* affectations and contexts (and sometimes resisted them),

---

[71] On the centrality of allegory in German baroque drama more generally see Walter Benjamin, *The Origins of German Tragic Drama*, trans. John Osborne (London: New Left Books, 1977), 159–235. See also Eric Chafe, *Tonal Allegory in the Vocal Music of J. S. Bach* (Berkeley, 1991), 1–25.

Example 4.18 J. S. Bach, *Fuga canonica*, from *A Musical Offering*, BWV 1079
(a) mm. 1–13
(b) mm. 49–78

I do not mean to minimize the uniqueness of *A Musical Offering*, a work that is much more than merely an object of delectation, more than ingenious table conversation. The entire collection far exceeds the limitations of fashionable musical discourse. Although I believe it would be a mistake to view Bach's explorations in this work as an attack on musical fashion (and, therefore, on the king's tastes), the collection is clearly out of the ordinary, even compulsive. Like Frederick the Great's domineering conversational style at table at Sans-souci, *A Musical Offering* takes up a viable *galant* topic (counterpoint) and seeks to control it completely. It is Bach's relentless investigation, manipulation, and domination of the royal theme in such a way that it pervades the collection so thoroughly, that returns us finally to the hermeneutic nexus between musical absolutism and political autocracy.

While Graupner, Telemann, Fasch, and the Bachs continued to compose canons, many reform-minded critics writing in the first half of the eighteenth century attacked strict compositional techniques such as those served up in large portions in *A Musical Offering*. But the

The autocratic regimes of A Musical Offering

Example 4.18 (cont.)

language they used in their critique of canon is important, for they frequently described the rigorous techniques of learned counterpoint as a subversion of the just political order of their metaphorical musical republic – a republic they idealized as akin to the conditions prevailing in Rome prior to the depredations of power-hungry rulers such as Caesar and the ensuing corruptions of empire. No stranger to the sometimes turbulent politics of his own republic of Hamburg, Mattheson described canon as nothing less than a "violent dictator" (gewaltiger Dictatore),[72] who maintained his reign because of the abject nature of his "slavish" (sclavisch) followers.[73] Lifelong resident of a relatively democratic Hanseatic city, Mattheson characterized the true source of political authority in music as the two unassuming burghers Mr. Hearing and Mrs. Melody (Herr Auditus und Frau Melodica), and it is this couple that incites the musical populace to "throw off the yoke of powerful canon."[74] Taking up the same metaphor, Heinichen, employee of a despotic regime in Saxony less efficient in its autocratic control than Frederick's, attacked the devotees of learned music as "potentates of counterpoint" (Contrapuncts-Potentaten) and personified the discipline itself as a tyrant who had long subjugated the aural faculty, the true musical sovereign.[75] The figurative language used to challenge the supremacy of canon was a mixture of the subversive and the utopian, as when Heinichen hoped for a revolution that would establish a new "musical republic," and return to the "oppressed ear the sovereignty of its realm."[76] Mattheson, who had dedicated the *Mithridat* to Frederick the Great two years after the publication of *A Musical Offering*, would hardly have failed to note the aptness of presenting a collection of excessively controlled canons to an autocratic titan of Frederick's stature. In his book, Mattheson calls Frederick a "magnanimous ruler" but claims that Alexander and Caesar were – especially compared to the musically inclined Solomon and his "even better father" David – a "pair of reckless tyrants" (ein Paar tollkühner Tyrannen), a characterization that Frederick, (and perhaps Bach?) would vehemently have disagreed with.[77] For Mattheson, tyranny in politics, as in music, was to be singled out and fought against.

These critiques of canon were, of course, meant to be inflammatory and had been fundamentally motivated by a desire for the reform of musical pedagogy, a much needed corrective to the hocus-pocus of teachers

---

[72] Mattheson, "Die canonische Anatomie," in *Critica musica*, 2 vols. (Hamburg, 1722–25; reprint, Amsterdam, 1964), I, 341.
[73] Ibid., 247.   [74] Ibid., 364.
[75] Heinichen, *Der General-Bass in der Composition* (Dresden, 1728), 7.
[76] Ibid., 4; trans. in George J. Buelow, *Thorough-Bass Accompaniment according to Johann David Heinichen*, rev. edn. (Ann Arbor, 1986), 311.
[77] Mattheson, *Mithridat*, 261.

like Buttstett (see p. 66 above) and an alternative to the kind of onerous tuition that Mattheson and some of his contemporaries had had to endure. As for the harsh words on counterpoint penned by the widely respected Heinichen, Kirnberger suggested that the author himself did not really believe them, but had simply adopted his scathing tone for polemical purposes; after all, Heinichen and Mattheson, like Frederick, enjoyed pleasing music when it was complemented, but not overwhelmed, by artifice. Still, the political resonance of these metaphors could not be ignored: the obedience of the devotees of canon to the canonic devices that held them in their thrall was, in this view, harmful both to musical culture and to the musical style it spawned. But the potentially destabilizing implications of these treatises remained confined to the musical world. There was virtually no public political critique in Germany, though in sublimated form political rhetoric pervaded music theory and the history tales told on the opera stage.

While the eighteenth century witnessed the relentless growth of centralized authority in monocratic regimes across German-speaking Europe, it paradoxically became a commonplace of political philosophy to reject the implications of autocracy, however fully realized its controlling apparatus might already be. Even Frederick, whose *Anti-Machiavel* was ushered into print with the help of Voltaire just as the young prince ascended the Prussian throne in 1740, could claim in that treatise that "no sentiment is more inseparable from our being than that of liberty" and assert, as well, that the sovereign is "the first servant of the people."[78] At the same time, however, organization and obedience – in the military and in society – were Frederick's chief obsessions; in *Les principes généraux de la guerre* (General Principles of War), published soon after his triumph in the Second Silesian War, the king boasted that "Roman discipline now exists only with us," in Prussia.[79] The fact that control and domination, a repeated concern of Heinichen and Mattheson, could restrict freedom is irrelevant here: indeed, the poet and friend of C. P. E. Bach Gotthold Ephraim Lessing wrote in a private letter of 1769 (two years after C. P. E. Bach had left Berlin for Hamburg) that if one were to "raise his voice for the rights of the subjects and against the exploitation and despotism as nowadays is being done even in France and Denmark... [one] would find out very soon which is the most enslaved country of Europe."[80] Equally as damning was Hugh Elliot, the British ambassador in Prussia towards the end of Frederick's reign, who likened his monarchy to "a vast prison in the center of which

---

[78] Frederick the Great, *Anti-Machiavel*, 34, 71.
[79] Quoted in Asprey, *Frederick the Great*, 389.
[80] G. E. Lessing, *Sämmtliche Schriften*, XXVII (Berlin, 1794), 257; quoted in Hans Rosenberg, *Bureaucracy, Aristocracy and Autocracy: The Prussian Experience, 1660–1815* (Cambridge, Mass., 1958), 41–42.

appears the great keeper, occupied in the care of his captives."[81] In spite of its self-serving rhetoric, the pervasive oppression and all-consuming militarism of Prussian benevolent despotism was undeniable.

But to the extent that it could further his position or that of his family, there is no reason to think that the absolutist-minded Bach was averse to Frederick's personal mission or to the autocratic project more generally. In his humanistic education, in his trips to the Dresden opera, in his daily religious study, in his reading of the books in his theological library with their frequent Lutheran diatribes against papal authority as a usurpation of temporal privilege, in his relations with his employers, Bach was everywhere confronted with issues of liberty and oppression. As I have suggested, his exposure to progressive music theory made him aware of current aesthetic debates; the language of these debates, so saturated with political metaphor, would not have been obscure to him, and he would have known that usurpation, tyranny, and domination formed one of the most powerful complex of meanings surrounding counterpoint. It is more than coincidence that Bach's desire for absolute control of his musical material is nowhere more palpable than in a work dedicated to a man equally committed to like goals in politics. Both men were intent on dominating their subjects.

Even before history and an unmatched skill in counterpoint brought him face to face with Frederick the Great, Bach had been attuned to the rhetoric of absolutism. As early as his tenure in Mühlhausen in 1707–08, Bach had sought a position which would place him at the head of a musical establishment capable of what he called a "well-regulated church music" – a description of such a musical establishment made in terms of a standing army, the true locus of absolutist power.[82] This was also his view of the musical forces at his disposal in Leipzig. And if, as Mattheson asserted, *inventio* depended on fire and spirit, *dispositio* on a sense of order, and *elaboratio* on cold-bloodedness, then *A Musical Offering* brings the latter to the fore to an extent surpassing any of Bach's other lengthy investigations into learned techniques: here was a thoroughly "well-regulated" music akin to absolutist ruthlessness.

Paradoxically, it was Bach's distance from the Prussian scene and his relatively independent and secure position as a municipal employee, albeit a frequently dissatisfied one, which allowed him the freedom to construct his elaborate representation of absolutist power. The often idealized portrayals of heroic rulers which populated Frederick's Berlin opera notwithstanding, it is equally paradoxical that although the *galant* style of Berlin was the everyday fare of the absolutist regime, this music,

---

[81] Quoted in Rosenberg, *Bureaucracy, Aristocracy and Autocracy*, 41.
[82] Siegele, "Bach and the Domestic Politics of Electoral Saxony," 27.

The autocratic regimes of A Musical Offering

in all its courtliness and grace, was not capable of a true allegorical representation of monarchic power. Rather, it took the single-mindedness, detachment, submissiveness, and genius of Bach to produce this apotheosis of the Prussian monarchy. Where the Prussian Kapellmeister Graun was forced to submit his arias to the king for approval – an approval which was not always forthcoming – Bach suffered no such crippling control, and therefore created a work that could amplify the meaning and importance of a royal command presented in the form of a learned subject ideal for contrapuntal investigation. Bach used his creative gifts both to glorify the Prussian king and to advance, if only in a small way, the autocratic project. In addition, Bach benefited personally from the prestige associated with his widely publicized encounter with the greatest German king; indeed, the meeting with Frederick the Great was to become a defining event in his historical legacy (see Chapter 6).

Of course Bach should not be condemned for paying tribute to Frederick. After all, Lutheran theology urged obedience to the state; as Calov put it in the preface to his edition of Luther's German Bible, Christians should remain "subject to the governing authorities" (Romans 13:1) as long as they "do not bear the sword in vain."[83] Frederick's own autocratic program depended on the creation of a pliant Lutheran bureaucracy whose members, intent on their advancement and, like Bach, eager for the spoils they could pick up, also paid lip service to Lutheran theological tenets which pointed up the futility of the entire enterprise of social control and its hierarchies. It is wrong to say that the historical figure Bach – an amalgam of real religious devotion and learning, worldly ambition, musical perfectionism, and political opportunism – was not interested in the benefits of power and unaware of the meanings that could attach themselves to his music. The acute tension between Bach's public actions and his private biblical jottings gives to *A Musical Offering* a vital hermeneutic richness and, if nothing else, helpfully tarnishes the mythical image of Bach the independent, insubordinate, Romantic artist.

When Bach was given the chance to play for and dedicate a collection to the dominant absolute monarch in Germany, he did so in supremely controlled and controlling musical discourse, which took the royal fiat as a point of departure. Elaborating the royal theme was for Bach both a challenging and a satisfying musical project: monarchic subordination and artistic ambition were not mutually exclusive, for it was the intense compositional activity itself which yielded this most submissive tribute to the greatest German monarch of the age. In the lavishly appointed exemplar that he sent to Frederick, Bach added two inscriptions which

---

[83] Robin Leaver, *J. S. Bach and Scripture* (St. Louis, 1985), 179.

make explicit the significance of the canonic techniques employed. In the inscription to the augmentation canon (no. 4), Bach warmly acknowledges the monarchic program of the piece: "As the notes increase [i.e., the note values in augmentation] so may the fortune of the king." Bach provided the *canon per tonos* (no. 5) with an equally ardent epigram: "And as the modulation rises, so may the King's Glory," an allegorical interpretation of the canonic ascent through all the keys as a representation of increasing monarchic ambitions and their realization. But it was equally true that with his demonstration of such compositional mastery Bach's own glory also grew. Bach could, metaphorically and literally, bow before the king while presenting him with something that would glorify Frederick, God, and himself. Indeed, Bach had done his job well, for a portion of Frederick's fame now rests not only on the talents for war and statecraft praised by Bach in the dedication to *A Musical Offering*, but on the counterpoint that follows.

5

Bach the machine

At the clavichord Bach is virtually still.[1] He plays effortlessly, the movements of his fingers "hardly perceptible." Those fingers not in action remain motionless, "quietly in position." The rest of his body takes even "[less] part in his playing." His hands do not contort or register any strain even in the most difficult passages. He is capable of "the most perfect accuracy in performance," whether sight-reading the work of another composer or improvising at his most fantastical. Does he affect the interpretive facial expressions later recommended by his son C. P. E. Bach in his celebrated essay on keyboard playing? One doubts it. The elder Bach plays expressively but his body expresses nothing. He is the picture of efficiency.

The physician turned philosopher Julien Offray de La Mettrie, who took up asylum in Frederick the Great's Berlin soon after Bach's appearance there in 1747, wanted to know how humans could be capable of such miraculous performance: "Glance at a violinist. What suppleness! What agile fingers! His movements are so rapid that they hardly seem to follow one another."[2] What interplay of faculties, what chain of mental impulses and physical reactions could explain such a display? Not only for La Mettrie but for his critics as well, it was musical performance that most dramatically problematized the relationship between mind and body.

The controversial but influential views of the great Pietist doctor Georg Ernst Stahl, attending physician to the Prussian king from 1715

---

[1] The account is based on Forkel's Bach biography: see *NBR*, 433.
[2] Julien Offray de La Mettrie, *Machine Man and Other Writing*, trans. and ed. Ann Thomson (Cambridge, 1996), 31–32.

to 1734, held that the soul was directly responsible for all the motions of the body, that the Cartesian dichotomy of mind and body was invalid. Bach stayed with Stahl's son, also called Georg Ernst and also a leading doctor, during his trips to Berlin in 1741 and 1747. A Privy Councillor to Frederick the Great, the younger Stahl was an avid collector of Bach's music; he certainly heard Bach play during one or both of his Berlin visits, though it is not known if Stahl was present at the famous meeting with Frederick the Great. Following his father's theories, Stahl would have explained Bach's phenomenal abilities as a performer and improviser as a vivid demonstration of the soul in action. The extemporaneous formation of musical ideas and their instantaneous realization were not distinct activities, but part of the same, holistic process. The range of improvisatory conceits hit upon by Bach – from the astonishing modulations, brilliant passage-work, and pathetic recitatives of his free fantasias to the more structured and contrapuntally complex fugues and chorale elaborations – and their expression through the precise movement of feet and fingers were part of a single, though admittedly complex, operation. The physical was inseparable from the spiritual.[3]

In his 1747 book *L'Homme machine* – a scandalous work which led to his flight from Holland to the court of Frederick the Great – La Mettrie disagreed: "That great chemist [Stahl] wanted to persuade us that the soul alone was the cause of all our movements. But that is the talk of a fanatic, not a philosopher." In considering the spectacle of the agile violinist described above, La Mettrie "[begs], or rather [defies] the Stahlians, who know so well everything that our soul can do, to tell [him] how it could possibly execute so rapidly so many movements, happening so far from it in so many different places." La Mettrie summons yet another bravura musician as further proof of the inadequacies of Stahl's theories; to claim that the soul is responsible for these minute and swift actions "is like supposing that a flautist could play brilliant cadenzas on an infinite number of holes he does not know, on which he cannot even put his fingers."[4] La Mettrie's decision to use a flute player in his argument is not accidental. He knew of and had certainly seen a mechanical flautist that had been available for viewing in Paris in the late 1730s and early 1740s. How then would La Mettrie explain Bach's unerring performance at the clavichord or organ? Bach is a machine.

In 1746, the year before the appearance of *L'Homme machine*, the parfumier and glove-maker Pierre Dumoulin left his native Lyons and

---

[3] Johanna Geyer-Kordesch, "Georg Ernst Stahl's Radical Pietist Medicine and its Influence on the German Enlightenment," in *The Medical Enlightenment of the Eighteenth Century*, ed. Andrew Cunningham and Roger French (Cambridge, 1990), 67–87, esp. 72–78.

[4] La Mettrie, *Machine Man*, 32.

headed north towards Germany to exhibit three remarkable automata – two mechanical musicians and a duck – constructed by the celebrated engineer Jacques de Vaucanson. By December of 1746, Dumoulin was in Frankfurt touting Vaucanson's inventions, and within a year he had probably made his way to Hamburg where a 1747 installment of the *Hamburgisches Magazin*, a publication oriented towards "men of high taste" and aimed at popularizing significant scientific developments from across Europe, printed the first surviving German translation of Vaucanson's own technical account of the flute-player.[5] The younger Stahl was a subscriber;[6] the magazine was also available in Leipzig and commented on by readers there.[7] In 1748 another German version of Vaucanson's memoir was published in Augsburg where the automata may also have made appearances. Dumoulin would spend the next several years displaying Vaucanson's inventions in Germany. In 1752 and 1753 he was in Nuremberg, and in 1754 Frederick the Great's brother-in-law, the Margrave of Bayreuth, offered Dumoulin 12,000 florins for the three automata, but, in the end, could not produce the necessary cash; by late 1755, having received a 3,000-florin advance from a Russian sponsor, Dumoulin and the machines had set off for St. Petersburg.[8]

One of the musical figures in Dumoulin's tour was dressed like a dancing shepherd and, by Vaucanson's own account, could play "twenty Tunes, Minuets, Rigaudons, and Country-dances" on a pipe (*flageolet*) held to its mouth with one hand while it beat on a tabor with the other.[9] The extraordinary duck was capable of all the movements of a living animal, the most remarkable of which were internal:[10] it could dabble greedily at handfuls of corn offered to it, after which "The Matter digested in the Stomach is conducted by Pipes, quite to the Anus, where there is a Sphincter that lets it out," once it had been transformed by the automaton's ingenious gastro-intestinal apparatus into stinking excrement.[11]

However amusing and scientifically revealing this duck may have been – it was eagerly examined by engineers and physiologists across Europe – the questions it raised had to do with the metaphysical as

---

[5] *Hamburgisches Magazin*, 6 vols. (Hamburg and Leipzig, 1747–67), II, 1–25.
[6] *Verzeichniß des Naturalien-Cabinets, der Bibliothek, Kupferstiche und Musikalien ingleichen der mathematischen, physikalischen und optischen Instrumente des seligen Hofraths und Doct. Med. Herrn Georg Ernst Stahl* (Berlin, 1773), 112.
[7] *Hamburgisches Magazin*, II, unpaginated preface.
[8] André Doyon and Lucien Liaigre, *Jacques Vaucanson: mécanicien de génie* (Paris, 1966), 92.
[9] Jacques de Vaucanson, *Le mécanisme du fluteur automate* (Paris, 1738), 21; trans. J. T. Desaguliers as *An Account of the Mechanism of an Automaton, or Image playing on the German-Flute* (London, 1742), 23.
[10] Doyon and Liaigre, *Jacques Vaucanson*, 52.
[11] The duck's digestive capacities were later proven to be fraudulent; thus reports of the gastronomic miracle proved to be, well, canards.

much as the mechanical. In opposition to Cartesian physiologists, who saw animals as machines having at most a "sensitive soul" capable of basic perception of pain, for example, but lacking even the least complex of the intellectual faculties, German philosophers of the mid-eighteenth century willingly granted that beasts were animated by a spirit ultimately traceable to God. Some went further still. The Halle professor G. F. Meier's "Essay on a new conception of the souls of animals," the second edition of which appeared in 1752 in the aftermath of La Mettrie's *L'Homme machine*, hypothesized that the souls of animals might attain the same spiritual standing as men, perhaps even immortality.[12] This problem exercised a group of Bach's academic colleagues in Leipzig, who considered the question of "Whether the Souls of Animals Have Understanding" and published their findings in 1742 in a pamphlet edited by Johann Heinrich Winckler, then a professor of Latin and Greek at Leipzig University.[13] A parishioner at the Thomaskirche, Winckler had been an instructor at the Thomasschule in Leipzig in the 1730s, and it was during this period that Winckler, now remembered chiefly as the leading Newtonian in Germany and a member of the British Royal Academy, wrote the libretto for Bach's lost cantata "Froher Tag, verlangte Stunde" (BWV Anh. I 18) performed in 1732 for the dedication of the renovated school building. But if Vaucanson could so convincingly duplicate the internal and external movements of an animal, what was the purpose of endowing that animal with a soul? Ironically claiming himself a true Cartesian, La Mettrie's answer was simple: animals may not be anything but machines, but neither were humans, a claim encapsulated in the ironic title of his *Animals More than Machines* of 1750.[14]

However important the conclusions to be drawn from the duck were for German metaphysics, they were not nearly as thought-provoking as the questions raised by the third member of Dumoulin's unlikely trio, Vaucanson's first and most famous invention, the one he had triumphantly presented to the Royal Academy of Sciences in Paris in 1738: a faun which played the transverse flute. Here was a figure capable of efficient, exacting, and astonishing musical performance. It was clearly a machine yet it approximated the uniquely human gift for music with startling verisimilitude. The frontispiece of the published account of the workings of the flute-player deliberately plays on the confounding of the natural and the artificial (Figure 5.1). While the raised curtain

---

[12] G. F. Meier, *Versuch eines neuen Lehrgebäudes von den Seelen der Thiere* (Halle, 1749). See also Frederick Albert Lange, *The History of Materialism*, trans. E. C. Thomas, 3 vols. (London, 1877–92), I, part 2, 136.

[13] Johann Heinrich Winckler, *Die Frage, ob die Seelen der Thiere Verstand Haben?* (Leipzig, 1742). This essay was apparently included in a 1745 collection entitled "Philosophische Untersuchungen von dem Seyn und Wesen der Thiere" also edited by Winckler. See Lange, *Materialism*, 136.

[14] See La Mettrie, *Machine Man*, 34.

Figure 5.1 Frontispiece, Jacques de Vaucanson, *Le mécanisme du fluteur automate* (1738)

framing the top of the image suggests the theatrical, the woodlands visible through the pillars of the open-air rotunda reveal the proximity of these machines to the untamed, or at least gently managed, natural world beyond. The flute-playing faun, nearly six-and-a-half feet tall, sits on a roughly hewn bolder, a further evocation of the pastoral, of an unforced and welcoming realm which belies the artificiality of Vaucanson's invention itself.[15]

What this engraving cannot convey is just how compelling the automata were once the marvelous mechanism hidden inside the figures and in the large pedestals on which they sat sprang into action. The faun was not a completely stiff, unmoving machine, but an astonishingly realistic figure which actually played a wooden flute; indeed, it could manage any transverse flute put into its hands.[16] It had fingers with leather pads that stopped and unstopped the holes of the instruments; it had lips and a tongue and a throat through which came a variable breath. In attempting to simulate human musical performance on the flute the ambitious Vaucanson had set his sights high: from a technological viewpoint, a dynamically more uniform instrument such as the harpsichord or organ, machine-like in the consistency of its own mechanism, would have been much easier for a machine to play. As Vaucanson acknowledged in his account of the automaton, the mouth of a flute-player does not remain fixed, as it does in the other wind instruments, but can, and should, be constantly changed by opening and closing the lips as well as altering their distance from, and angle with, the mouthpiece of the flute. Because of these variables the instrument was "capable of a very great Number of Perfections, which are wanting in other Wind-Instruments."[17] With its moving lips Vaucanson's flute-player could achieve a fine control of pitch and a range of dynamic nuances, including the faintest of echoes. That Vaucanson was able to produce a convincing facsimile of human performance on this most difficult and subtle instrument was a testament to the masterful engineering concealed within: three sets of three bellows produced different wind-pressures; a series of levers and pulleys allowed the lips to protrude and to change the size of the windway; they also controlled the action of the tongue capable of varied articulations, and the movement of the fingers covering the holes of the flute – all these carefully constructed parts were governed by a precisely pinned cylinder boasting a diverse repertory. With this tour-de-force of mechanics, Vaucanson claimed that his figure could produce motions like "those of a Living Person."[18]

The impact that Vaucanson's faun had on German musicians can perhaps be measured by the studied coolness with which Frederick the Great's teacher and the greatest flute virtuoso of his generation, Johann Joachim Quantz, commented on the machine. Writing in 1752, while

---

[15] For more on Vaucanson's automata and mid-eighteenth-century music aesthetics see Annette Richards, "Automatic Genius: Mozart and the Mechanical Sublime," *Music & Letters* 80 (1999): 366–389.

[16] Doyon and Liaigre, *Jacques Vaucanson*, 49.   [17] Vaucanson, *Account*, 4.

[18] Ibid., 16.

Dumoulin was still touring in Germany, Quantz presents as a futuristic fantasy a scenario he had most likely seen in Berlin or, at the very least, heard reports of from none other than Frederick the Great, one of Vaucanson's most ardent admirers. (With Voltaire's help Frederick had tried to lure Vaucanson and his automata to Berlin back in 1740, but even the lucrative offer of 12,000 livres a year could not convince Vaucanson; the rebuffed Prussian King promptly set about organizing his own factory for the construction of musical automata.)[19] Quantz writes that

> With skill a musical machine could be constructed that would play certain pieces with a quickness and exactitude so remarkable that no human being could equal it either with his fingers or with his tongue. Indeed it would excite astonishment, but it would never move you; and having heard it several times, and understood its construction, you would even cease to be astonished. Accordingly, those who wish to maintain their superiority over the machine, and wish to touch people, must play each piece with its proper fire.[20]

While admitting that a complex automaton such as that constructed by Vaucanson could surpass the accuracy and speed of human performance, such a machine could never be endowed with the subjectivity necessary for meaningful musical expression. In short, cogs and pulleys and levers could not simulate the discernment of good taste and the intensity and refinement of convincing performance. A machine could mimic human motions but it could not reproduce or elicit human emotions. Yet the admonitory tone of Quantz's closing suggests that the threat posed by machine performance was a real one. Quantz's counter-attack against the ferociously accurate machine and the inferences that might be drawn from it abjures the mechanical for the metaphysical: if performance was a form of communication between the soul of the player and that of the listener, then a soulless machine could never achieve human profundity. But with the increasing realism of the counterfeit, human musicians would now be harder pressed to convince, to win over their audience, to differentiate themselves from the machine. For Quantz, as for so many others, to confront the flute-playing faun was to confront the troubling proposition that having a human soul might not be a requirement for the enjoyment and understanding of music; worse than that, the soul might not exist at all.

The concept of materialism, according to which all phenomena, including the operation of human mental faculties, resulted from the interaction of matter, was anathema to almost all German theologians

---

[19] Doyon and Liaigre, *Jacques Vaucanson*, 136–137.
[20] Johann Joachim Quantz, *Versuch einer Anweisung die Flöte traversiere zu spielen* (Berlin, 1752; reprint, Kassel, 1953); trans. Edward R. Reilly as *On Playing the Flute* (London, 1985), 131.

and musicians on account of its implications for the immortality of the soul and therefore, too, for the entire enterprise of Christianity. Materialism had already been decried in Germany as an "altogether erroneous idea and false concept,"[21] and "an evil sect among the philosophers"[22] before the appearance there of La Mettrie's *L'Homme machine* and Vaucanson's flute player. But the publication and dissemination of *L'Homme machine* and the harboring of its author in Berlin required rebuttal comparable to Quantz's dismissal of Vaucanson's faun. Predictably, two responses to La Mettrie soon appeared in Leipzig. *Widerlegung des L'Homme Machine* (Leipzig, 1749) by one Magister Frantzen contested La Mettrie's claims with wide-ranging biblical citation, while D. B. L. Tralles' *De machina et anima humana* argued that although mental activity may well correspond to physical states, thought was nevertheless a product, ultimately, of nothing less than divine will.[23] Tralles cited the specifically human talents for mathematical calculation, conversation among friends, religious activity, and, to be sure, music as proof of the immaterial soul.[24] Rare were philosophers such as Georg Friedrich Meier of Halle, who rejected the tenets of materialism, but did so without fear or fury, somewhat condescendingly likening the demonization of its followers to the taunting of a blind man who denies the existence of colors.[25] Meier had already published a book in 1743 entitled *Beweis, dass keine Materie denken könne*, and produced a second edition in 1751, a temperate commentary on the furor over La Mettrie's *L'Homme machine*.[26]

Just as music figured prominently in La Mettrie's materialism, it was crucial to the arguments of his opponents. Assigned by Luther a status nearly equal to that of theology, music not surprisingly played a prominent part in the defenses of the soul made by La Mettrie's Lutheran respondents. What has since become a cliché – "a musician must have soul"[27] – was in the middle of the eighteenth century a central axiom of anti-materialist thought as it related to music. As Bach devotee and Lutheran clergyman Johann Michael Schmidt, who had perhaps been a student of Bach's in the 1740s, explained in a chapter entitled "How Necessary A Soul is to a Musician" from his 1754 book *Musico-Theologia*, that "through mere organism no consciousness is possible, be it as

---

[21] Johann Georg Walch, *Philosophisches Lexicon* (Leipzig, 1726), col. 1747.
[22] Heinrich Adam Meißner, *Philosophisches Lexicon* (Bayreuth, 1737), 363.
[23] For further reactions in Germany to *L'Homme machine* see Lange, *History of Materialism*, I, part 2, 124–150.
[24] D. B. L. Tralles, *De machina et anima humana* (Leipzig, 1749), 229.
[25] G. F. Meier, *Gedanken von dem Zustande der Seele nach dem Tode* (Halle, 1746), 78.
[26] G. F. Meier, *Beweis, dass keine Materie denken könne*, 2nd edn. (Halle, 1751).
[27] Schmidt, quoted in Friedrich Wilhelm Marpurg, *Historisch-kritische Beyträge zur Aufnahme der Musik*, 5 vols. (Berlin, 1754–62; reprint, Hildesheim, 1970), I, 346–357, III, 356.

artfully made as one would like."²⁸ Evincing a common Orthodox distrust of the senses, Schmidt acknowledged that music appeals to the body, but argues that it is really through the soul that humans gain a deeper understanding of the art as well as of God. Thus the main requirement of the composer is intellectual: "he must be able to think deeply and concentratedly."²⁹ This is not the animated musical performance described by La Mettrie, but the learned man at his composing desk. Bach the composer is not a machine. Echoing Tralles, Schmidt likened the contrapuntal complexity of Bach's *Canonic Variations* to "the most difficult demonstration in geometry,"³⁰ and cited the miraculous contrapuntal music of Bach as a refutation of both La Mettrie and Vaucanson:

> Not many years ago it was reported from France that a man had made a statue that could play various pieces on the flute, placed the flute to his lips and took it down again, rolled its eyes, etc. But no one has yet invented an image that thinks, or wills, or composes or even does anything at all similar. Let anyone who wishes to be convinced look carefully at the last fugal work of the above-praised Bach, which has appeared in copper engraving, but which was left unfinished because his blindness intervened, and let him observe the art that is contained therein; or what must strike him as even more wonderful, the chorale which he dictated in his blindness to the pen of another: *Wenn wir in höchsten Nöthen seyn*. I am sure that he will soon need his soul if he wishes to observe all the beauties contained therein, let alone wishes to play it to himself or to form a judgment of the author. Everything the champions of materialism put forward must fall to the ground in view of this single example.³¹

Music and immortality both demand the soul. But for opponents of materialism such as Schmidt it was the dynamic mental associations involved in discovering intricate contrapuntal correspondence that could never be matched by any machine. And yet even this was perhaps not beyond the reach of mechanical simulation, at least according to the materialists. La Mettrie took Vaucanson's automata as a sign of things to come: "if it took Vaucanson more artistry to make his flautist than his duck, he would have needed even more to make a speaking machine, which can no longer be considered impossible."³² If the flexible requirements of language could be conquered by the machine, the intangible nuances of musical performance and the complex mental associations required by intricate composition could as well.

Indeed, the role of mechanism in musical composition and the viability of capturing the subtleties of performance were of great interest to musicians and critics in the middle of the eighteenth century. Inspired by

---

[28] J. M. Schmidt, *Musico-Theologia* (Bayreuth, 1754), 195. Schmidt's book was well received by musicians, chief among them the Bach advocate Marpurg, who praised the work and excerpted its opening in his *Historisch-kritische Beyträge*.
[29] Schmidt, *Musico-Theologia*, 150. [30] Ibid.
[31] NBR, 361. [32] La Mettrie, *Machine Man*, 34.

a mathematical calculating machine devised by Leibniz, Mizler invented a mechanism which he claimed could computationally determine the proper chords to be played above any given bass-line. He had a prototype fabricated from the best-quality brass, milled to minute tolerances, and then produced the machines and tried to sell them. Advertising the merits of his invention in an April 1738 installment of his journal, *Die musikalische Bibliothek*, Mizler effused over the pedagogical value of his thorough-bass machine, especially when used alongside his newly published book on the subject. To entice prospective buyers, Mizler even offered to throw in a handy carrying case.[33]

Mizler's bald attempt to flog his thorough-bass machine provided an irresistible target for his nemesis on the current music journalism scene, Johann Adolph Scheibe. Having recently let loose his considerable satiric talents on J. S. Bach, Scheibe now turned them on Mizler, belittling not only his pomposity but also his apparent faith in mechanically generated truth. Writing in the April 1739 issue of *Der critische Musikus* as a certain "Ventoso," Scheibe grandly announces a new invention, noting the exact minute of his epiphany – 12:33 p.m. on July 20, 1737 (Scheibe archly dated his "Ventoso" article August 1737, that is, more than half a year before Mizler's announcement of his thorough-bass machine).[34] Predictably, the construction of the apparatus itself sounds quite like that of Mizler's machine. But this contraption promises much more: on the first of its two circular tables are all the rules of composition, which, according to our inventor turn out to number exactly 150 in total. In the center of this circular table is a needle which points to all the rules which must be taken into account to compose a given piece. When in a diagnostic mode, the needle either spins frenetically round the dial pointing to all the rules that are being violated, or, in the case of musical excellence, remains respectfully still. This needle can also divine the genre and emotional affect of the piece, as well as judge the composer's powers of invention and the broader scope of his imagination. Equipped with a separate needle, the second table has an inner and outer circle: on one are written the names of all the composers, and on the other words such as good, bad, mediocre, horrible, and turgid. (These were many of the same negative adjectives deployed two years earlier by Scheibe in his attack on Bach.) Here, in absurd caricature, is musical understanding as pure mechanism, the complexities of music reduced to tables, the infinite gradations of taste and affect calibrated on a metal plate. After describing how a tube from the device is held up to the ear – the machine can be used as a kind of interface between music

---

[33] Lorenz Christoph Mizler, *Neu-eröffnete musikalische Bibliothek* (Leipzig, 1739–54; reprint, Hildesheim, 1970), IV, 78.

[34] Johann Adolph Scheibe, *Critischer Musikus*, rev. edn. (Leipzig, 1745; reprint, Hildesheim, 1970), 298–391, at p. 299.

and perception – Scheibe/Ventoso reveals the secret behind its working: the readings of the device are actually the product of an Arabian talisman. Behind this ludicrous rationalist project lurks an exotic magic, the ghost of hermeticism: unbridled reason – represented here by the musical mathematician Mizler and his thinking thorough-bass gadget – could lead to a kind of blindness akin to irrational beliefs in occult science. In spite of its flippancy, however, Scheibe's satire tacitly recognizes the emerging possibility that technological advance might have applications to music; at the very least the implications of machines in music would have to be considered. Vaucanson had constructed a convincing (and threatening) mechanical flute-player; Scheibe had now imagined a mechanical critic. No more was heard in Mizler's journal about his thorough-bass machine.

Scheibe considered yet another musical machine in 1752 when he saw a device by which keyboard improvisations could be mechanically written down on a paper roll; invented by F. E. Unger, this so-called fantasy machine had been inspired by a similar one exhibited before the Royal Academy in London in 1747.[35] The German version was probably seen by C. P. E. Bach, Quantz, and numerous other musicians in Berlin, who seemed to have agreed that it was ultimately a failure, incapable of capturing nuances such as trills and unable to reproduce the more elusive qualities of expression. This machine, too, had only highlighted the uniqueness of human musical performance and composition (as improvisation). Scheibe is both specific in his criticism of the fantasy machine – the stiffness of the keyboard action, which among other deficiencies, was unable to register ornaments – and expansive regarding its faults: a machine such as this one could never capture the essence of music, since there is more to composition and indeed performance than the mere notation of pitch and duration. Only "thinking machines" could ever match the elasticity of the human faculties, and such machines were held to be an impossibility by all but the most ardent materialists, those cast in the mold of La Mettrie.

Or were they? Mizler's machine was already a step towards mechanistic duplication of human thought in the realization of thoroughbass. The idea of creating a device that could generate music automatically, held an undeniable appeal: hence the attraction of C. P. E. Bach's "Einfall, einen doppelten Contrapunct in der Octave von 6 Tacten zu machen, ohne die Regeln davon zu wissen" (Invention by which Six Measures of Double Counterpoint can be Written without a Knowledge of the Rules), published around 1757.[36] This musical amusement

---

[35] See Annette Richards, *The Free Fantasia and the Musical Picturesque* (Cambridge, 2001), 77–81.

[36] Trans. in Eugene Helm, "Six Random Measures of C. P. E. Bach," *Journal of Music Theory* 10 (1966): 139–151.

is presented on four fold-out pages of Marpurg's *Historisch-kritische Beyträge zur Aufnahme der Musik*,[37] and at first glance appears to be a seemingly random assortment of single notes and forbidding crosses (Figure 5.2). The composer's accompanying instructions outline how, by following a simple, and to all appearances arbitrary, algorithm a perfectly good piece of double counterpoint at the octave can be obtained, and without any knowledge of its workings: pick six random numbers; apply the first number to the first table (there are different tables for the soprano and bass parts), counting forward by nine until the first measure is complete; proceed in the same way until all six measures have been filled up with the proper note values. Astoundingly, a perfectly good piece of mechanically correct invertible counterpoint results, no less charmingly persuasive than the one generated by C. P. E. Bach's own randomly chosen numbers (Example 5.1). The conceit is representative of the mid-century interest in dice games which create viable pieces from pre-fabricated material; Bach's self-generating double counterpoints are rather more recherché – if one can say such a thing about a trifle like this one – than even lighter pieces like the minuets and polonaises which J. P. Kirnberger deconstructed so that amusement-seekers could reconstruct them while at dice.[38]

Utterly insignificant when compared with his father's late works, C. P. E. Bach's "Einfall" nonetheless reproduces the kind of contrapuntal relationships that three years earlier Schmidt had said could only be the product of human intellect. There was no denying that the "Einfall" was a geometrical demonstration, albeit a modest one, of the fact that mechanical operations might indeed be able to produce the kinds of results considered impossible by Tralles, Schmidt and other critics of materialism. Part of the fun, of course, of this ingenious fabrication, lies in the uncovering of the secret, the moment in which the byzantine apparatus is exposed, to the delight of those previously befuddled: Marpurg reveals that Buch simply composed nine different invertible counterpoints over a given harmonic pattern, then cut up each one and spread them out at nine-measure intervals. But once in place, the algorithm yields unfailingly grammatical and intricate music: the real genius in the game is that no ingenuity is required of the players. And the number of pieces created from this permutational scheme is inexhaustible; Marpurg calculates the total to be in the hundreds of billions. If being able to reproduce a process mechanically proved irrefutably that that process had been understood, then C. P. E. Bach had made a clever and not insignificant step towards simulating the complex faculty of human invention.

[37] Marpurg, *Historisch-kritische Beyträge*, III, 167–181, at pp. 175–181.
[38] J. P. Kirnberger, *Der allzeit fertige Menuetten- und Polonoisenkomponist* (Berlin, 1757); see O. E. Deutsch: "Mit Würfeln komponieren," *Zeitschrift für Musikwissenschaft* 12 (1929–30): 595.

Figure 5.2 Invertible Counterpoint "Device," C. P. E. Bach, *Einfall, einen doppelten Contrapunct in der Octave von 6 Tacten zu machen, ohne die Regeln davon zu wissen* as printed in F. W. Marpurg, *Historisch-kritische Beyträge zur Aufnahme der Musik*, vol. I (1755)

Example 5.1 C. P. E. Bach, A randomly generated six-measure piece in invertible counterpoint, H. 869

Example 5.2 C. P. E. Bach, Contrapuntal combinations of a four-note theme, selection, from F. W. Marpurg, *Abhandlung von der Fuge*, vol. II (1754)

In the *Abhandlung von der Fuge* Marpurg includes another interesting exercise by C. P. E. Bach: an extended examination of the contrapuntal possibilities of a four-note subject, presented in various degrees of stretto and in various combinations of diminution, retrograde, melodic and harmonic inversion (Example 5.2). Marpurg prints C. P. E. Bach's investigation into this short theme in order to provide an example for the student of the nearly limitless potential of the basic material when considered by an imaginative and well-trained musical mind. Laid out with impressive pedagogical rigor are the kind of insights that, according to his son, J. S. Bach would have when listening to an improvising organist embark on a fugal subject, predicting the operations that could be performed on the theme and nudging his son when the player made good on those possibilities.[39] Clearly, though, as C. P. E. Bach shows in his examination of the four-note theme, there are more contrapuntal inventions here than could fit into any one piece or be presented extemporaneously by any organist. (Is it coincidence that C. P. E. Bach's soggetto is the same as the first four notes of his father's mighty E♭ "St. Anne" fugue, BWV 552/2, a piece which explores almost none of these possibilities?) With the addition of connective material, modulating appropriately in order to introduce the subject in various keys, a work of "deep reflection" could be literally pieced together by the contrapuntal mechanisms set up by the inventor. Indeed, as the "Einfall"

[39] *NBR*, 397.

Example 5.3   C. P. E. Bach, diminution canon, from J. P. Kirnberger, *Die Kunst des reinen Satzes* (1776–79)

showed, a seemingly infinite number of different such works might be generated automatically, within well-defined parameters.

C. P. E. Bach himself gives an example of what such contrapuntal mechanisms might yield in Kirnberger's *Die Kunst des reinen Satzes* (Example 5.3). This elaborate canon comes in the seemingly modest guise of a non-modulating binary-form piece with symmetrical eight-measure halves. The piece begins unproblematically as a simple canon at the lower fifth, with the bass as the *comes*. But in the bass in the fifth measure there is a covert shift in the canonic procedure: the descending broken triad is not only a faithful answer at the lower fifth to the material heard in the previous measure in the soprano, it is also the beginning of a *diminution* canon, a genre that had been deemed by most a theoretical impossibility, a contradiction in terms.[40] The soprano at this point (mm. 5–6) is also wonderfully ambiguous, for it now seems to follow the bass at the upper octave and thus to represent an inversion of the roles of *dux* and *comes*. Yet as the bass clips along in diminution it is heard (or perhaps only seen) to be following the soprano after all: the quarter-notes in the soprano from m. 5 on are delivered in only two measures (7 and 8) in the bass, it having suddenly shifted into high gear and accelerated to catch up with the soprano. The bass seems to speed up and the soprano to slow down, and the whole affair concludes astonishingly in the same measure. Kirnberger, in his commentary, applauded C. P. E. Bach for creating a novel genre of canon and he appends an example based on Bach's by J. C. F. Fasch, C. P. E. Bach's former colleague at Frederick the Great's court. In fact the novelty of C. P. E. Bach's canon is based on a contrapuntal sleight-of-hand: on inspection, each half of the piece is revealed to be a diminution canon after all, as can be seen simply by omitting the first five notes of the bass, and the first eight

---

[40] Marpurg, *Abhandlung von der Fuge*, II, 109.

notes of the soprano in the second half. C. P. E. Bach's trick is to insert a segment of imitation at the lower fifth in the bass at the start of the piece in order to mislead the listener into thinking that another procedure is being employed. When the diminution canon actually begins there is a marvelous confusion of the frame of reference, a surprising repudiation of what had apparently been the controlling contrapuntal technique. The fact that the second half of the soprano itself begins with the head motive adds to this confusion, which arises as a result of the precision of the canonic ratios and the grammatically coherent music they yield. The effect of this overabundance of signs is that the counterpoint itself appears to be controlling the order of events; counterpoint itself seems to be the agent that disturbs the temporal and intervallic relationships between the voices, with several permutational possibilities available and one or another arbitrarily engaged at any moment. It is as if the contrapuntal operations are automatically generating the musical material. Like Vaucanson's automata these contrapuntal constructs are products of human genius which, once fabricated, seem to run on their own, to think for themselves. The performing machine had challenged the performer; the thinking composition machine now challenged the composer to distinguish himself from "unthinking matter."

In adducing Bach's late contrapuntal works to refute La Mettrie's materialism and its embodiment in Vaucanson's flautist, Schmidt predictably emphasized the intellectual over the physical, privileging ineffable mental processes over the purely mechanical and reproducible. While he does not overtly dismiss the validity of mechanistic performance, Schmidt seems less concerned with matters of expression than Quantz and, like him, admits that such machines could perhaps equal, or even surpass, the precision of performances delivered by the marvelous "springs of the human machine," as La Mettrie put it.[41] But for Schmidt it is self-evident that the purely mechanical duplication of contrapuntal thought is impossible, C. P. E. Bach's collection of intellectual curiosities notwithstanding. That *Wenn wir in höchsten Nöthen sein* was bound up with Bach's death was no doubt significant to Schmidt, since it allowed him to use this chorale setting as a kind of musical proof of the soul's immateriality, a pre-condition for its departure from the body and ascent to heaven. The body left behind by the soul was itself considered, by all but the Stahlians, to be merely an automaton, more complex than Vaucanson's faun, to be sure, but a mechanism nonetheless. (This dualism was a basic tenet of medical thought in Leipzig during Bach's lifetime and would have been reflected in the education of the Bach family friend Benjamin Gottlob Faber, the medical student to whom Bach

---

[41] La Mettrie, *Machine Man*, 28.

dedicated the eponymous canon of 1749, the year that Faber delivered his inaugural dissertation at the university.) For Schmidt, counterpoint separates the man from the machine, and, in the case of the deathbed chorale, the formulation of contrapuntal insights by the composer dramatizes this very separation of mind from body, spirit from matter. It is partly for this reason, perhaps, that Schmidt repeats the myth promulgated by Bach's heirs, that the old man had composed the last chorale extemporaneously, a spontaneous demonstration of counterpoint that is a fitting prelude to eternity. Stately, even grave, the piece becomes for Schmidt a projection of the mind at work. The same is true for Bach's last collection, the *Art of Fugue*, which, because Bach was at work on it at the time of his death, also harmonizes with the overall eschatological tone of Schmidt's interpretation. Indeed, since Bach had, according to Schmidt, recently taken his place in the choir of angels, it is not surprising that his final contrapuntal works – the *Art of Fugue*, the *Canonic Variations*, the deathbed chorale – confirm the loftiness of his thoughts, and therefore the immortality of his soul, and ultimately the fallacy of La Mettrie's materialism.

Given Schmidt's theological inclinations, it is not surprising that he singles out *Wenn wir in höchsten Nöthen sein*, rather than the startlingly mechanistic canons that precede it in the 1751 printed edition of the *Art of Fugue*. The Canon at the Octave and an earlier, shorter version of the augmentation canon were completed by about 1742, but the other two – the Canons at the Tenth and Twelfth, which appear only in the posthumous print – might well be Bach's last newly conceived and completed composition, and the set of four canons was perhaps intended by Bach to conclude his final collection.[42]

The *Art of Fugue* canons make a startling new contribution to the continuing story of counterpoint: they are bravura keyboard pieces made up purely of canonic material. Bach had, of course, included demanding keyboard canons in the *Canonic Variations*, and, at the beginning of the 1740s, in the Goldberg Variations. In these collections, however, the canons themselves were enmeshed within a larger fabric of voices and a generally more welcoming texture, anchored by the chorale melody itself in the *Canonic Variations*, or in the case of the Goldberg Variations, the progress of the bass-line. The *Art of Fugue* canons are more uncompromising in their use of counterpoint; canonic artifice and virtuosic display are equally audible, and indeed are inseparable. Many of the critiques of learned music we have encountered centered on the overweening specificity of the devices employed because, it was argued, they precluded the free, natural associations found in convincing

---

[42] Gregory Butler, "Ordering Problems in J. S. Bach's *Art of Fugue* Resolved," *Musical Quarterly* 69 (1983): 44–61.

music – they were, as Mattheson put it, too "algebraic," the equation of *dux* and *comes* producing automatic music lacking the natural charms of fluid, unforced melody.[43]

What I will argue in my analysis of these curious pieces is that in them Bach exaggerates the mechanistic, self-generating aspects of canonic writing, and that he does so, significantly, in the context of lengthy canons that have the dimensions and aspect of more naturalistic, if you will, "lifelike" genres such as the duetto and invention. Through these means, Bach explores the gap between the fluidity of natural thought and expression on the one hand, and the inflexibility and ungainliness of music based on quasi-mathematical formula on the other. The contrapuntal equations he solves on the local level create larger forms that proceed in ways similar to the progress typical of less contrapuntally rigorous pieces; but these uncanny similarities only draw greater attention to their essential difference. They may seem at first to be "normal" but the educated human mind soon perceives them to be otherwise: that is, to be awkwardly, eerily, and profoundly unlike the kind of musical discourse they approximate so well. My readings of these canons does not depend on claiming that Bach was commenting directly on the celebrated musical machines of his day or that he was responding to the perceived threat of materialist philosophy, although he likely was aware of both matters. Rather, I hope to show that the *Art of Fugue* canons investigate some of the same metaphysical issues raised by Vaucanson and others, issues that so unsettled musicians across Germany during the middle of the eighteenth century. And just as Vaucanson's faun revealed to contemporaries so much about the mechanism of flute playing and the nature of human musicianship, so Bach's last canons might be seen as deeply personal, even eccentric, summation of the meaning of counterpoint in musical composition generally and, more specifically, in Bach's own work.

Throughout the *Art of Fugue* canons Bach emphasizes the canonic restrictions by continually introducing gestures that highlight congruity between *dux* and *comes* across the many-bar temporal displacement that separates them.The periodicity intrinsic to canonic writing is particularly pronounced in the Canon at the Twelfth where the subject itself is highly profiled and given to internal differentiation (Example 5.4). Bach delineates the beginning of the theme with a full measure of triplets then, after the first half-note, reverts to duple time and a generally eighth-note pulse. This triplet motion, whether heard in one voice or divided between the hands, is reserved – with one important exception – for the beginning of each eight-bar contrapuntal unit. The start

---

[43] Johann Mattheson, *Critica musica*, 2 vols. (Hamburg, 1722–25), I, 239.

Example 5.4 J. S. Bach, Canon at the Twelfth in Counterpoint at the Twelfth, from *Art of Fugue*, BWV 1080/17, mm. 1–17

of each new musical unit is unequivocally signalled, and the piece proceeds by unambiguously articulated eight-bar phrases. Likewise, the Canon at the Tenth exhibits a similarly regular division into four-bar segments with the starting point of each new contrapuntal unit marked by distinctive leaps (e.g., an octave, m. 25 = 29, or tritone, m. 33) or shifts in the rhythmic surface (again into sixteenth notes at m. 33, then back to eighths at m. 36); the chromaticism (as at mm. 18 into 20) is easily traced to the correlative spot when the *comes* takes it up four measures later.

In the sprawling *Canon per augmentationem contrario motu* Bach is even able to highlight some of the internal connections as the distance between the *dux* and *comes* relentlessly expands. Making the two canonic voices refer intelligibly to one another across a great, and ever-increasing, temporal distance is at least one explanation for Bach's extensive use of chromaticism in the piece. But since Bach employs not only augmentation but also contrary motion, what goes up must come

Example 5.5   J. S. Bach, *Canon per Augmentationem in Contrario Motu*, from *Art of Fugue*, BWV 1080/14, mm. 15–21; 33–47

down: thus the descending chromatic line in the bass in m. 34 is an unmistakable reminder of that prior, determinant event, the first appearance of the rising chromatic line in measures 15 and 16 (Example 5.5). The second skein of chromaticism in the soprano comes soon after this (mm. 19–20) and the speed of these figures necessarily changes in the *comes* (eighth notes in the soprano answered by quarters in the bass); the spacing between the two occurrences of chromaticism in the bass also lengthens. The serpentine chromatic descent in m. 29 in the right hand, answered in m. 47, has the same effect. The distension of the temporal fabric is vividly dramatized as we hear, particularly in the recurring chromaticism, the piece augmenting before our ears; we are made aware of the generating contrapuntal principle, one which was almost completely inaudible in Bach's other mighty augmentation canon, that in the *Canonic Variations*. Of course, good pedagogical reasons can be found for this kind of clarity in the context of a didactic work like the *Art of Fugue*, since one of the goals of the collection, after all, is to demonstrate plainly to students the interrelationships which govern learned composition. But given their putative complexity, the *Art of Fugue* canons are surprisingly clear: they display their confining contrapuntal parameters proudly, even amidst the otherwise distracting virtuosity of the keyboard playing.

In the case of an infinite canon, periodicity on a large scale translates into perpetuity: a perpetual canon is by definition cyclic. Bach presents the Canons at the Octave and the Tenth as if they were infinite, with their inseparable *dux/comes* pairs ceaselessly brought back to their beginnings by the repeat signs. In point of fact, however, the Canon at the Octave is the only one that is authentically perpetual. The Canon at the Twelfth appropriates the canonic emblem of perpetuity (the repeat sign) but diverges from the complete parallelism between the voices required by the genre: it is not, strictly speaking, a perpetual canon at all. The Canon at the Octave, on the other hand, could have been printed enigmatically, on a single line, with a sign to mark the entry of the *comes*, since the *dux* alone contains the entire piece within itself, including the crucial material that connects back to the beginning of the piece and makes the piece infinite. (It is also presented in this cryptic format in the autograph version.)

Although equipped with the markers of perpetuity, the Canon at the Twelfth, like the Canon at the Tenth and the augmentation canon, is actually two canons (or, thought of in another way, two solutions to a single canon) stitched together (Figure 5.3). This can be noticed in the left hand which repeats itself in the second half of both the Canons at the Tenth (compare Example 5.7, m. 44 and Example 5.11, m. 1) and Twelfth (Example 5.6). These twin solutions are made possible because all three canons are written in double counterpoint, and Bach organizes the pieces to reflect this fact: the first half presents the original counterpoint (the *Hauptcomposition*); the second half delivers the inversion (the *Verkehrung/evolutio*). Bach connects these two elements by means of short bridges and, in the case of the Canon at the Twelfth, he includes a transition back to the beginning, which renders the piece infinitely repeatable, though the level of contrapuntal artifice required is not as difficult as that involved in the truly perpetual canon at the octave. The

Bach and the meanings of counterpoint

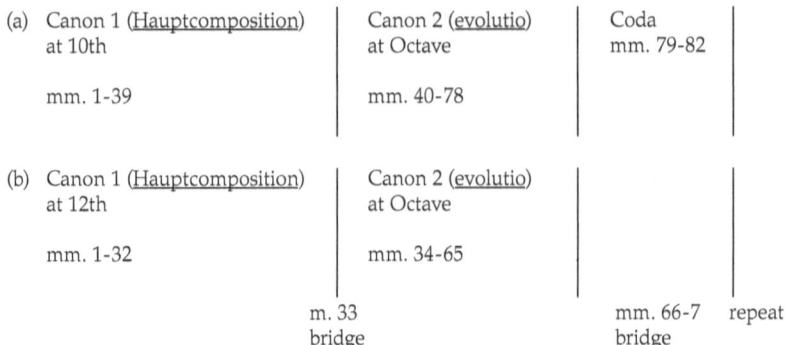

Figure 5.3 *Hauptcomposition/evolutio* scheme for Canons at the Tenth and Twelfth from *Art of Fugue*, BWV 1080/16 and BWV 1080/17

Example 5.6   J. S. Bach, Canon at the Twelfth, from *Art of Fugue*, BWV 1080/17, mm. 1–3; 42–44

augmentation canon is the most obvious manifestation of this mirror-like disposition: the first half of the piece has the faster moving part in the right hand; then at m. 53 this material is given to the left hand and the entire piece is repeated with the voices inverted and with a four-measure concluding coda.

The reasons for writing a canon at the twelfth which is also invertible at the twelfth and, likewise, one at the tenth that is invertible at the tenth are to be seen in the dispositions of these pieces. As Figure 5.3 suggests, the *Verkehrung* (inversion) of a canon at the twelfth written according to the rules of counterpoint at the twelfth will be a canon at the octave. Of course, one could reverse this ordering: as Marpurg pointed out in the *Abhandlung von der Fuge*, in a two-part piece of double counterpoint one can treat either voice as the principal one, since "it is one and the same thing."[44] But using the opposite ordering of the solutions to the canon would shift the piece out of the tonic at the close. Thus, in the case of the Canon at the Twelfth the concluding half of the piece would have one voice in the dominant and one in the tonic (or one voice in the subdominant and one in the tonic). Because this ordering precludes tonal closure it is clearly not viable. Bach's title – Canon at the Twelfth in Counterpoint at the Fifth (i.e., Twelfth) – therefore suggests the disposition of the piece; any sufficiently advanced student of counterpoint would realize that Bach had constructed two canons in one, the second canon being an automatic by-product of the first. But what this disposition does is shift the tonal ambiguity from the second half of the piece to the first half: in the first solution – the *Hauptcomposition* – there is a palpable tonal friction between the two voices, a friction theorists such as Marpurg acknowledge by describing such pieces as bi-tonal. The clear establishment of the key of the piece is superseded by the canonic requirements, "normal" musical syntax is subordinated to the contrapuntal mechanism.

This knitting together of *Hauptcomposition* and *evolutio* was not Bach's invention; we have already seen it in other places, such as the *Praeludium* from the *Musicalisches Kunstbuch* where Johann Theile melds two solutions to a piece of double counterpoint at the twelfth into a coherent and quite lovely movement. But Bach takes this same principle of expansion to massive lengths, and, in contrast to Theile, does not add any extraneous voices which disguise the contrapuntal inversion. Each of the canons in double counterpoint is, in effect, a large-scale projection of the inversion tables found in almost all contrapuntal treatises. Figure 5.4a shows the table for inversion at the twelfth from Berardi's *Documenti armonici*, a book which circulated widely in Germany and was probably known to Bach, even copied out by him.[45] The longest such exercises ever conceived, these invertible canons can be thought of as contrapuntal heuristics extended through time; the Canon at the Twelfth will, theoretically, oscillate unceasingly between either half of the inversion table. The intervals in the first half of the piece (*Hauptcomposition*; mm. 1–32) are converted to those from one side of Berardi's table to the other in the second half (the *evolutio*; mm. 34–65): ignoring octave displacements, a unison becomes a twelfth, a second an eleventh, and so forth. Unlike Contrapunctus 9, which integrates invertible counterpoint

---

[44] Marpurg, *Abhandlung von der Fuge*, II, 177.
[45] Kirsten Beißwenger, *Johann Sebastian Bachs Notenbibliothek* (Kassel, 1992), 341–342.

Bach and the meanings of counterpoint

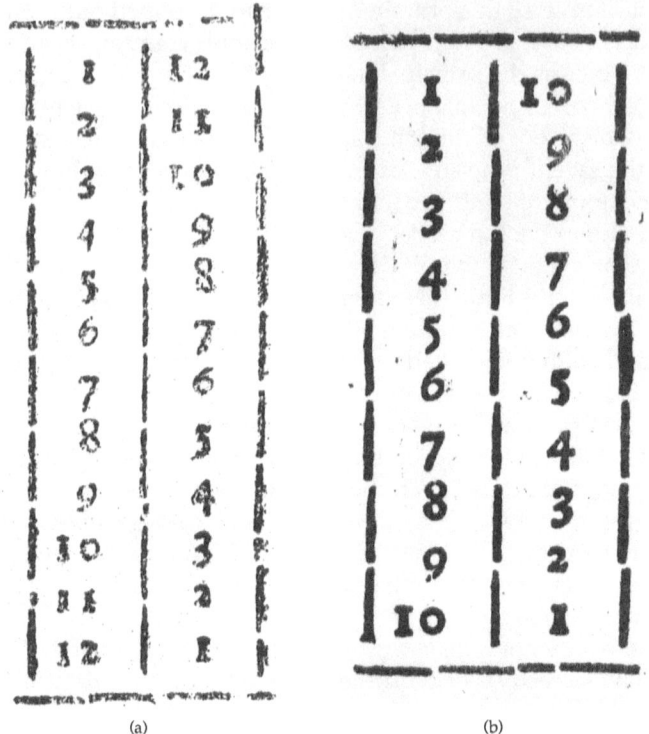

Figure 5.4 (a) and (b) Inversion tables for invertible counterpoint at the twelfth and tenth from Anglo Berardi, *Documenti armonici* (1687)

at the twelfth into the course of the piece, the contrapuntal mechanism of the Canon at the Twelfth determines the musical argument – indeed, the mechanism is the argument. This is what I mean by describing such music as overtly schematic.

In Bach's canons the specific algorithm employed (inversion at the twelfth, tenth, octave) fixes not only the overall scheme but also the local intervallic relationships, and hence, the sound of the piece. One of the most important things that the inversion table reveals about counterpoint at the twelfth is that thirds become tenths and vice-versa; a run of parallel tenths produces perfectly viable, though uninteresting, double counterpoint at the twelfth. This means that these "sweet" imperfect consonances will dominate the writing: in Bach's Canon at the Twelfth the intervals on all but two of the downbeats in the first half of the piece, and therefore in the second half as well, are thirds. Because thirds are mirrored by thirds, and are allowed to pervade the counterpoint, the two solutions to the canon (the *Hauptcomposition* and its *Verkehrung*) sound quite similar even when the voices are inverted, and even though the polarity between the D minor (*dux*) and A minor (*comes*), evident in the first half of the piece, is resolved so that both voices are in the tonic in the second half.

Whereas the inversion algorithms produce homogenization in the case of counterpoint at the twelfth, they produce differentiation in counterpoint at the tenth. A quick look at the inversion table for counterpoint at the tenth discloses the main problem that one must confront when using this technique: parallel thirds become forbidden parallel octaves on inversion, and parallel sixths become parallel fifths. This is a serious hurdle to overcome when writing a bicinium, which so typically relies to varying degrees on parallel thirds (although one could note that the opening section of the F major Duetto from *Clavierübung III* introduces none of them – yet another signal of its disquieting perfectionism). The inversion algorithm also converts the sweet imperfect consonances of the sixth and third into empty-sounding fifths and octaves. This has important consequences, as can be seen in the first contrapuntal matrix of Bach's Canon at the Tenth: it employs mostly fifths and octaves and thus sounds much less antique and less severe when it is inverted in the second half of the piece (Example 5.7). The unique qualities of counterpoint at the tenth explain the pervasiveness of perfect intervals in Bach's Canon at the Tenth and give it a quality unusual for the music of the period. The obligations of the counterpoint are heard in each ungainly, antique-sounding progression, as, for example, in the succession of perfect intervals in mm. 5–6. Unfaltering in its application of contrapuntal rules, it nonetheless sounds stilted, even as if something were lacking. It is certainly because of this propensity for empty sonorities that

Example 5.7   J. S. Bach, Canon at the Tenth, from *Art of Fugue*, BWV 1080/16, correspondence between *Hauptcomposition* and *Verkehrung*, mm. 5–8; 44–47

Example 5.8 Canon at the Tenth, with parallel thirds added to left hand, mm. 5–6

counterpoint at the tenth is rarely left in an unadorned two-voice state; indeed, its reliance on perfect intervals is precisely the reason that it so easily admits of the addition of one or two voices in thirds, which theorists such as Marpurg encouraged in order to ameliorate this emptiness. Just such an addition to the contrapuntal matrix from mm. 5–8 illustrates this kind of decorative technique (Example 5.8). That Bach would extend a bare-bones essay in double counterpoint at the tenth to such lengths speaks to the unyielding intensity of his investigation. The contrapuntal constraints are not allowed to reside deferentially in the domain of *Augenmusik*, but are brought to the sounding surface of the work. The eerily archaic sound of the piece is a constant reminder of its inherent restrictions. The piece constantly confronts the listener with the algebraic equation which fixes the *dux* and *comes* on the local level, and *Hauptcomposition* and its *evolutio* on the large-scale framework.

The inversion algorithms contribute in one other way to the mechanistic quality of the piece. As I pointed out above, the Canon at the Twelfth draws particular attention to its periodicity by announcing the beginning of each new contrapuntal matrix with the flurry of eighth-note triplets, the same rhythmic pattern with which the theme itself begins. This triplet activity extends over the entire first measure of the eight-bar units and is almost always confined to this measure and divided between the hands (Example 5.4). This can be heard already in m. 9, where the *comes* first enters: the triplet action necessarily begins in the right hand but is immediately taken up by the *dux* as well, which, astonishingly, imitates at the octave. What started out as a canon at the twelfth at the distance of eight measures suddenly gives the impression of bolting into a canon at the octave at the distance of only a half measure with the *dux* following the *comes*. Not only has the piece reverted to a much quicker temporal interval of imitation than the length of the subject suggests, but the entire frame of reference has been momentarily inverted. What should be an expansive contrapuntal exposition is suddenly brought back to a more immediate relation and therefore punctured. Bach is a master at creating these kinds of canons-within-canons. In the Canon at the Twelfth from the *Art of Fugue*, this "internal canon" is not a particularly complex feat of contrapuntal ingenuity, since, as

Bach the machine

outlined above, parallel thirds produce parallel tenths (i.e., thirds) when inverted at the twelfth. But the effect is no less unexpected. Similar internal canons at various intervals of imitation, always preceded by a rest in the following voice, crop up every eight bars through the rest of the piece. As noted above, the gesture has the effect of reinforcing the periodicity of the canon by clearly marking the beginning of each new eight-bar contrapuntal matrix; this signpost is so unfailingly regular as to appear almost automatic. But just as important, these imitative relationships confuse the ordering of voices (*dux* becomes *comes*, and vice versa) and momentarily subvert the dominant interval of imitation.

Such subversions create an acute confusion at important structural points in the piece. At m. 33 this figure begins for the first time on the second half of the bar; m. 34 is in fact an "extra measure" inserted to connect the first *Hauptcomposition* and the *Verkehrung*, i.e., the canon at the tenth with the canon at the octave (Example 5.9). The appearance of the subject leading in the soprano (it acts as the *comes* beginning in m. 34) is not only anticipated by the seemingly premature triplets in the right hand but it is also obscured by them. The audibility of this crucial juncture is further weakened by the intimation of a deceptive cadence on the downbeat of m. 34 – the precise point at which the soprano assumes control over the canonic discourse. The establishment of a discernible canonic ordering is also vitiated when the bass races after the soprano in a canon at the lower octave, imitating the right hand for two groups

Example 5.9   J. S. Bach, Canon at the Twelfth, from *Art of Fugue*, BWV 1080/17, mm. 33–43 of triplets rather than the usual one. Things are even more drastically confused by the fact that the first (and only) full cadence in the piece at m. 42 (it is also a cadence to the tonic) lends greater weight to the bass entry of the subject, making it appear to lay claims to being the *dux*, when it is actually the *comes* at this point. In other words, it is easy to miss the soprano entry at m. 34 and then mistake m. 42 for the return to the beginning, or at least to assume that the bass is still the leading voice. The peculiarities of the counterpoint add to the perplexity: that m. 42 repeats m. 9 with the voices inverted and still in parallel thirds recalls the opening matrix, but with an unsettling sense of displacement. Finally, this point of connection between the two solutions of the canon is complicated by the way the left hand harmonizes the entry of the subject in the right hand using counterpoint at the twelfth. This contrapuntal relationship will be inverted for the bridge back to the beginning after the second solution has concluded, but in this context it also produces a continuation of imitation at the twelfth – another internal canon – across m. 36 and into m. 37, with the right hand functioning as the *dux*.

The bridge leading back to the beginning is even more convoluted. Extending over three measures, this passage consists of the longest run of triplets in the entire piece (Example 5.10). It begins at m. 66 (the inversion of the analogous spot, m. 33) with an internal canon at the octave in counterpoint at the twelfth and at the space of a half-note.

Example 5.10 J. S. Bach, Canon at the Twelfth, from *Art of Fugue*, BWV 1080/17, mm. 66–72

When the actual subject reenters at m. 68 in the left hand, surrounded by the rapid exchange of the head motive between the voices, the right hand is still leading the canon at the octave, which could have been continued *ad infinitum*. The momentum derived from these triplets is a result not just of their increased velocity but of the accelerated pace of canonic imitation: digital speed brings with it contrapuntal speed, and it is this mechanical cooperation which propels the piece towards perpetuity, that is, back to the beginning. Finally in the second half of m. 68 the bass escapes this vortex with its run of an entire measure of triplets, but because of the profusion of internal references the exact point at which the bass takes over – i.e., the beginning of the repeat of the entire canon – is deliberately clouded. The ambiguity persists, for the soprano pursues the internal canon at the twelfth across the bar-line into m. 69, following the bass at the distance of a half-note. The soprano finally concludes the uninterrupted stretch of triplets divided between the voices with its eighth-notes at the second half of m. 69, leaping up to the high a^2, only then to begin following the bass in yet another internal canon at the octave for mm. 70 and into 71 (this is analogous to the passage just discussed in mm. 35 and 36). The churning out of contrapuntal operations creates not the rhetorical force of, say, a fugal stretto, but the confusion that comes with an excess of signs. Bach introduces no cadences, no rests, no rhythmic differentiation which would make the formal layout of the piece clear, and the superfluity of imitative relations, especially in the bridge, gives the impression that the operations of counterpoint have taken over, automatically hitting upon short-term relations which go against the grain of the larger contrapuntal designs. Indeed, the passage verges on the aleatoric, the algorithms producing a dizzying array of canonic relationships in rapid succession.

Bach gives counterpoint the appearance of controlling musical events even more firmly in the Canon at the Tenth. The title itself announces that this will be an odd piece, for writing a canon at the tenth has important ramifications for tonal organization since the answer will not enter at a more normal interval of imitation (octave or fifth) and so will immediately trouble any sense of harmonic stability. Indeed, the theme begins in the expected D minor but when the *comes* enters it sounds out starkly in F major, while the *dux* cleaves to D minor beneath it (Example 5.11). Thus the contrapuntal mechanism overrides the accepted goal of establishing the key. From the outset Bach deploys the contrapuntal operations inherent in invertibility in order to undermine the usual logic of an imitative piece. As is often stressed in German theoretical writings on the subject, invertible counterpoint and canon are closely related: a piece of invertible counterpoint necessarily yields a canon if one simply places the counterpoint after the theme, a procedure not unlike that used in the crab canon from *A Musical Offering*.

Example 5.11 J. S. Bach, Canon at the Tenth, from *Art of Fugue*, BWV 1080/16, mm. 1–21

Thus mm. 5 through 8 in the bass will fit contrapuntally with the opening form of the subject and can therefore produce a perfectly serviceable eight-measure canon (Example 5.12); Bach demonstrates this fact at m. 40, the point at which the right hand assumes the role of *dux*; the bass-line here is simply a decorated version of the first harmonization of the theme, that is the bass in mm. 5 through 8. Example 5.12 is a canon at the octave rather than one at the tenth, and because no dissonances are used on strong beats this four-bar passage is invertible at the octave and the tenth, as the addition of thirds in Example 5.8 has already shown.

The bi-tonal entry of the *comes* in F major is already odd enough, but Bach then immediately demonstrates in the succeeding contrapuntal

Example 5.12 Eight-measure canon at the octave, based on J. S. Bach, Canon at the Tenth, from *Art of Fugue*, BWV 1080/16, mm. 1–8 and 42–43

matrix (mm. 9–12; Example 5.11) that the theme and its counterpoint are invertible at the octave. But this demonstration comes too early, for this is a contrapuntal operation that should rightly be reserved for the second half of the piece, for the *Verkehrung*; what the premature inversion does is to reverse the order of *dux* and *comes*: it is a purposefully disorienting move, for suddenly at m. 9 we hear a canon at the octave with the bass now seeming to follow, not lead, the soprano. At the beginning of the third contrapuntal matrix (m. 13), Bach archly implies that he is willing to continue with this inverted *dux/comes* scheme and head off into an epic *canon per tonos*, which is what he would have had to do had he continued this pattern. Instead, Bach introduces sixteenth notes and chromaticism in the next contrapuntal matrix beginning in m. 17; these anticipate the virtuosic display of sixteenth-note runs and twisting chromatic touches that come to dominate the piece.

Given the disposition of the Canon at the Tenth, we know that there will be more confusion in the second half with the inversion of the voices. Yet the matrix beginning in m. 48 sounds eerily familiar, indeed it is identical to the material which begins at m. 5, and suggests perhaps to the perceptive listener that we have returned to the beginning, with the bass in m. 44 (see Example 5.7). The next two contrapuntal matrices are also taken from the opening of the piece, and merely introduce a few chromatic alterations. Thus for a considerable stretch the same material is presented in the same order, even though the roles of *dux* and *comes* have been reversed. Although the *Verkehrung* (a canon at the octave) is well under way, the identical nature of the material makes it seem as if the piece has already cycled back in on itself. This kind of uncanny regression is what happens when an inversion canon that has already been folded back on itself is inverted. These temporal distortions and inversions, occurring both over longer frames of reference (*Hauptcomposition* imported into the *Verkehrung* and vice versa) and on a more local level (*comes* doubling back on *dux*), continually undermine the sense of forward progress and rational ordering; it is as if they were generated automatically by the contrapuntal algorithms rather than by the deep reflections of the composer. Indeed, there is a marked affinity between the confusions of the canon at the tenth and the odd little diminution canon (Example 5.3), so like clockwork, that C. P. E. Bach sent to Kirnberger. Like C. P. E. Bach's "device" for generating a piece of invertible counterpoint, the weirdly interchangeable construction of Bach's Canon at the Tenth exploits the modular nature of contrapuntal techniques. In the Canon at the Tenth this modularity leads to continual reversals of canonic hierarchies, and the piece is therefore a vertiginous exercise in constantly shifting the contrapuntal frames of reference by means of the seemingly automatic, almost arbitrary, illogical application of the rules of invertibility.

After the first 39 bars have been repeated (in the *evolutio*), Bach concludes the piece with what is one of the most mechanistic-sounding passages in his oeuvre (Example 5.13). At m. 79 he notates a bizarre shift in tempo: the running figures in the right hand are suddenly slowed down by a rate of 3:2, while the left hand delivers the syncopated subject

Example 5.13 J. S. Bach, Canon at the Tenth, from *Art of Fugue*, BWV 1080/16, mm. 77–82

(in inverted form) at an accelerated rate, twice as fast as at the opening. Thus the piece simultaneously speeds up and slows down. Even the articulation is precisely indicated here, and the markings added by Bach draw attention to the tempo change with their awkward off-beat relation to the suddenly shifting meter. Yet the deceleration in the right hand is only momentary, since in the next measure (80) it too speeds up without warning, its outburst of thirty-second notes now joining in the regulated accelerando already introduced by the left hand. If Bach were following the norms of musical expression, the piece should be slowing down here in preparation for the close, yet it bolts ahead, as if a higher gear ratio had been peremptorily engaged.

Schmidt stressed that mechanical musicians could not think at all, let alone deeply, and therefore could never begin to fathom the intricacies of counterpoint. As one moves through the *Art of Fugue* it is the canons that first confront one with impressively demanding passage-work as well as the tightest contrapuntal operations: with the chance to exercise one's facility at the keyboard come the most restrictive musical conditions. By bringing the "deep" contrapuntal structure to the surface of the *Art of Fugue* canons, Bach allows glitter and substance to reside within the same musical material, and be heard on the same level. The canons are the most contrapuntally rigorous pieces in the *Art of Fugue*, while at the same time being the most superficially brilliant. In this way they dramatize the tension between thinking and playing, between reflection and action: virtuosic flamboyance becomes the byproduct of contrapuntal mechanism.

The conflation of contrapuntal technique and keyboard technique is challenged few times in the collection, but dramatically so at the close of the Canon at the Octave (Example 5.14). From m. 99 on the right hand

Example 5.14 J. S. Bach, Canon at the Octave, from *Art of Fugue*, BWV 1080/15, mm. 95–103

freely harmonizes the left hand, which executes the leading-tone trill first heard in the *dux* in m. 98. But how will Bach provide an acceptable cadence if the lower voice is confined to the leading tone rather than the dominant? Perpetual canons must contravene their internal rules in order to come to an end at all: the canon can only be stopped by being interrupted. Bach could, for example, have written more extended, more expansive ending in which both voices freely attempt to find harmonically viable closure. Instead he ends the piece abruptly with the right hand physically breaking free from the canonic armature and flamboyantly crossing over the left hand in order to deliver the mandatory full cadence that brings the piece to an almost shockingly abrupt close – a fiercely defiant gesture of virtuosic hauteur. But defiance can also be an admission of defeat. The burst of belated freedom, a last-ditch effort to realize a cadence, only confirms the total control exercised in all the foregoing material.

The closely managed tempo change at the end of the Canon at the Tenth leads to a similar confrontation (see again Example 5.13). After the notationally accelerated passage described above, the piece comes to an unexpected halt at the fermata and its call for a cadenza. This sudden relaxation renders the prior exertion of contrapuntal authority more striking: it is as if Bach is asking the player to distinguish himself from the composer's contrapuntal machine. This is the only cadenza in the collection and it is a contest which in intellectual terms – or to use Schmidt's words, "geometrical" terms – the player will lose; nothing even approximating the preceding contrapuntal complexity could possibly be delivered spontaneously. Suspension of pulse and the concomitant demand to improvise are the antithesis of the unrelentingly controlled and motoric canon in which this space for unmediated inspiration is carved out. The seemingly unassuming fermata is the chasm between the complete freedom embodied in fantastical improvisation and the absolute control required of canonic imitation. With the fermata Bach brings mechanism and spontaneity into irreconcilable confrontation, the exact and unfailing operations of counterpoint momentarily held in abeyance to make way for the discursive and fallible insights of the improviser. Which is superior: the man or the machine? Or perhaps Bach wants to dramatize the unbreachable rift between the two, and in so doing highlight the mechanistic quality of the canon itself.

As the last of the last – the final segment of Bach's crowning collection – the *Art of Fugue* canons are in this respect a fitting conclusion to a decade, even a life, of work: in fabricating these contrapuntal machines with ultimate precision and then letting them loose at high speed, Bach had in a way removed himself from his music. He had produced pieces in which the compositional mechanisms are seemingly allowed to determine the succession of musical events, pieces in which the workings of double counterpoint and canon seem, at times, to "think" for themselves. With their internal references and disconcerting accelerations these pieces seem to imply a mechanically generated, quasi-independent will – they suggest, especially in the Canon at the Tenth, that the machine is thinking for itself. But of course this is nonsense, and what both these pieces do, like Vaucanson's flute player, is astonish and confuse with their illusion of the real. Just as the secret of C. P. E. Bach's automatic contrapuntal machine is divulged by Marpurg in his commentary, one of the points of the exercise – which has an important pedagogical result – is to draw the student behind the game itself and to an admiration of the creator and his creation, the traces of the man behind the machine. In approximating more accessible genres like the keyboard duet and the two-part invention so closely, the canons only demonstrate how uncannily different they are. Like the relationship between Vaucanson's faun and the human flute-player Quantz, the closeness of these canons to "real" music only brings their fundamental difference into greater relief.

Compared to the once-favored narrative of Bach's last years as a retreat from the world, a rejection of current trends and practices in favor of a self-absorbed abstraction, I prefer this story: among his very last works is a set of canons in which Bach presents an automatic, self-referential music; in these pieces I hear Bach playing at fabricating mechanistic composition, producing not so much music as meta-music, not so much compositional thought as a picture of the objects of compositional thought and how they might be automatically strung together, yet still grammatically coherent. Bach presents a counterfeit of "real" music, an imposture of a "real" composer, compelling in its manifest arbitrariness, sublime awkwardness, and nearly perpetual energy.

More than a retreat from the contemporary musical world, the *Art of Fugue* canons might be thought of as a distancing from the self, a maneuver that allowed for a different kind of self-knowledge, a reflective examination of the great contrapuntal project as a whole, and the purpose to which counterpoint could be put. This critical look at the self combines those admittedly Romantic attributes with which Forkel described Bach at the close of his 1802 biography: "the main tendency of his genius [was] to the great and sublime" but he was also capable of an elevated humor; this "cheerfulness and joking" were those of a sage.[46] That a learned humor again impinges on the realm of Bach's counterpoint – a discipline characterized by many eighteenth- and twentieth-century commentators as an unremittingly pedantic, or at least serious, undertaking – is perhaps another reason for the critical uncertainty that has marked reception of these pieces. To appreciate the

[46] NBR, 477.

learned humor of the canons is to appreciate the heights to be attained by playing the games of the contrapuntal enterprise and the mental and physical athleticism they require.

Before we leave Bach at his clavichord, endlessly circling through his Canon at the Tenth, let us remember that what the counterfeiter counterfeits is not the thing produced – a duck, a faun, an intricate piece of music – but himself.[47] As Vaucanson so brilliantly demonstrated, one could be said to understand a phenomenon or process if one could build a machine that could reproduce it: this was a compelling mode of articulating knowledge taking shape in Bach's last years as can be seen in the works of Mizler, Scheibe, C. P. E. Bach and their musical computing machines simulating and/or satirizing figured bass, critical judgment, intricate counterpoint. The *Art of Fugue* canons are the ultimate reproduction, or perhaps reinvention, of the efficient and unfailing performer and the inexorable contrapuntal framer: they brilliantly create a counterfeit Bach, and are thus among his greatest achievements.

[47] For more on this line of argument and the following point about understanding a process by reproducing it mechanically see Hugh Kenner, *The Counterfeiters: An Historical Comedy* (Bloomington, 1968; reprint, Baltimore, 1985), 25–26, 170–174.

6

Physiognomies of Bach's counterpoint

Few would contest the claim that the greater part of Bach's legacy derives from his mastery of counterpoint, for this is the dominant theme in Bach reception beginning with the obituary of 1750: "If ever a composer showed polyphony (*Vollstimmigkeit*) in its greatest strength, it was certainly our late lamented Bach."[1] Indeed, Bach's nineteenth-century afterlife as a colossus of the Western musical canon was born of his primacy in counterpoint. Perhaps it is not surprising that Bach's unique brand of musical complexity became an unapproachable and irreproachable standard in an increasingly complex world of unceasing technological advance. But however much his ingenuity at dealing with multiple themes and his ability to synthesize seemingly disparate musical concepts in a single work might have suggested the image of the modern industrial manager or enterprising inventor, Bach's historical persona was insulated from such comparisons. As Theodor Adorno argued, this most modern of composer's music became an anachronism, returned by the nostalgic historicist imagination to a place safely within the boundaries of the theological age in which it was originally composed.[2]

Inasmuch as the meanings of Bach's music are inseparable from those of counterpoint – a fact made clear over two-and-a-half centuries of Bach reception – it is certainly relevant here to survey the course of their entwined development since his death. In this way I hope to avoid the kind of blinkered approach to Bach's music so maligned by Adorno. In this book I have so far tried to place Bach and his most complex

---

[1] *NBR*, 305; *BD* III, 87.
[2] Theodor Adorno, "Bach Defended against His Devotees," in *Prisms*, trans. Samuel Weber and Shierry Weber (Cambridge, Mass., 1981), 133–146, at 135–136.

compositional techniques in at least something of their original context – an admittedly historicist project. But I have also hoped that these efforts would help us to contextualize our own historical perspective on his work; I have attempted not only to reanimate his music in its contemporary aesthetic environment, but to investigate the highly malleable meanings from which it has derived so much of its cultural potency. The metaphors used in describing Bach and his counterpoint after 1750 and the diverse causes in which these metaphors have been enlisted also help to bring the issues at stake in the earlier eighteenth-century reception of Bach's strict music into greater focus. One of the most striking results of this hermeneutic exchange is to highlight the fluidity of the meanings that have attached themselves to Bach's contrapuntal works ever since he composed them.

My study of the meanings of Bach's counterpoint began at his deathbed. I would like to conclude it by following his funeral procession – family and friends, along with the students and faculty of the Thomasschule – out through the Grimma Gate and to his burial spot. I begin my account of the posthumous meanings of Bach's counterpoint with the search for his body.

Bach's bones

Bach was buried on July 31, three days after his death, on the south side of the Johanniskirche outside the walls of the city of Leipzig. The place of his interment was not accidental. Some of the most intense confessional conflicts surrounding the introduction of the Evangelical faith in Leipzig in the 1530s had to do with rites of burial, and especially where dead bodies were to be buried. Indeed, the main impetus for the Reformation had come as a response to a complex of corrupt practices associated with death and dying: the charging of fees for special masses for the dead, for intercessory prayers, and for indulgences intended to procure the remission of damnable sins for those in purgatory.[3] Before the Reformation the dead were buried within the the city walls – that is, close to the living; the dead were neither out of sight nor out of mind, and the state of their souls remained a central concern to the survivors. Thus they also represented a financial resource to be exploited by the clerical establishment.

With the official acceptance of the Evangelical faith in Leipzig in 1539, burial outside the city walls became the norm, sanctioned both theologically and as a matter of public health since putting more bodies into the already overcrowded intramural churchyards was rightly thought

---

[3] Craig Koslofsky, *The Reformation of the Dead: Death and Ritual in Early Modern Germany, 1450–1700* (New York, 2000), 40–77.

to increase the threat of disease. The physical removal of the dead to a location outside the social geography of everyday life was a crucial concern of the Reformation: Lutherans were offered no way of intervening on behalf of their dead, and could not become vulnerable to corrupt practices associated with death. The dead were not to be forgotten, but they were to be separated both spiritually and physically from the living.

Anticipating his own burial during his final illness, Bach would have expected God to look after his posthumous body, and he would have hoped that the oak casket in which it was to be buried would be his only resting place until the Last Day, when his rotting corpse would be raised up and transfigured into its heavenly form. Indeed, Bach's bones would have remained in the ground where they were put on July 31, 1750, had his beliefs about the dead body retained their currency. Instead, however, a new faith, science, had its own designs on Bach's remains, undeterred by the beliefs once held by the dead man himself. If Bach's bones could be found they would be exhumed and the remaining biological characteristics of his genius elucidated. Spurred by an emerging sense of national pride, the nineteenth century saw the remains of famous historical figures, among them Kant, Schiller, Raphael, and Beethoven, exhumed, examined and analyzed, and then placed in new, more prominent "final resting places" that allowed for easier access and worshipful pilgrimage, often in the shadow of a newly designed monument.

By the nineteenth century Bach's burial place was without a marker; prevailing scholarly opinion in the 1890s held that there had never been one.[4] This made the task of finding his remains difficult, given the numbers of bodies that had been buried around the Johanniskirche. Oral tradition had it that Bach's grave was six paces from the south door of the church; this was the spot where choristers from the Thomasschule had long sung every year on the anniversary of Bach's death.[5] In spite of their interest in finding Bach's actual grave site and remains, many were not hopeful. In 1880 Spitta claimed that the grave had been obliterated and would be impossible to locate.[6] Gustav Wustmann, director of the Leipzig city archives, had been among the most eager to find Bach's grave and in his extensive research into the subject had discovered in the Johanniskirche's account books that Bach had been buried in an oak casket, one of only twelve such caskets out of the 1,400 containing Leipzigers who had died in 1750; this narrowed down the hunt for his remains considerably. But in spite of his work, Wustmann, too, became convinced that there was little chance of finding Bach's grave.

---

[4] Wilhelm His, *Johann Sebastian Bach: Forschungen über dessen Grabstätte, Gebeine und Antlitz* (Leipzig, 1895), 4.
[5] Christoph Wolff, *Johann Sebastian Bach: The Learned Musician* (New York, 2000), 453.
[6] Philipp Spitta, *Johann Sebastian Bach*, trans. Clara Bell and J. A. Fuller Maitland, 3 vols. (London, 1889), III, 276.

The chairman of the Johanniskirche vestry, Pastor Tranzschel, did not give up hope, however. During the rebuilding of the church in 1894 he ordered excavations in the graveyard, directing some of the workers to dig down to about eight feet in the area where Bach's grave was thought to have been. On October 19 Tranzschel summoned Leipzig forensic expert and craniologist Wilhelm His to the excavation site. His described the scene as an enormous hole filled with "heaps of bones, some in many layers lying on top of each other, some mixed in with the remains of coffins, others already smashed by the hacking of the diggers"[7] – a grim tableau worthy of Müller and other Lutheran writers on the earthly fate of the posthumous body. In such chaos Bach's coffin certainly would not be found; as yet only remnants of pine coffins were to be seen at the site. The workers were now ordered to dig more carefully and look for signs of an oak casket. At eleven in the morning on October 22 they came upon one; the casket had collapsed around the skeleton, bits of wood mashed around the bones. His began sifting through the remains, and quickly established that they belonged to a young woman of diminutive stature. But before disappointment could set in, another oak casket was found, the opening of which had to wait until after the workers had had their lunch. In inclement weather perfect for the Gothic scene, a dark-clad pastor and an anatomist with his trusty anatomic assistant stood over a jumbled pit of bone, mud, and wood in which men dug with picks and shovels as the second casket was pulled from the ground. His and his assistant Dornfeld removed the skull from the casket and slowly, too, the bones. They could quickly see that the skeleton belonged to an elderly man. The skull was "sturdy and of strong features" – a protruding jaw, relatively lowset eye sockets, sharply angled base of the nose (Figure 6.1). His could barely believe his good luck: after inspecting less than a dozen skulls in the bone-strewn mud of the graveyard, littered with so many skulls of "indifferent form" which precluded any investigation into their origins, he had found a remarkable specimen, the skeleton that must have belonged to a man of distinction. Given His's initial reaction, it hardly comes as a surprise that his subsequent "scientific" research conducted over the winter would prove to him and other enthusiasts of such national relics that these were Bach's remains.[8] But what of the third oak casket also unearthed in the morning of the 22nd, the skull inside smashed beyond recognition and therefore unsuitable for scientific study? His does not entertain the possibility that it could have been these that were Bach's bones. Indeed, a satire published in Leipzig in 1906 raised this very real possibility and vehemently criticized His for a shoddy, self-serving science,

---

[7] His, *Johann Sebastian Bach: Forschungen über dessen Grabstätte, Gebeine und Antlitz*, 4.
[8] Ibid., 4–6.

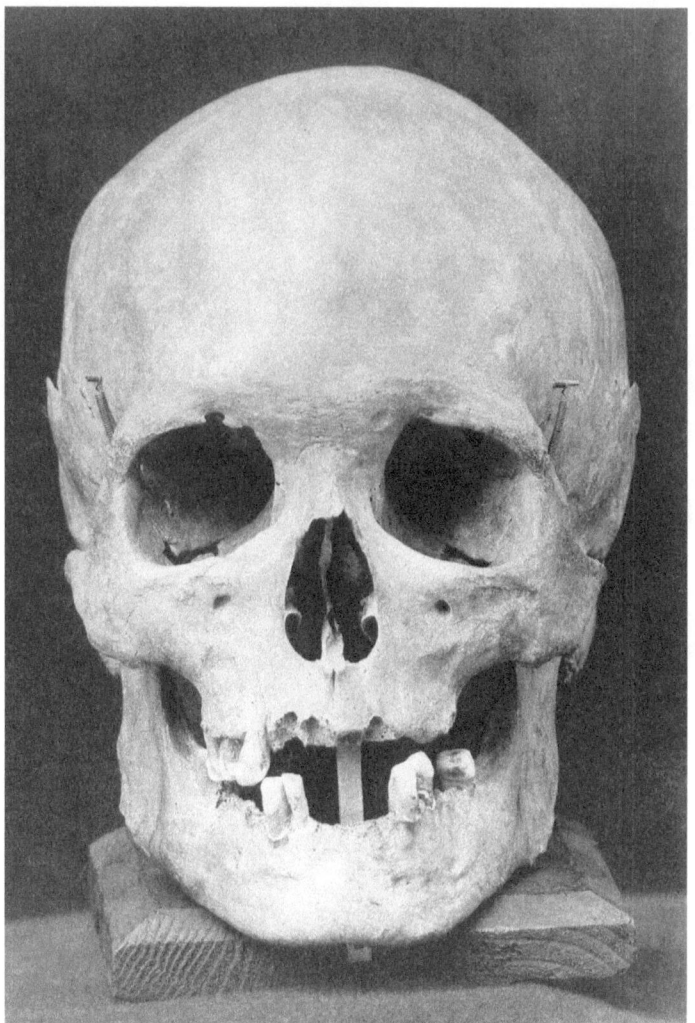

Figure 6.1   Bach's skull; photographs from Wilhelm His, *Johann Sebastian Bach: Forschungen über dessen Grabstätte, Gebeine und Antlitz* (1895)

clouded by a nationalist ideology that aimed only at validating foregone conclusions.[9]

Nonetheless, His presented his report to the Leipzig city council in March of the following year, and soon after that published a more detailed, "scientific" article in the journal of the Royal Saxon Society

[9] D. V. [Ernst Klotz], *Das fragwürdige Todtenbein von Leipzig. Satire auf die tieftraurige Historie vom Leben, Sterben und Ausgrabung der Gebeine J. S. Bach's* (Leipzig: Paul de Wit, 1906).

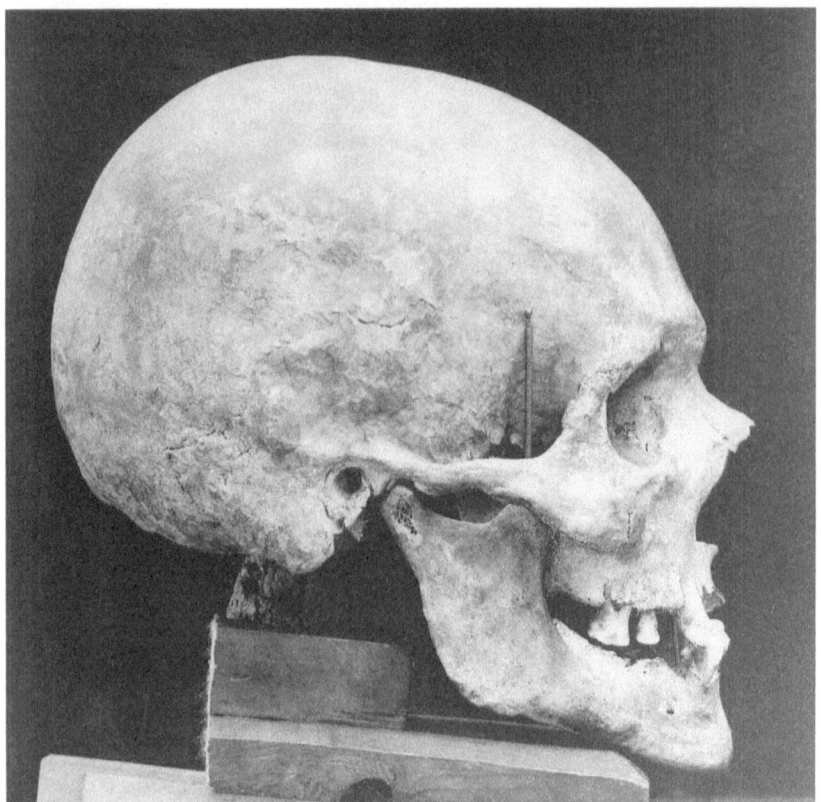

Figure 6.1 (cont.)

of Sciences. His's method for confirming that he had in fact found Bach's bones was a circular one: the authenticity of the skull would be established if it allowed for the reconstruction of a face that corresponded sufficiently to the surviving portraits, in particular those by E. G. Haußmann. Here was wish-fulfillment masquerading as scientific research, a ritual that not surprisingly had the end result of verifying the enthusiasts' desires to "prove" that they were in fact in possession of this significant relic of national patrimony. The commission charged with finding Bach's body, a group that included His, Tranzschel, Wustmann, and the sculptor Karl Seffner (called into make a bust of Bach based on the skull) reported to the Leipzig city council in a signed statement, that the authenticity of Bach's bones had been established "to the highest degree of probability."[10]

---

[10] His, *Johann Sebastian Bach: Forschungen über dessen Grabstätte Gebeine und Antlitz*, 16.

His had set to work on the bones, free of "all biases" and "false concerns for piety" (falsche Pietätsrücksichten) in the discovery and examination of "scientifically significant relics."[11] But even before subjecting the remains to technical inquiry, His had strong opinions about the skull. He was, after all, not only a leading anatomist but an expert in phrenological categories, having contributed important studies to the discipline.[12] Thus he was able to cite his own work in interpreting the prominent features of the skull: the deeply-set base of its nose; the bridge of the nose jutting forward in a "bold" (kühn) manner; the eye sockets small; and the cheek bone "strongly developed" (stark entwickelt). Taken together, these characteristics "presented an uncommonly powerful (kräftig) expression" – that is, the undeniable aspect of genius.

As was fitting for a sober researcher, there was no room in His's work for the humor of Mattheson's metaphorical dissection of canon: the real skeleton of Germany's greatest contrapuntist was to be treated with utter seriousness and care, the new magic of forensic science revealing the vital truths it contained. Heeding the anatomist's contempt for religious squeamishness, and answering instead to the higher calling of science, His carefully dissected Bach's skull (Figure 6.2). Now a plaster replica of the brain could be cast in the cranial cavity and its features analyzed. Bach's temporal lobe (Schläfenwindung), thought to be responsible for acoustical cognition, was seen to be particularly well developed.[13] The temporal bones (Schläfenbeine) were carefully cross-sectioned with a small jig-saw so as to minimize the loss of irreplaceable bone mass (Figure 6.3). After painstakingly measuring the openings in the temporal bone, His sent his data to the leading expert on the osteology of the temple and ear, his colleague Herr Prof. Dr. Adam Politzer in Vienna. Politzer was impressed by "Bach's" temple, in particular by the impressive size of the fenestra rotunda – the opening between the middle ear and the cochlea. Other peculiarities of construction led Politzer to pronounce its features to be "very rare" indeed.[14] These were exceptional bones that must have belonged to an exceptional person – a striking confirmation, it seemed, that they had once been part of Bach. Further comparative research, suggested His, should be done on the temporal bones of other (dead) composers, though His lamented the deplorable fact that on the exhumation of Beethoven's remains for his removal to Vienna's central cemetery, his temporal bones had been sawed out of the skull and then preserved in alcohol. Unfortunately, they had subsequently disappeared, apparently sold off to an English doctor – a great loss for science and culture.

---

[11] His, "Johann Sebastian Bach's Gebeine und Antlitz," *Abhandlungen der Königlich Sächsischen Gesellschaft der Wissenschaften* 37 (1895): 381–420, at 391.
[12] Ibid., 387.   [13] Ibid., 400.   [14] Ibid., 397.

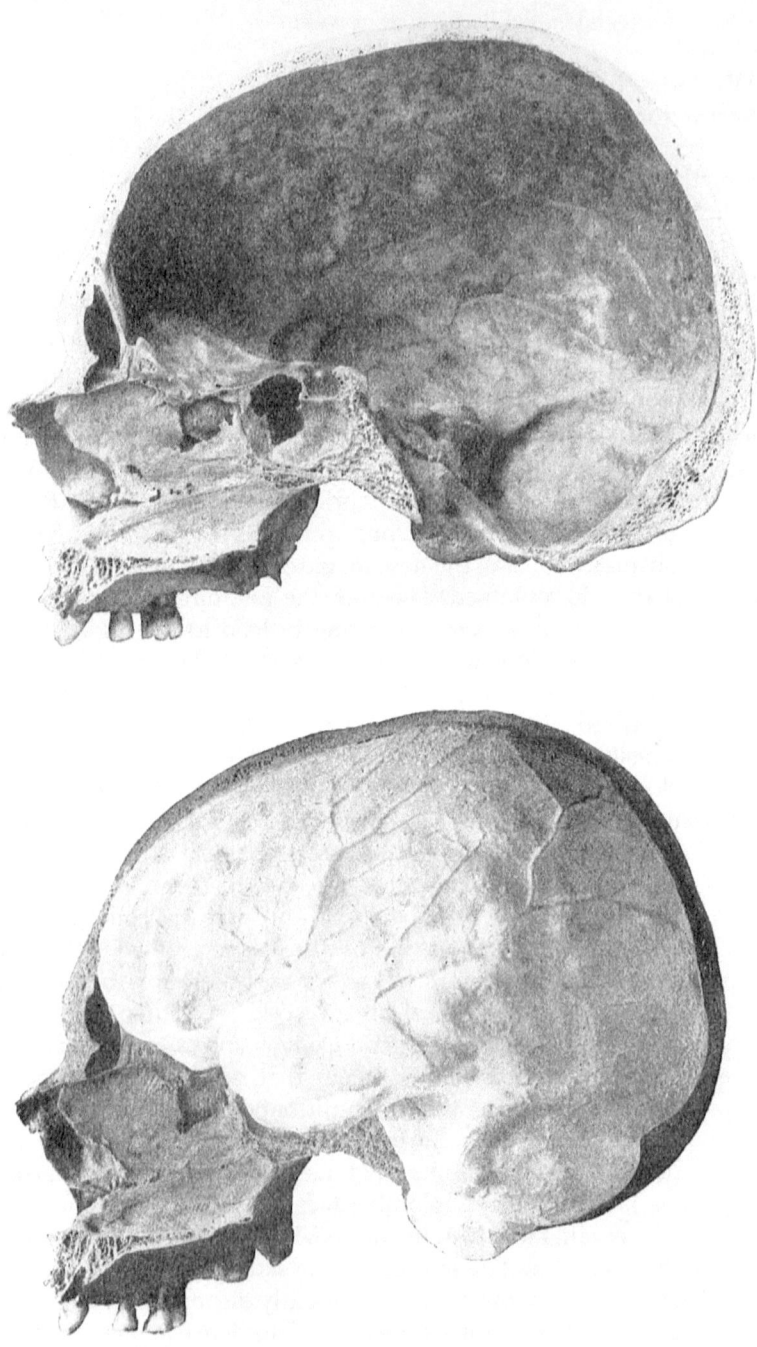

Figure 6.2   Bach's skull dissected; photographs from His, "Anatomische Forschungen über Johann Sebastian Bach's Gebeine und Antlitz" (1895)

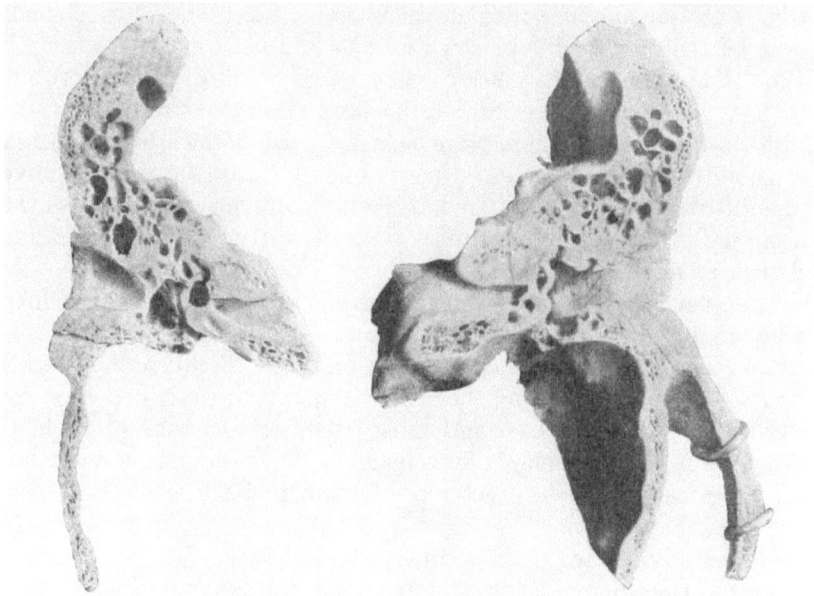

Figure 6.3   Bach's temporal bones, cross-sectioned; from His, "Anatomische Forschungen über Johann Sebastian Bach's Gebeine und Antlitz" (1895)

Just as important as the analysis of the formation of Bach's brain was the project to establish the literal expression of his genius as well as his character: to reconstruct Bach's face. For this the thickness of the flesh (Weichtheile) in all the regions of the face had to be established scientifically.[15] Over the winter of 1894–95 His began his own *Weichtheile* researches with a grim eagerness, probing the faces of thirty-seven corpses with a sewing needle and measuring the depth of the flesh, from the surface of the skin to the bone. All but four of the corpses were male: nine bodies "consumed by disease" came from the penitentiary, the remaining twenty-eight were "corpses of healthy suicides." The inmates were for the most part emaciated; the suicides by contrast were generally "well-nourished" or "robust" (kräftig). The averages of the measurements of the regions of the face were computed and then compared with the more cogent data from the faces of the eight elderly men who had died while still in fairly good condition. With the data thus meaningfully compiled into illuminating categories, His perceived clear

---

[15] Some scholarly work on this topic had been done: the immediate model for the analysis of the remains and the method for establishing a viable "Profilemethode" had been the attempts made a decade earlier to reconstruct the faces of Schiller and Raphael from their unearthed skulls. Ibid., 403.

trends establishing the median thickness of the tissue. A face could now be sculpted on the plaster cast that had been made of the Bach skull. And if the result accorded reasonably with the historical portraits then it would further verify that the skull was Bach's. Whereas these historical potraits had heretofore been the result of the artists' skill and sensibilities, His now believed that a bust of Bach based on objective scientific data could be created, a likeness which would surpass the accuracy of any of the historical portraits on which its verification depended in the first place.

The relevant *Weichtheile* averages were given to the sculptor Seffner, who would follow the measurements precisely in his three-dimensional reconstruction of Bach's head (Figure 6.4). The discoverers of Bach's bones were awe-struck by the result. Wustmann described the bust as "undoubtedly the best and most trustworthy image of Bach."[16] Wustmann, His, and many others believed that a previously undreamt of, historically elusive, exact reproduction of Bach's face had been achieved (Figure 6.5).

His's study leading to the reconstruction of Bach's face had cited the research of Germany's leading forensic expert on skulls and facial tissue, Hermann Welcker from nearby Halle. Himself a music-lover, Welcker was very interested in the nature and authenticity of the famous bones recently disinterred in Leipzig's Johanniskirche cemetery, and offered to review the work done by His and Seffner. Beginning in the 1860s Welcker been called on to verify numerous portraits of great historical figures – Raphael, Dante, Schiller, and Kant – by comparing these images against scientific measurements he had made on their exhumed skulls. Like His, of course, Welcker had done all his research into the thickness of facial tissue exclusively on corpses. But in November of 1895, little more than a year after Bach's casket was pulled from the muddy Johanniskirche churchyard, a scientific breakthrough was made that had potentially crucial implications for the field of forensic facial reconstruction: Wilhelm Roentgen discovered the X-ray. Within a few months, Welcker had eagerly strapped himself in front of an X-ray gun and was subjecting his head to thirty 30-second doses of the particles; in between each dose he waited, motionless, as the apparatus cooled down before the next blast. After this gruelling hour – one wonders whether the session might have hastened his death, which came the following year – the 74-year-old anatomist now had an image of his own skull and used it to verify his so-called geometrical profiling method, itself based on the claim that the thickness and contour of living tissue related to the skull in the same way that the tissue of recently dead corpses

---

[16] Gustav Wustmann, *Bilderbuch aus der Geschichte der Stadt Leipzig* (Leipzig, 1897), 64.

Physiognomies of Bach's counterpoint

Figure 6.4 Bach's skull with "scientifically accurate" face; from His, *Forschungen über dessen Grabstätte, Gebeine und Antlitz* (1895)

did. Turning his attention promptly to Bach's skull, Welcker endorsed the His/Seffner reconstruction save for a small caveat having to do with their interpretation of the thickness of the tissue at the bridge of the nose. The leading figure in the field of forensics had now pronounced

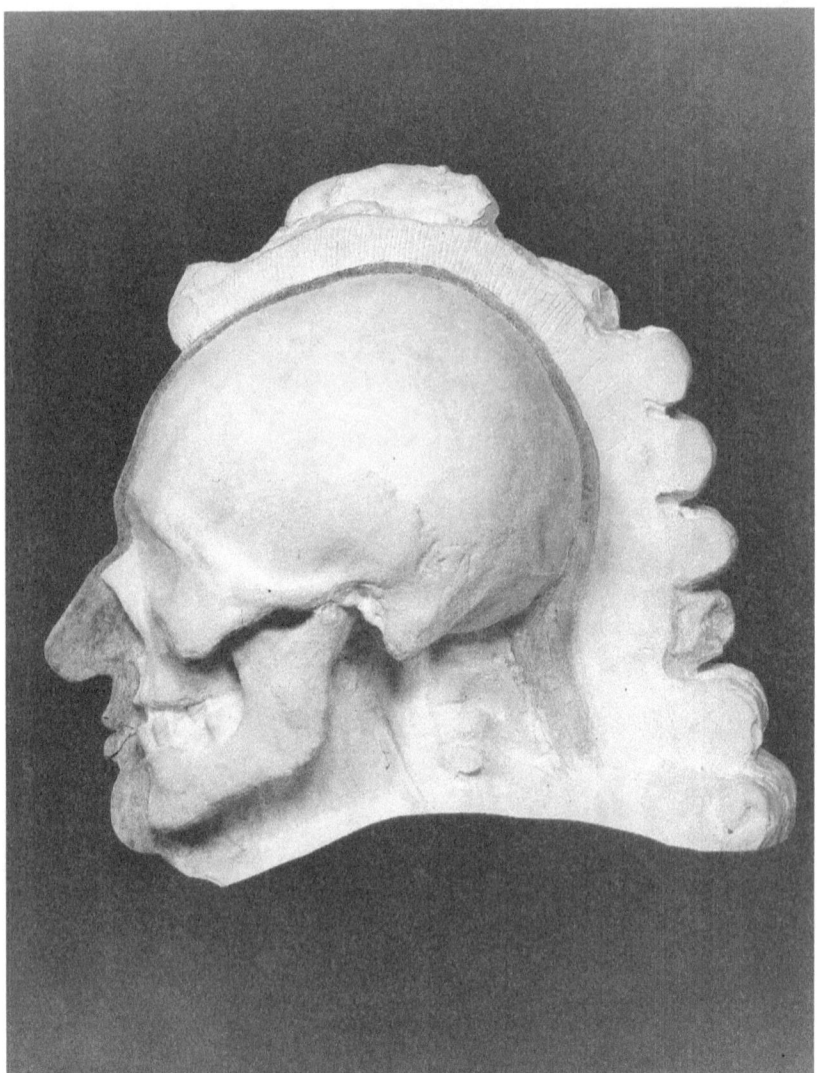

Figure 6.4 (cont.)

favorably on the authenticity of the Leipzig skull: it was certainly Bach's.[17]

---

[17] Joachim-Hermann Scharf, "Hermann Welckers Bedeutung für die Identifizierung der Gebeine Johann Sebastian Bachs," *Bach-Jahrbuch* 51 (1965): 5–9. See also Scharf, "Die historische Röntgenaufnahme zur Kontrolle der Rekonstruktion des Antlitzes Johann Sebastian Bachs," *Bach-Jahrbuch* 58 (1972): 91–94. For a summary of the history of Bach's exhumation, the subsequent peregrinations of his bones, and some of the studies

Figure 6.5   Karl Seffner, Bust of Bach (1895)

Even before this approbation His had claimed a status as the foremost expert on Bach's countenance, the man with the unparalleled knowledge of the specifics of his bone structure and the scientifically calibrated flesh thickness. Various collectors sent portraits of Bach to His for his inspection hoping that he would authenticate them. In His's

done on them, see Reinhard Ludewig, *Johann Sebastian Bach im Spiegel der Medizin: Persönlichkeit, Krankheiten, Operationen, Ärzte, Tod, Reliquien, Denkmäler und Ruhestätten des Thomaskantors* (Grimma, 2000), 51–67.

assessment of one portrait he received from a certain Herr Bormann phrenology, physiognomy, and aesthetics flow together in frothy confluence: "the bloated distended, insipid and smug face of Bormann's picture with its flat eyes is... not that of a man of Bach's immense power and depth"[18] – a less than flattering assessment of an heirloom that had apparently been in the Bormann family's possession for nearly a hundred years. A great man, a German genius, necessarily had a striking countenance, a bold and determined look about him. The rather negative assessment by His and Wustmann of the two Haußmann portraits, and their elevation of the Seffner bust, reveal something of the image they implicitly, unconciously sought: one senses that they believed Haußmann's portraits were not quite heroic enough, not quite German enough; the character it indicated was somewhat too furtive. Instead, it was the new bust by Seffner that gave true form to the hero Bach, an idealized, accurate, scientific representation of Germany's greatest composer.

With the bust completed and the data assembled and published, Bach's remains, cleaned and arranged in anatomically correct configuration (Figure 6.6), were laid in a newly made sarcophagus of hulking, heroic proportions, and placed in a tomb below the altar of the Johanniskirche. Instead of the decaying morass of bone, earth, and wood that had been the the skeleton's surroundings in the ground outside the Johanniskirche, Bach's remains were now installed in an austere and seemingly permanent mausoleum. The new tomb could be visited, the remains honored, their symbolic value reflected upon. Indeed, Bach's new sarcophagus was used as the final image for Robert Haas's 1928 book on the baroque, this newly interred Bach encapsulating an age, or, as Hass put it, "the entire baroque cultural imagination" (die ganze barocke Geisteskultur). Haas was then a professor at the University of Vienna and he would join the Nazi party in 1933, still five years before the Anschluss. For him the bones were a sign of past greatness and of a greatness still to come.

But the Johanniskirche was not to be Bach's final resting place; the remains would be moved yet again before the Last Day. The church was bombed in the Second World War, but the vault was not destroyed, Bach's remains lying safely in their thick stone box. In 1949, on the eve of the 200th anniversary of Bach's death, the skeleton was moved to the Thomaskirche in the center of Leipzig. There it could be duly worshipped. Following the 1950 commemorative address by Christian Marenholz, then chair of the Neue Bach-Gesellschaft, on the entombment of Bach's remains in his former place of employment, a group of state and religious dignitaries placed a wreath on the bronze plaque that marked Bach's new "final resting place." Reporting on the Leipzig Bach

---

[18] His, "Johann Sebastian Bach's Gebeine und Antlitz," 419.

Physiognomies of Bach's counterpoint

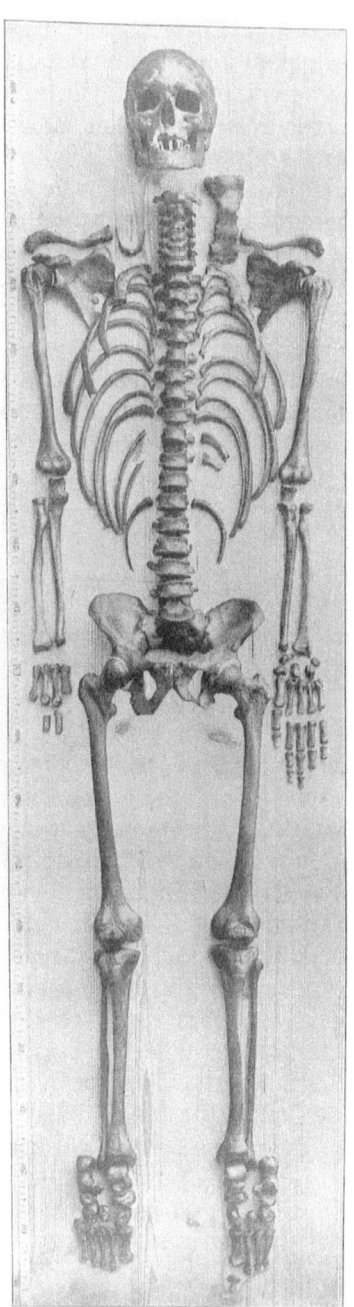

Figure 6.6   Bach's skeleton; from His, "Anatomische Forschungen über Johann Sebastian Bach's Gebeine und Antlitz" (1895)

Festival for the West German magazine *Musik und Kirche*, the musicologist Walter Blankenburg noted that in the celebrations of the 200th year of Bach's birth the Thomaskirche had become a place of pilgrimage from morning till night, with many lavish funeral wreaths placed on his sarcophagus. A performance of Bach's contrapuntal masterpiece, the *Art of Fugue*, was clearly obligatory in such a landmark Bach festival, one that, as Blankenburg noted, took place in a devastated Germany. Hearing the *Art of Fugue* in this house of pilgrimage, with Bach's wreath-laden tomb in view no doubt added to the intensity of the reaction following the cataclysmic breaking-off of the final Contrapunctus. Blankenburg heard in the "seconds of silent stillness which the thousands spontaneously raised up... undoubtedly something more than a sentimental state of excitement."[19] Then, emerging from the hushed reverence of mass emotion came the deathbed chorale *Vor deinen Thron*, Bach's intimate *ars moriendi* transformed into a cathartic spectacle for a divided nation.

Prussian fugues

At the time of the 1950 Leipzig Bach Festival the belief that it had indeed been Bach's remains before which so many officials and worshippers had placed their wreaths was still based on His's work – that is, largely on nineteenth-century phrenology and physiognomy. As with religious relics, verification of authenticity had little to do with the symbolic value of the remains, and as a symbol they were now indispensable. Inspired nonetheless by the events of the 1950 Bach festival, the former Nazi party member Heinrich Besseler undertook a new examination of the 1894 plaster cast of the skull in cooperation with the Berlin anatomist Hermann Stieve (as well as the opthalmologist Ernst Engelking) in the hope – shared by His – of evaluating the authenticity of the extant portraits. In a book based on these forensic studies, *Fünf echte Bildnisse Johann Sebastian Bachs* (Five Authentic Portraits of Johann Sebastian Bach), Besseler of course refers to His's work: but where His had claimed only that the bones in question were almost certainly Bach's, Besseler himself could emphatically pronounce after the conclusion of his research that "today there is no longer any doubt that this is the skull of Johann Sebastian Bach" (Figure 6.7).[20] Besseler's book is cleansed of overtly racist views, but in spite of its seemingly more convincing scientific apparatus, it indulges in a good deal of pseudo-science and

---

[19] Walter Blankenburg, "Deutsche Bach-Feier Leipzig 1950," *Musik und Kirche* 20 (1950): 165–169, at 167.

[20] Heinrich Besseler, *Fünf echte Bildnisse Johann Sebastian Bachs* (Kassel, 1956), 18; see also 59. The grand claims for the authenticity of Bach's bones continued to be doubted by Georg von Dadelsen in his review of Besseler's monograph in *Die Musikforschung* 10/2 (1957): 314–320, esp. 316.

Physiognomies of Bach's counterpoint

questionable physiognomy, citing such works as Fritz Lange's notorious *Die Sprache des menschlichen Antlitzes* (The Language of the Human Countenance; Munich, 1937) and other transparently racist tracts.[21] (Following the war Besseler had been exonerated in the denazification proceedings in the West, but his appointment was not renewed at Heidelberg University because of his marking of Jewish books; two years before the 1950 Leipzig Bach Festival he had removed himself to the Soviet zone.)[22] Besseler described the earliest portrait stemming from Bach's tenure in Weimar 1708–17 as nothing less than "a document from the period in which genius breaks through (*Durchbruchszeit des Genius*)." Besseler is in fact more confident even than His in his reading of this portrait: "the worldly openness in the countenance recalls youthful pictures of Goethe. The prominent forehead bespeaks originality and uncommon mental powers."[23] In spite of his reliance on a complex of disturbing assumptions about the relationship between physical appearance and character, Besseler painstakingly avoids any mention of Germanness, except for his statement that the capacity of the skull (1479.5 square centimeters) falls exactly on the "German" average. Still Bach evinces clear Germanic (read Aryan) characteristics: the portraits confirm that Bach's eyes are the required blue; the skeleton shows that his muscles are strong, especially in the arms.[24] Besseler's description of the Haußmann portrait in Leipzig barely refrains from reverting to the rhetoric of Germanic racial profiling, the foundations of which are still discernible behind the generally unobjectionable descriptive language: this portrait shows Bach "at the peak of his manly power, conscious of his achievement."[25] The bones confirmed his vigor; in the wake of the war it was not prudent to emphasize the Germanness of that vigor or the Germanness of the bones.

The idea that manliness in music derived from counterpoint – a discipline that Germans, and especially Bach, had safeguarded – was firmly embedded in Bach reception. This trope originates even before Forkel's biography of Bach, undertaken, as Forkel wrote in his preface, "to contribute to the honor of the German name," since "the works which Johann Sebastian has left us are an invaluable national patrimony, with which no other nation has anything to compare."[26] Even before such claims were made, Bach was being held up as a great defender of national music, the most vigorous upholder of traditional, indeed, timeless, musical values which were represented quintessentially by counterpoint.

---

[21] Fritz Lange, *Die Sprache des menschlichen Antlitzes* (Munich, 1937). In the book Bach makes a cameo as a proto-Nazi, the characteristics of his face indicating "the character of a powerful fighter and leader" (eine kraftvolle Kämpfer- und Führernatur). (195) See Besseler, *Fünf echte Bildnisse*, 22, 61.

[22] Pamela Potter, *The Most German of Arts: Musicology and Society from the Weimar Republic to the End of Hitler's Reich* (New Haven, 1998), 247.

[23] Ibid., 26. [24] Ibid., 60. [25] Ibid., 68. [26] NBR, 419.

Bach and the meanings of counterpoint

Figure 6.7 Bach portraits and skull; from Heinrich Besseler, *Fünf echte Bildnisse Johann Sebastian Bachs* (1956)

Physiognomies of Bach's counterpoint

Figure 6.7 (*cont.*)

If, as Marpurg often asserted, the period following Bach's death was marked by a precipitous decline in musical standards and culture, then the cause of this decline was that the typical composer had become a slave to taste and the fleeting pleasures of catchy melody-making. But, writes Marpurg, "speak to him of a canon, [and] he is seized by a cold shudder. He considers that century barbaric in which this part of composition was particularly cultivated."[27] Marpurg goes on: "mention the word fugue" to a rising opera composer and "he makes the sign of the cross," as if about to be set upon by a vampire.[28] Thus the shallow composer is not only unskilled and ignorant but most likely Catholic as well. Similarly, in the second volume of his *Abhandlung von der Fuge* Marpurg satirizes the slavishly modern musicians, who know nothing more than how

> to combine various modish trimmings with second-hand melodies, which every year give birth to different fashions, because they are based on the caprice of men, not on the eternal laws of nature. An advantage of counterpoint is that it is not based on the changeable style of the day and its wretched traits, which creates a dubious taste; at the present time there is neither a German, nor a French, nor an Italian counterpoint, while at the same time all nations agree that counterpoint is truth in music.[29]

Mastery of and dedication to counterpoint – a particularly German, indeed, a particularly Bachian predilection – had been inscribed as a universal. If counterpoint was timeless truth, it was the Germans who were largely responsible for attending to its continued cultivation. Above all, it had been Bach who had codified the universal laws of music (i.e., counterpoint), which, as he had admirably shown, were adaptable to wholesale stylistic developments and across various national traditions.

In Marpurg's preface to the second edition of the *Art of Fugue*, published the same year as the first volume of the *Abhandlung von der Fuge*, Bach the defender of German masculinity strides forth in muscular outline, a titan among the weak and effete who lack the resolve of the contrapuntal master: without knowledge of counterpoint "the manly element which should prevail in music remains quite absent from it." Indeed, "fugues and counterpoints" make up the essential, German defense "against the spreading rubbish of womanish song (*weibisches Gesang*)"; counterpoint is the fortified border against incursions of undesirable elements from the south, the defense against the dissipation of manly, German traditions. Even for the wide-ranging and cosmopolitan-minded Johann Mattheson, Bach's *Art of Fugue* was in the first instance

---

[27] Friedrich Wilhelm Marpurg, *Abhandlung von der Fuge*, 2 vols. (Berlin 1753–54; reprint, Hildesheim, 1970), II, ii.
[28] Ibid.   [29] Ibid., 30–31.

proof of the primacy of the German contrapuntal tradition over that of the French and Italians.[30]

Even if the debased melody-making of Italian opera had insinuated itself into every corner of the German homeland, the eternal truths of music were embodied in Bach's work where they would be safe, an untouchable ideal of musical purity, a national relic in themselves. Thanks largely to Bach's legacy-makers, beginning with Marpurg and continuing through to modern musicology, counterpoint has formed a pillar of the western musical canon. The fashioning of Bach as the last great contrapuntist was not just a myth about musical style, but one of national pride. Counterpoint was the most powerful hormone driving Bach's virility – the virility that makes Seffner's bust so heroic, the virility that pervades Marpurg, Forkel and much of the ensuing two-and-a-half centuries of Bach criticism.

Predictably, Philipp Spitta's seminal biography finds Bach's greatness nourished by his German roots and defined in no small part by his mastery of the national traditions of counterpoint; Bach's contrapuntal works – here Spitta is referring to the *Musical Offering* canons, "[penetrate] even to the deepest source of harmony," they are "a monument of strict writing which will endure for all time."[31] These foundational contrapuntal verities are among the crucial elements which, as Spitta puts it on the last page of his study – itself a monument not only to Bach but to the founding of the discipline of musicology – render it "[impossible] that Bach should be forgotten so long as the German people exist."[32]

Counterpoint as an anchor in the choppy seas of stylistic change had been posited as far back as Zarlino, and in the seventeenth century by his followers in north Germany. Thus Heinrich Schütz, in the preface to his collection of motets, *Geistliche Chormusik* (1648), recommended that "Before [the young composer] proceeds to the concerted style, [he] bite into this hard nut in which the true kernel and the true foundation of a good counterpoint is to be sought."[33] Hans Joachim Moser's 1936 biography of Schütz likens this pedagogical program to that of Bach, and claims that "we can observe [in this preface] a thoroughly German tendency towards a sense of responsibility for one's craftsmanship" that for Moser brings to mind Wagner's Hans Sachs and his respect for and cultivation of time-honored German traditions and rules.[34] Brahms's desire to prove himself at counterpoint, even after his early successes as a composer, similarly reflects the notion that canon, above all else, was

---

[30] BD III, 13.   [31] Spitta, *Johann Sebastian Bach*, III, 186.   [32] Ibid.
[33] Heinrich Schütz, *Neue Ausgabe Sämtlicher Werke*, V, ed. Wilhelm Kamlah (Kassel, 1955), vi.
[34] Hans Joachim Moser, *Heinrich Schütz: sein Leben und Werk* (Kassel, 1936; trans. Carl Pfattreicher, St. Louis, 1959), 494; trans., 581–582.

an immutable measure of composerly skill, a rite of passage: the real truth to be found in music was a German truth.[35] In Beethoven's 1808 plea for the overdue publication of the Bach complete edition, in a letter reprinted by Schumann in the *Neue Zeitschrift für Musik* in 1837, Bach is the "progenitor of harmony" (Urvater der Harmonie), which is to say of counterpoint.[36] A. B. Marx, writing in 1838, is more explicit: he proclaims the German *Volk* uniquely blessed to have Bach as a national musical hero; Bach's music is the alpha and omega of compositional pedagogy, and as the later Germanic symphonists Haydn and Beethoven would prove, Bach's art was decisive in the ultimate "victory of polyphony over homophony."[37]

The true ugliness of such essentialisms, begun with Marpurg and flourishing in the nineteenth century, was revealed at its starkest with the rise of national socialism. Given the populist ideology of the Nazis it is not surprising that musicologists active in Germany during the Third Reich often emphasized the more rustic side of Bach over his more intricate music. Hence the 1935 biography by Joseph Müller-Blattau has facing the title-page a facsimile not of one of the formidable – and relatively inaccessible – contrapuntal works such as the *Art of Fugue*, but instead of the opening of the Peasant Cantata. Nonetheless, that counterpoint was an organic part of the Germanic musical spirit was not in question. In Moser's 1935 study of Bach's life and works – a book which takes as its lengthy epigram Wagner's description of Bach's triumph over the foreign influences dominating German music – counterpoint lies at the center of the musical universe, so that the obsession of seventeenth-century German composers such as Schütz with Italian music led them to the "most distant point (the aphelion) from counterpoint."[38] The "historical necessity" (geschichtliche Notwendigkeit) of returning to the true reference point of music is left to Bach and Handel.

For many commentators of the 1930s the meeting of Bach and Frederick the Great signalled the ultimate realization of the potential of the German people. The year 1936 marked the 150th anniversary of Frederick the Great's death, and to commemorate the event the *Zeitschrift für Musik* published a series of articles on Frederick's musical

---

[35] David Brodbeck, "The Brahms–Joachim Counterpoint Exchange: or, Robert, Clara, and 'the Best Harmony between Jos. and Joh.'" in *Brahms Studies 1* (Lincoln, Nebr., 1994), 30–88, esp. 30–42. See also Reinhard Schäftertons, "Johannes Brahms und die Musik von Johann Sebastian Bach," in *Bach und die Nachwelt*, ed. Michael Heinemann and Hans-Joachim Hinrichsen, 3 vols. (Laaber, 1997–2000), II, 198–224, at pp. 213–17.

[36] Ludwig van Beethoven, Letter of January 15, 1801, reprinted in *Neue Zeitschrift für Musik* 6/2 (1837): 76. See also Hans-Joachim Hinrichsen, "Johann Nikolaus Forkel und die Anfänge der Bachforschung," in *Bach und die Nachwelt*, III, 192–253, at p. 239.

[37] Adolph Bernhard Marx, *Die Lehre von der musikalischen Komposition*, 2 vols. (Leipzig, 1837–38), II, 164. Quoted in Hinrichsen, "Johann Nikolaus Forkel und die Anfänge der Bachforschung," 241.

[38] Hans Joachim Moser, *Johann Sebastian Bach* (Berlin, 1935), 21–22.

life; not surprisingly, Bach and *A Musical Offering* figured prominently in many of the essays. In the series' first article, "Frederick the Great and Music," Richard Münnich honored the Prussian monarch for "instilling in German hearts the seeds of a new, richly forward-looking national feeling (*ein zukunftsreiches Nationgefühl*)," and for leading the proto-German state of Prussia to European prominence. Frederick's taste for the Italian style, like his cultivation of the French language in preference to German, was undeniably tragic (tragisch), but attributable to the distractions and overwhelming workload of kingship.[39] Yet in spite of these odd proclivities the meeting with Bach and the ensuing drama of counterpoint provided a defining moment in Frederick's own musical career. Surrounded by Bach's students and admirers in his own musical establishment, Frederick yearned for such a meeting: "it is no wonder that the king became more and more eager to meet this miracle-man."[40] In an article on "Frederick the Great and Johann Sebastian Bach," Fritz Müller claimed that Bach's entrance at the Potsdam palace was not that of a "clumsy and ignorant cantor" but that of "a world-wise artist" (weltgewandter Künstler) who had become hardened through long but successful battles against various authorities.[41] Indeed Bach was, according to Müller, covetous of a title from Frederick, that of Prussian Court Composer, an honorific that would supersede the one he already held from the Saxon royal house.

Rudolf Steglich, who among his other contributions to Nazi musicology would later attempt to develop a model for evaluating a musical work's acceptability to the Nazi state,[42] disagreed vehemently with Müller's claim, unauthenticated by any historical source, that Bach had been in pursuit of a fee or an honorary title from Frederick. This was not the way heroes dealt with one another. The dedication of *A Musical Offering* was proof enough of Bach's purity of motive since it was nothing less than "a monument of strong and upright, thoroughly manly, sincere national-German (*nationaldeutsch*) sentiment" and a reflection of his "pure and robust hero-worship."[43] Even more incontestable proof

---

[39] Richard Münnich, "Friedrich der Große und die Musik," *Zeitschrift für Musik* 103 (1936): 913–916.

[40] Ibid., 915.

[41] Fritz Müller, "Friedrich der Große und Johann Sebastian Bach," *Zeitschrift für Musik* 106 (1936): 931–933.

[42] Potter, *The Most German of Arts*, 53.

[43] Rudolf Steglich, "Nochmals: Friedrich der Große und Johann Sebastian Bach," *Zeitschrift für Musik* 106 (1936): 1368–1370, at 1369. Contemporary source studies confirmed Bach's worship of the proto-Führer, Frederick the Great. Georg Kinsky incorrectly claimed that the hand-written title-page of one of the surviving prints of *A Musical Offering* was in Bach's autograph and represented an early version of the dedication – "A Humble Offering of Thankfulness" (Ein schuldiges Opfer der Dankbarkeit). Here was even more blatant hero-worship. See Georg Kinsky, *Die Originalausgaben der Werke Johann Sebastian Bachs* (Vienna–Leipzig, 1937), 114.

of Bach's selflessly German and undeniably masculine bearing was the music itself, particularly the Prussian Fugues, a designation, says Steglich, that Bach himself invented. In response to claims for Bach's disinterested service to the proto-German state, Müller pointed out that Bach consistently sought honorary titles and never signed his name as a "simple cantor" (simpler Kantor).[44] Müller concludes his reply to Steglich with a statement that was presumably rather unpopular if not downright transgressive in an era of hero-worship and at a precise moment of national reverence – the 150th anniversary of Frederick's death: "For my part I treasure the great master [Bach] ever higher, the more I see that he was simply a man as we all are. And that holds also for Frederick the Great!"[45]

Even more extreme in linking Frederick and Bach, and in reading *A Musical Offering* as an expression of the Prussian militaristic ethos, was Alfred Burgartz's 1931 article on "The Prussian Style in Music," in which Burgartz claimed that "Bach's fugues and Frederick's battle plans are spiritually united."[46] Battles are won through "external deployment" (Entfaltung) of collective will without "individual freedom" being extinguished; so are fugues, in which the independent voices, like individual soldiers in battle fight for a single goal. Indeed, Bach's fugues are an "idealized confluence of popular feeling" (ideale volkhafte Zusammenfassung) in which contrapuntal forces "march to the most precise, even beat" like troops in massed formation. They carry out the orders of the theme "in the most sober Prussian uniform."[47] Needless to say, Burgartz argued that such complex and disciplined music stood in stark contrast to the eruptive, dramatic style of the south.

Before we conclude from all this that Burgartz crossed the boundaries of legitimate interpretation and violated respectable precedent, let us return to Forkel on fugue. In his *Allgemeine Geschichte* of 1788 Forkel characterized fugue as "the most splendid, most perfect, and greatest genre for the expression of individual sentiments," in which artful combination of discrete voices could represent "the general concurrence of an entire people, in the expression of a feeling"; fugue, therefore, may be thought of as "the most splendid, moving and great spectacle (*Schauspiel*)."[48] The collective power of fugue swamps that of even the most emotive melody: "What can a single person do against an

---

[44] Fritz Müller, "Unterstellung? Verunglimpfung? Geschichtswidrigkeit?" *Zeitschrift für Musik* 106 (1936): 1370–1372.
[45] Ibid.
[46] Alfred Burgartz, "Der Preussische Stil in der Musik," *Die Musik* 26/10 (1931), 721–723.
[47] Ibid., 722. See also Christa Brüstle, "Bach-Rezeption im Nationalsozialismus: Aspekte und Stationen," in *Bach und die Nachwelt*, III, 114–153, at pp. 142–143.
[48] J. N. Forkel, *Allgemeine Geschichte der Musik*, 2 vols. (Leipzig 1788–1801; reprint, Graz, 1967), I, 48.

entire people? As little as a single aria against a fugue. Aria constitutes only a part of fugue, just as a single person is just part of the people (*das Volk*). The *Volk* embodies many individuals, and fugue many arias. The aria is only a part of fugue, just as a single person is part of the *Volk*."[49] (One wonders if Burgartz knew this passage from Forkel's history.) For Forkel, of course, Bach was the greatest practitioner of fugue, and therefore also for Forkel (and for Burgartz) the most adept of composers at giving musical expression to the unified spirit of a people. It would, of course, be preposterous to accuse Forkel of fascist tendencies *avant la lettre*, but it is certainly worth noting, nonetheless, that the antecedents for the chilling Bach hermeneutics of the 1930s can clearly be discerned in his work. I am also aware that my interpretation of *A Musical Offering* – that Bach and Frederick the Great shared a sometimes ruthless approach to their respective arts – comes to conclusions that are not as dissimilar to those of Burgartz as I would like them to be; I am equally aware that to think along lines that converge on fascist and proto-fascist hermeneutics threatens to poison any hearing of Bach's counterpoint. My intent was rather to portray Bach as a canny participant in eighteenth-century structures of power and to argue that his music reflects this. The fact that Bach's contrapuntal works could spawn such militaristic imagery speaks to Bach's determination to bring diverse elements – the proudly independent course of individual voices that is the hallmark of his polyphony – into a powerful unity. But as I have also tried to show, simply because discipline is a first principle of Bach's counterpoint does not make the musical result agressive or covertly pernicious. Still, I cannot deny that my own attempt at a kind of historicist criticism of *A Musical Offering* is haunted by the dark readings of the 1930s.

More terrifying still is the 1941 wartime Bach biography by Karl Hasse, Director of the Hochschule für Musik in Cologne. Hasse's final chapter examines the historical effect (Auswirkung) of Bach's music; it moves from a survey of nineteenth-century Bach reception, much of it emphasizing Bach's Germanness, through to Reger, who is held to be the bridge between Brahms and Wagner, and one who lives Bach's counterpoint. Along the way Hasse alights on Johann Ludwig Tieck's favored image of Bach's works as medieval cathedrals[50] – a

---

[49] Ibid. The idea that counterpoint could represent the unified efforts of a population was also taken up by A. B. Marx, who argued that the "power of polyphony" (die Macht der Polyphonie) lay in the fact that individual voices not only contributed to the whole, but were energized by it, while remaining independent contributors to the interplay of ideas. Marx, *Auswahl aus Sebastian Bach's Kompositionen* (1853), quoted in Michael Heinemann, "Paradigma Fuge: Bach und das Erbe des Kontrapunkts," in *Bach und die Nachwelt*, I, 104–189, at p. 184.

[50] Johann Ludwig Tieck, quoted in Karl Hasse, *Johann Sebastian Bach: Leben, Werk und Wirkung* (Cologne, 1941), 177.

long-standing trope of Bach as gothic and primordially German. The trope continues into the twentieth century, not least in the Bach aesthetics of Heinrich Besseler, who lectured on the topic of Bach and the middle ages during the 1950 Bach festival.[51] For Marpurg it is counterpoint which summons among vacuous composers thoughts of barbaric, medieval times. For Hasse (via Tieck) the solidity, earnestness, and ornament of Bach's music is comparable to ancient abbeys with the riot of detail prevented from flying off into excessive emotional display by its contrapuntal organization. Hasse praises Philipp Kämpfer for rebutting the "barren formalism" (kahle Formalaesthetik) of the francophone biographies of Albert Schweitzer and André Pirro; hitting on a pun of particular resonance in Nazi Germany, Hasse calls the appropriately named Kämpfer's biography a "German book of struggle" (ein deutsches Kampfbuch) which promotes the idea that Bach's music is a "manifestation of the manly, upright German spirit."[52]

Hasse closes his own book in an unforgettably chilling way, with a letter from a young composer, Johannes Paul Thilman, then serving as a soldier at the front. The soldier's life has led Thilman to find strength in the unity of his regiment, like the individual voice in Burgartz's reading of Bach's fugues, a subject that answers to the commands of the leader/composer. In the "astonishing" push through Belgium and France Thilman has an epiphany which comes from not only witnessing, but being a part of, "the frictionless cooperation of all the diverse troops, the brilliant organization that is also to be perceived, if rarely, in music."[53] (After the war Thilman became a respected professor of composition at the Dresden Hochschule, but it is difficult not to recall his euphoric account of the spiritual force of the German army when reading his 1949 book on polyphony in which he returns yet again to the old trope that counterpoint's governing ideology is that it requires the submission of individual voices to a collective unconscious; indeed Thilman goes so far as to assert that a newly energized polyphony manifesting such ideals would metaphysically parallel the creation of a utopian – i.e., socialist – post-war society.[54]) This triumphant oneness of the German army not only serves, in Hasse's view, as a metaphor for the power of Bach's music but is in fact an embodiment of that same spirit, which, Thilman claims, ensures "the immortality of the German River of Life" (Unvergänglichkeit des deutschen Lebensstromes).[55] This is Bach's analogy between "well-regulated" music and a military force taken to its extreme (see p. 170): Burgartz's Prussian fugal columns have become Panzer divisions.

[51] Blankenburg, "Deutsche Bach-Feier Leipzig 1950," 166.
[52] Hasse, *Johann Sebastian Bach*, 181. [53] Ibid., 199–200.
[54] Johannes Paul Thilman, *Probleme der neuen Polyphonie* (Dresden, 1949).
[55] Hasse, *Johann Sebastian Bach*, 200.

A comparative history of musical revolutions

Reflexively described as abstract and therefore often marginalized, strict counterpoint has inspired some of the most socially resonant language in the history of Western European music criticism, a discourse which speaks, in fact, for its centrality and relevance. In all its contexts – alchemical, Enlightened, gustatory, avant-garde, reactionary – and whether it captivates or angers, it is a rich resource for metaphor. In the bourgeois musical revolution promoted by Mattheson, Heinichen, and some of their contemporaries, complex counterpoint was a symbol of reaction, and the discipline required of it, both from the composer and from the contrapuntal voices themselves, was to be resisted in order to allow greater freedom for musical expression. The denial of the rights of melody in favor of larger, group goals was to be fought against rather than submitted to. In the Third Reich, by contrast, counterpoint could represent a powerful tributary of the great German River of Life, a force as much biological as metaphysical, which subsumed the intentions of the composer and the contribution of individual contrapuntal voices into a larger goal paralleling the adherence of these elements to a national will. Counterpoint meant selfless obedience.

Yet even while strident nationalistic sentiment was gathering around Bach, and his contrapuntal formations were being drafted into military service, the anti-fascist critic Theodor Adorno was using counterpoint to attack precisely these fascist aesthetics. "Bach Defended Against his Devotees" is, in effect, a polemic against the kind of interpretations to be realized so fully later in Hasse's biography; as Adorno put it, "Reaction, deprived of its political heroes, takes complete possession of the composer whom it long had claimed as one of its own." The nostalgic, Germanic Bach is the fabrication of "all those who, having lost either the ability to believe or the desire for self-determination go in search of authority, obsessed by the notion of how nice it would be to be secure." (This sounds like nothing so much as Mattheson at his polemical best, attacking counterpoint and contrapuntists.) Like the soldier Thilman, such devotees of Bach want to share in the inextinguishable German life-force; as Adorno sardonically noted, "They have made [Bach] into a composer for organ festivals in well-preserved Baroque towns." But for those who abhor the reduction of Bach to ideology, the internal, autonomous relationships in Bach's music – especially its contrapuntal rigor – resist the nascent commodification of music and burst through the "narrow theological horizon" of his time and the workaday conditions of his professional life.[56]

Likewise, in the music of the Second Viennese School counterpoint could act as a progressive force: Adorno claims invertible counterpoint

[56] Adorno, "Bach Defended Against his Devotees," 135–146, at p. 135.

as one of the agents that – note the political metaphors – aid atonality, in subverting the "hegemony" of harmonic control by "[negating] the traditional status of the bass line."[57] Individual voices could now become truly free of harmonic restrictions. Rather than subjugation, counterpoint becomes an important means of developing variation, as Schoenberg himself wrote in a commentary on his Serenade, Op. 24; for the "technical tools of the [twelve-tone] method" include "inversions and retrograde inversions, diminutions and augmentations, canons of various kinds, and rhythmic shifts to different beats," all of which contribute to true musical liberation – that is, to "the emancipation of the dissonance."[58] The Nazi musicologist Hans Joachim Moser had stressed in his 1935 book on Bach that Bach's counterpoint was not "absolutely linear counterpoint" but "harmonic," implying a kind of dedication to a healthy organic unity.[59] The only true example of linear counterpoint, says Moser, had been what he derisively calls the "inflation atonality" (Inflationsatonalität) of 1923, the year in which the deutschmark sank to four million to the dollar, and Schoenberg completed the Serenade, op. 24, among other works. What was for Moser a use of counterpoint that portended dissolution and despair created for Schoenberg a music of emancipation, marking out a path towards freedom, subjectivity, artistic autonomy. Webern's orchestration of the six-part Ricercar from *A Musical Offering* is a further reflection of this impulse; "the emancipation of the motive" which, in bringing out the kaleidoscopic color and heteronomous psychology of the contrapuntal voices, deflates the collectivist drama Forkel saw in fugue, or the military metaphors developed by Burgartz.[60] One could even say that Webern's version of the Ricercar argues for a kind of democratic alternative to a Bach-as-battle-plan aesthetics.

It is hardly surprising that over a period of two hundred years the same techniques could be interpreted in contradictory ways: they could be read as signs of political reaction or democratic progress, as mystical reflections of the "unfathomability of music," or as a catalog of music at its most rational and scientific. It seems as if in interpreting contrapuntal music in Bach's time and into the twentieth century, listeners and critics could not but see and hear individual voices working in concert, or, from another point of view, voices forced to labor together against their wills: the same procedures, indeed the same pieces of music, could be interpreted by different writers as signs of both dependence and

[57] Theodor Adorno, *Quasi una Fantasia*, trans. Rodney Livingstone (London, 1992), 214.
[58] Arnold Schoenberg, *Style and Idea*, ed. Leonard Stein (London, 1975), 91.
[59] Moser, *Johann Sebastian Bach*, 28.
[60] Carl Dahlhaus, "Analytische Instrumentation: Bachs sechsstimmiges Ricercar in der Orchestrierung Anton Weberns," in *Bach-Interpretationen*, ed. Martin Geck (Göttingen, 1967), 197–206, at p. 206.

independence. Claiming themselves to be more enlightened and rational than the occult-minded contrapuntists of the seventeenth and early eighteenth centuries, progressive writers and composers were no less likely to react to the allegorical power of complex music. The same was true of German nationalist Bach criticism and its opponents. In all these cases counterpoint could not be understood without recourse to metaphor. As malleable and multi-faceted as the contrapuntal techniques they sought to describe, these metaphors draw attention to the fact that musical revolutions are as much about words as they are about music. Indeed, counterpoint repeatedly breaks through the confines of autonomous isolation and reveals itself to be as much social practice as compositional technique. The rules might be mastered, but the need to impose a broader meaning remains, and this cannot be achieved without vibrant words and vivid mental imagery – without a broad sense of context. Paradoxically, the articulation of this most well-defined and restrictive set of compositional principles – claimed by so many to represent an objective musical reality, the purest of abstractions – constitutes both research into the infinities of combinatorial possibility and exploration into the limitless richness of musical meaning. Like Bach's bones, any contrapuntal framework is nothing but a set of physical data until it is likened to non-musical things, until it becomes one kind of allegory or another. It becomes meaningful only when stories are told about it.

In light of the often controversial position of counterpoint within musical thought during Bach's own lifetime, it was of course to be expected that its significance and meaning would undergo continual change after his death. One crucial transformation, still being wrought in our own time, relates to the perpetual contest between relativism and idealism that lies at the heart of "Die canonische Anatomie," as well as so many other aesthetic disputes of the early Enlightenment: Is counterpoint an absolute whose precepts remain unaltered by the ceaseless change in musical style? Or, as Mattheson argued, are these rules merely human constructs, and as such of no particular epistemological value? The former position is that of the elitist upholder of traditions – the forlorn Bokemeyer and, perhaps, Bach himself. I recognize that my own book has been full of relativizing gestures which to a certain degree attempt to bring Bach and his counterpoint down from the lofty summit on which they have been so safely ensconced with the help of generations of Bach's admirers. This project was motivated by a belief that Bach's most complex music might be better understood by trying to grapple with it as one of his contemporaries might have done, that is, as someone for whom Bach's contrapuntal insights retained a very real currency and vivid significance. Indeed, what I hope to retrieve in my own study of Bach is some part of the immediacy and wonder counterpoint held for his colleagues and admirers. Even while historicizing and relativizing

Bach's achievement, I also recognize his unmatched mastery of the intricacies of counterpoint, from the minutiae of dedication canons to the sprawling, virtuosic essays of the *Art of Fugue*. As long as there are those who appreciate counterpoint, Bach's will be the gold standard. This statement is hardly controversial now, and it does not stray much from the position held by the writers of Bach's obituary as well as legions of subsequent commentators on his music. But in spite of its status as an ideal, it is important to remember that Bach's counterpoint, above that of any other composer, has been put to the most diverse ideological uses, both ennobling and pernicious. It is incumbent upon us to recognize the lasting value inherent in the contrapuntal endeavor; to be liberated by and respectful of its restrictions; to accept the fact that its meanings can be slippery, but also rewarding; and to cherish its potential for profound beauty.

SELECT BIBLIOGRAPHY

Adlung, Jacob. *Anleitung zu der musikalischen Gelahrtheit*. Erfurt, 1758; reprint, Kassel, 1953.
Adorno, Theodor W. "Bach Defended Against His Devotees." In *Prisms*. Trans. Samuel Weber and Shierry Weber. Cambridge, Mass., 1981, pp. 133–146.
Quasi una fantasia. Trans. Rodney Livingstone. London, 1992.
Althaus, Paul. *The Theology of Martin Luther*. Trans. Robert C. Schulz. Philadelphia, 1966.
Ariès, Philippe. *The Hour of our Death*. Trans. Helen Weaver. New York, 1981.
Asprey, Robert. *Frederick the Great: The Magnificent Enigma*. New York, 1986.
Bach, C. P. E. *Sei sonate per cembalo*. Berlin, 1742; reprint, New York, 1986.
  Versuch über die wahre Art das Clavier zu spielen. 2 vols. Berlin, 1753, 1762; reprint, Wiesbaden, 1954. Trans. William J. Mitchell as *Essay on the True Art of Playing Keyboard Instruments*. London, 1974.
Bach, Johann Sebastian. *Neue Ausgabe sämtlicher Werke*. Leipzig and Kassel, 1954–.
Becher, Johann Joachim. *Chymischer Glückshafen*. Frankfurt, 1682; reprint, Hildesheim, 1974.
Beer, Johann. *Musicalische Diskurse*. Nuremberg, 1719.
Beißwenger, Kirsten. *Johann Sebastian Bachs Notenbibliothek*. Kassel, 1992.
Benary, Peter. *Die deutsche Kompositionslehre des 18. Jahrhunderts*. Leipzig, 1960.
Berardi, Angelo. *Documenti armonici*. Bologna, 1687; reprint, Bologna, 1970.
Berend, Fritz. *Nicolaus Adam Strungk (1640–1700): Sein Leben und seine Werke*. Hanover, [1915].
Bernhard, Christoph. *Tractatus compositionis augmentatus*. In *Die Kompositionslehre Heinrich Schützens in der Fassung seines Schülers Christoph Bernhard*, 2nd edn. Ed. Joseph Müller-Blattau. Kassel, 1963, pp. 40–121.
  Tractatus compositionis augmentatus. Trans. Walter Hilse as "The Treatises of Christoph Bernhard." *Music Forum* 3 (1973): 31–196.
Besseler, Heinrich. *Fünf echte Bildnisse Johann Sebastian Bachs*. Kassel, 1956.
Birnbaum, Johann Abraham. "Unpartheyische Anmerkungen." In *BD* II, 296–306.
  "Verteidigung Bachs gegen Scheibes Angriffe." In *BD* II, 440–60. Also reprinted in *Critischer Musikus*, rev. edn. Ed. Johann Adolph Scheibe. Leipzig, 1745; reprint, Hildesheim, 1970, pp. 900–1031.
Blankenburg, Walter. "Deutsche Bach-Feier Leipzig 1950." *Musik und Kirche* 20 (1950): 165–169.
Boeldicke, Johann. *Gründliche Anweisung zur hermetischen Wissenschaft und Bereitung der philosophischen Tinctur*. Leipzig, 1723.

Select bibliography

Bokemeyer, Heinrich. *Elaboratio dissonantiarum nach den Fundamental Reguln des sel. Herrn Theile.* Manuscript. Staatsbibliothek zu Berlin, Mus. ms. theor. 130.

Bolin, Norbert. *"Sterben ist mein Gewinn": Ein Beitrag zur evangelischen Funeral-Komposition des Barock.* Kassel, 1989.

Bononcini, Giovanni Maria. *Musico prattico.* Bologna, 1673; reprint, New York, 1969.

Braun, Werner. "Bachs Stellung im Kanonstreit." In *Bach-Interpretationen.* Ed. Martin Geck. Göttingen, 1969, pp. 106–111.

Brodbeck, David. "The Brahms–Joachim Counterpoint Exchange: or, Robert, Clara, and 'the Best Harmony between Jos. and Joh.'" In *Brahms Studies 1.* Ed. David Brodbeck. Lincoln, Nebr., 1994, pp. 30–88.

Bruford, Walter. *Germany in the Eighteenth Century: The Social Background of the Literary Revival.* Cambridge, 1971.

Brüstle, Christa. "Bach-Rezeption im Nationalsozialismus: Aspekte und Stationen." In *Bach und die Nachwelt.* 3 vols. Ed. Michael Heinemann and Hans-Joachim Hinrichsen. Laaber, 1997–2000, vol. III, pp. 114–153.

Buelow, George J. "Mattheson and the Affektenlehre." In *New Mattheson Studies.* Ed. George J. Buelow and Hans Joachim Marx. Cambridge, 1983, pp. 394–395.

Thorough-Bass Accompaniment According to Johann David Heinichen, revised edn. Ann Arbor, 1986.

Bukofzer, Manfred. "Allegory in Baroque Music." *Journal of the Warburg Institute* 3 (1939–40): 1–21.

Music in the Baroque Era. New York, 1947.

Bünting, Heinrich. *Itinerarium sacrae scipturae... mit einem Büchlein de monetis mensuris.* 3rd edn. Magdeburg, 1589.

Buntz, Herwig. "Alchemie und Aufklärung: Die Diskussion in der Zeitschrift Parnassus Boicus (1722–1740)." In *Die Alchemie in der europäischen Kultur- und Wissenschaftgeschichte,* Ed. Christoph Meinel. Wiesbaden, 1980, pp. 327–338.

Burgartz, Alfred. "Der Preussische Stil in der Musik." In *Die Musik* 1931: 721–723.

Burland, C. A. *The Arts of the Alchemists.* New York, 1968.

Burney, Charles. *The Present State of Music in Germany, the Netherlands, and United Provinces.* Vol. II. London, 1773; reprint of 2nd edn. (1775), New York, 1969.

Butler, Gregory. *Bach's Clavier-Übung III: The Making of a Print, with a Companion Study of the Canonic Variations on "Vom Himmel Hoch," BWV 769.* Durham, 1990.

"Ordering Problems in J. S. Bach's *Art of Fugue* Resolved." *Musical Quarterly* 69 (1989): 44–61.

Butt, John. "'A Mind Unconscious that it is Calculating'? Bach and the Rationalist Philosophy of Wolff, Leibniz and Spinoza." In *The Cambridge Companion to Bach.* Ed. John Butt. Cambridge, 1997, pp. 60–71.

Bach Interpretation: Articulation Marks in Primary Sources of J. S. Bach. Cambridge, 1990.

Music Education and the Art of Performance in the German Baroque. Cambridge, 1994.

Select bibliography

"J. S. Bach and G. F. Kauffmann: Reflections on Bach's Later Style." In *Bach Studies 2*. Ed. Daniel R. Melamed. Cambridge, 1995, pp. 47–61.
Buttstett, Johann Heinrich. *Ut, mi, sol, re, fa, la, tota musica et harmonia aeterna*. Erfurt, [1717].
Buxtehude, Dieterich. *Werke*. Vol. II. Klecken, 1926.
Cahn, Peter. "Christoph Graupners 'Kanons' als Versuch einer systematischen Imitationslehre." *Musiktheorie* 1/2 (1986), 130–136.
Cannon, Beekman C. *Johann Mattheson, Spectator in Music*. New Haven, 1947.
Carlyle, Thomas. *Frederick the Great*. 10 vols. London, 1875.
Chafe, Eric. *Tonal Allegory in the Vocal Music of J. S. Bach*. Berkeley, 1991.
Collins, Denis Brian. "Canon in Music Theory from c. 1550 to c. 1800." Ph.D. diss., Stanford University, 1992.
Dahlhaus, Carl. "Analytische Instrumentation: Bachs sechsstimmiges Ricercar in der Orchestrierung Anton Weberns." In *Bach-Interpretationen*. Ed. Martin Geck. Göttingen, 1967, pp. 197–206.
"Einleitung" and "Kritischer Bericht." In *Johann Theiles Musicalisches Kunstbuch*. Denkmäler norddeutscher Musik. Vol. I. Kassel, 1965, pp. vii–ix, 132–139.
"Zur Geschichte der Permutationsfuge." *Bach-Jahrbuch* 46 (1959): 95–110.
Dammann, Rolf. *Der Musikbegriff im deutschen Barock*. Cologne, 1967.
"Zur Musiklehre des Andreas Werckmeister." *Archiv für Musikwissenschaft* 11 (1954): 206–237.
David, Hans T. *J. S. Bach's Musical Offering: History, Interpretation and Analysis*. New York, 1945.
Dekker, Wil. "Ein Karfreitagsrätselkanon aus Adam Gumpelzhaimers *Compendium musicae* (1532)." *Die Musikforschung* 27/3 (1974): 323–322.
Dobbs, Betty Jo Teeter. *The Janus Faces of Genius: the Role of Alchemy in Newton's Thought*. Cambridge, 1991.
Dobbs, Betty Jo Teeter and Margaret C. Jacob. *Newton and the Culture of Newtonianism*. Atlantic Highlands, NJ, 1995.
Doyon, André and Lucien Liaigre. *Jacques Vaucanson: mécanicien de génie*. Paris, 1966.
Dreyfus, Laurence. *Bach and the Patterns of Invention*. Cambridge, Mass., 1996.
Eggebrecht, Hans. *Bachs Kunst der Fuge*. Munich, 1985; trans. Jeffrey L. Prater as *J. S. Bach's The Art of Fugue*. Ames, Iowa, 1993.
Falck, Myron. "Seventeenth-century Contrapuntal Theory in Germany." Ph.D. diss. University of Rochester, 1965.
Fasch, Johann Friedrich. *Canon. Sonata à 3* (F major). Ed. Hermann A. Moeck and Eitel-Friedrich Callenberg. Celle, 1957.
Trio-Sonate (D major). Ed. Albert Kranz. Munich–Leipzig, 1935.
Federhofer, Hellmut. "Johann Christoph Mizlers Kommentare zu den beiden Büchern des 'Gradus ad Parnassum.'" In *Johann Joseph Fux und Seine Zeit: Kultur, Kunst und Musik im Spätbarock*. Ed. Arnfried Edler and Friedrich W. Riedel. Laaber, 1996, pp. 121–136.
Fiebig, Folker. *Christoph Bernhard und der stile moderno. Untersuchung zu Leben und Werk*. Hamburg, 1980.

Fink, G. W. "Johann Philipp Förtsch." *Allgemeine Encyklopädie der Wissenschaften und Künste* I, pp. 46, 443–458.
Forkel, Johann Nikolaus. *Allgemeine Geschichte der Musik.* 2 vols. Leipzig, 1788–1801; reprint, Graz, 1967.
   Ueber Johann Sebastian Bachs Leben, Kunst und Kunstwerke. Leipzig, 1802; reprint, Kassel, 1982.
Förtsch, Johann Philipp. *Musicalischer Compositions Tractat.* Manuscript. Staatsbibliothek zu Berlin, Mus. ms. theor. 300.
   Von dem dreyfachen Contrapunct. Manuscript. Staatsbibliothek zu Berlin, Mus. ms. theor. 910.
Foucault, Michel. *The Order of Things.* New York, 1971.
Frederick the Great. *Anti-Machiavel.* Trans. Paul Sonnino. Athens, Ohio, 1981.
   Musikalische Werke. Vol. I. Ed. Philipp Spitta. Leipzig, 1889.
Frisch, Johann Leonhard. *Teutsch-Lateinisches Wörterbuch.* Berlin, 1741.
Fuhrmann, Martin Heinrich. *Die an der Kirchen Gottes gebauete Satans-Capelle.* Berlin, 1729.
   Musicalischer-Trichter. Frankfurt an der Spree, 1706.
Fux, Johann Joseph. *Gradus ad Parnassum.* Trans. Lorenz Mizler. Leipzig, 1742; reprint, Hildesheim, 1984.
Geier, Martin. *Kurze Beschreibung des. (Tit.) Herrn Heinrich Schützens, chur-fürstl. sächs-ältern Capellmeisters, geführten mühseeligen Lebens-Lauff.* Dresden, 1672; reprint, Kassel, 1972.
Geyer-Kordesch, Johanna. "Georg Ernst Stahl's Radical Pietist Medicine and its Influence on the German Enlightenment." In *The Medical Enlightenment of the Eighteenth Century.* Ed. Andrew Cunningham and Roger French. Cambridge, 1990, pp. 67–87.
Graun, Karl Heinrich. *Duetti, Terzetti, Quintetti, Sestetti, ed alcuni Chori.* 4 vols. Ed. Johann Philipp Kirnberger. Berlin, 1773–74.
Gumpelzhaimer, Adam. *Compendium musicae.* Augsburg, 1632.
Gurlitt, Willibald. "Die Kompositionslehre des deutschen 16. und 17. Jahrhunderts." In *Musikgeschichte und Gegenwart. Beihefte zum Archiv für Musikwissenschaft.* Vol. I. Ed. Hans Heinrich Eggebrecht. Wiesbaden, 1966, part 1, pp. 82–93.
Haas, Robert. *Die Musik des Barocks.* Potsdam, 1928.
Hamburgisches Magazin, oder Gesammelte Schriften aus der Naturforschung und den angenehmen Wissenschaften überhaupt. Hamburg and Leipzig, 1747–53.
Hasse, Karl. *Johann Sebastian Bach: Leben, Werk und Wirkung.* Cologne, 1941.
Hegel, G. W. F. *Aesthetics: Lectures on Fine Art.* 2 vols. Trans. T. M. Knox. Oxford, 1975.
Heinemann, Michael. "Paradigma Fuge: Bach und das Erbe des Kontrapunkts." In *Bach und die Nachwelt.* 3 vols. Ed. Michael Heinemann and Hans-Joachim Hinrichsen. Laaber, 1997–2000, vol. III, pp. 104–189.
Heinichen, Johann David. *Neu erfundene und gründliche Anweisung...zu vollkommener Erlernung des General-Basses.* Hamburg, 1711.
   Der General-Bass in der Composition. Dresden, 1728; reprint, Hildesheim, 1969.
Helm, Eugene. *Music at the Court of Frederick the Great.* Norman, 1960.
Hill, Robert. "'Der Himmel weiss, wo diese Sachen hingekommen sind': Reconstructing the Lost Keyboard Notebooks of the Young Bach and

Handel." In *Bach, Handel, Scarlatti: Tercentenary Essays*. Ed. Peter Williams. Cambridge, 1985, pp. 161–172.

Hinrichsen, Hans-Joachim. "Johann Nikolaus Forkel und die Anfänge der Bachforschung." In *Bach und die Nachwelt*. Ed. Michael Heinemann and Hans-Joachim Hinrichsen. 3 vols. Laaber, 1997–2000, vol. III, pp. 192–253.

His, Wilhelm. *Johann Sebastian Bach: Forschungen über dessen Grabstätte, Gebeine und Antlitz*. Leipzig, 1895.

"Johann Sebastian Bach's Gebeine und Antlitz." *Abhandlungen der Königlich Sächsischen Gesellschaft der Wissenschafte* 37 (1895): 381–420.

Hofstadter, Douglas. *Gödel, Escher, Bach: An Eternal Golden Braid*. New York, 1979.

Horn, Wolfgang. *Die Dresdner Hofkirchenmusik, 1720 bis 1745: Studien zu ihren Voraussetzungen und ihrem Repertoire*. Kassel, 1987.

Johnston, Gregory. "Rhetorical Personification of the Dead in 17th-Century German Funeral Music: Heinrich Schütz's *Musikalische Exequien* (1636) and Three Works by Michael Wiedemann (1693)." *Journal of Musicology* 9/2 (1991): 186–213.

Jung, Carl. *Psychology and Alchemy*. Trans. R. F. C. Hull. London, 1953.

Kauffmann, Georg Friedrich. *Harmonische Seelenlust* (1733–36). 2 vols. Ed. Pierre Pidoux. Kassel, 1951.

Kennan, Kent. *Counterpoint Based on Eighteenth-Century Practice*. 4th edn. Upper Saddle River, NJ, 1999.

Kenner, Hugh. *The Counterfeiters: An Historical Comedy*. Baltimore, 1985.

Kinsky, Georg. *Die Originalausgaben der Werke Johann Sebastian Bachs*. Vienna–Leipzig, 1937.

Kircher, Athanasius. *Musurgia universalis*. Rome: Francesco Corbelletti, 1650; reprint, Hildesheim, 1970.

Germaniae redonatus: sive artis magnae de consono et dissono ars minor. Trans. Andrea Hirsch. Schwäbisch Hall, 1662.

Kirnberger, Johann Philipp. *Der allzeit fertige Menuetten- und Polonoisenkomponist*. Berlin, 1757.

Die Kunst des reinen Satzes in der Musik. Berlin, 1776–79; reprint, Hildesheim, 1968.

Koslofsky, Craig. *The Reformation of the Dead: Death and Ritual in Early Modern Germany, 1450–1700*. New York, 2000.

Kuhnau, Johann. *Der Musicalische Quacksalber*. Dresden, 1700; reprint, Bern, 1992; trans. by James Hardin as *The Musical Charlatan*. Columbia, SC, 1997.

Kümmerling, Harald. *Katalog der Sammlung Bokemeyer*. Kassel, 1970.

La Mettrie, Julien Offray de. *Machine Man and Other Writing*. Trans. Ann Thomson. Cambridge, 1996.

Lange, Friedrich Albert. *History of Materialism*. 2nd edn. 3 vols. Trans. Ernest C. Thomas. London, 1879; reprint, New York, 1974.

Lange, Fritz. *Die Sprache des menschlichen Antlitzes*. Munich, 1937.

Leaver, Robin. *Bach's Theological Library*. Neuhausen-Stuttgart, 1983.

"The Funeral Sermon for Heinrich Schütz." *BACH* 4/4 (1973): 3–17; 5/2 (1974): 22–35; 5/3 (1974): 13–20.

J. S. Bach and Scripture. St. Louis, 1985.

Leisinger, Ulrich. "Die 'Bachsche Auction' von 1789." *Bach-Jahrbuch* 77 (1991): 97–126.

Select bibliography

Lessing, Gotthold Ephraim. *Wie die Alten den Tod gebildet: eine Untersuchung.* Ed. Ludwig Uhlig. Stuttgart, 1984.
[Liebezeit, Christian]. "Vorrede." In *Aureum vellus oder Guldin Schatz und Kunstkammer.* Vol. V. Hamburg, 1709.
Ludwig, M. Christian. *Englisch – Teutsch – Französisch Lexicon.* Leipzig, 1706.
Luther, Martin. "Preface to the Burial Hymns (1542)." Trans. Paul Z. Strodach. In *Luther's Works.* Vol. LIII. Ed. Helmut T. Lehmann. Philadelphia, 1965, pp. 32–331.
"A Sermon on Preparing to Die." Translated by Martin H. Bertram; edited by Martin O. Dietrich. In *Luther's Works.* Vol. XLII. Philadelphia 1969, pp. 97–115.
"Two Funeral Sermons, 1532." Trans. John W. Doberstein. In *Luther's Works.* Vol. LI. Philadelphia, 1959, pp. 229–255.
Magner, Lois N. *A History of Medicine.* New York, 1992.
Maier, Michael. *Atalanta fugiens.* Oppenheim, 1618. Trans. Joscelyn Godwin in *Magnum Opus Hermetic Sourceworks* 22. Grand Rapids, 1989.
Chymisches Cabinet. Frankfurt, 1708.
Marissen, Michael. *The Social and Religious Designs of J. S. Bach's Brandenburg Concertos.* Princeton, 1995.
"The Theological Character of J. S. Bach's *Musical Offering.*" In *Bach Studies 2.* Ed. Daniel R. Melamed. Cambridge, 1995, pp. 85–106.
Marpurg, Friedrich Wilhelm. *Abhandlung von der Fuge.* 2 vols. Berlin, 1753–54; reprint, Hildesheim, 1970.
Historisch-kritische Beyträge zur Aufnahme der Musik. 5 vols. Berlin, 1754–62; reprint, Hildesheim, 1970.
Marshall, Robert. *The Music of Johann Sebastian Bach.* New York, 1989.
Marx, Adolph Bernhard. *Auswahl aus Sebastian Bach's Kompositionen.* Vol. II. Berlin, 1853.
Die Lehre von der musikalischen Komposition. Vol. II. Leipzig, 1838.
Marx, Hans Joachim. *Johann Mattheson (1681–1764): Lebensbeschreibung des Hamburger Musikers, Schriftstellers, und Diplomaten.* Hamburg, 1982.
Mattheson, Johann. *Behauptung der himmlischen Musik.* Hamburg, 1747.
Das beschützte Orchestre. Hamburg, 1717; reprint, Leipzig, 1981.
Bewahrte Panacea. Hamburg, 1750.
Critica musica. 2 vols. Hamburg, 1722–25; reprint, Amsterdam, 1964.
Das forschende Orchestre. Hamburg, 1721; reprint, Hildesheim, 1976.
Grundlage einer Ehren-Pforte. Hamburg, 1740; modern edn. Max Schneider. Berlin, 1910.
Inimici mortis verdächtiger Todes-Freund. Hamburg, 1747.
Mithridat wider den Gift einer welschen Satyr. Hamburg, 1749.
Die neuangelegte Freuden-Akademie. 2 vols. Hamburg, 1751–53.
Das neu-eröffnete Orchestre. Hamburg, 1713; reprint, Hildesheim, 1993.
Die neueste Untersuchung der Singspiele nebst beygefügter musikalischen Geschmacksprobe. Hamburg 1744; reprint, Leipzig, 1975.
Der vollkommene Capellmeister. Hamburg, 1739; reprint, Kassel, 1954; trans. Ernest C. Harriss as *Der vollkommene Capellmeister: A Revised Translation with Critical Commentary.* Ann Arbor, 1981.

Select bibliography

Gültige Zeugnisse über die jüngste Matthesonisch-Musicalische Kern-Schrifft. Hamburg, 1738.
XII Sonates à Deux & Trois Flutes sans Basse. Amsterdam, 1708.
Der Brauchbare Virtuoso. Hamburg, 1720; reprint, Florence, 1997.
Mautner, Martin-Christian. *Mach einmal mein Ende gut: Zur Sterbekunst in den Kantaten Johann Sebastian Bachs zum 16. Sonntag nach Trinitatis.* Frankfurt, 1997.
Meier, Georg Friedrich. *Beweis, dass keine Materie denken könne.* 2nd edn. Halle, 1751.
Gedanken von dem Zustande der Seele nach dem Tode. 2nd edn. Halle, 1749.
Versuch eines neuen Lehrgebäudes von den Seelen der Thiere. Halle, 1749.
Meinel, Christoph. "Alchemie und Musik." In *Die Alchemie in der europäischen Kultur- und Wissenschaftgeschichte.* Ed. Christoph Meinel. Wiesbaden, 1986, pp. 201–227.
Meißner, Heinrich Adam. *Philosophisches Lexicon.* Bayreuth, 1737.
Melamed, Daniel, ed. *Bach Studies 2.* Cambridge, 1995.
Meyer-Baer, Kathi. *Music of the Spheres and the Dance of Death: Studies in Musical Iconology.* Princeton, 1970.
Mizler, Lorenz Christoph. *Neu eröffnete musikalische Bibliothek.* Leipzig, 1739–54; reprint, Hildesheim, 1970.
Mohr, Rudolf. *Protestantische Theologie und Frömmigkeit im Angesicht des Todes während des Barockzeitalters hauptsächlich auf Grund hessischer Leichenpredigten.* Marburg, 1964.
Der unverhoffte Tod: theologie- und kulturgeschichtliche Untersuchungen zu aussergewöhnlichen Todesfällen in Leichenpredigten. Marburg, 1982.
Moser, Hans Joachim. *Heinrich Schütz: sein Leben und Werk.* Kassel, 1936.
Johann Sebastian Bach. Berlin, 1935.
Müller, Fritz. "Unterstellung? Verunglimpfung? Geschichtswidrigkeit?" *Zeitschrift für Musik* 106 (1936): 1370–1372.
Müller, Heinrich. *Geistliche Erquickstunden.* Frankfurt, 1700.
Vermehrter und durchgehends verbesserter Himmlischer Liebes-Kuß oder Göttliche Liebes-Flamme. Nuremberg, 1732.
Müller-Blattau, Joseph. *Geschichte der Fuge.* 3rd edn. Kassel, 1963.
Münnich, Richard. "Friedrich der Große und die Musik." *Zeitschrift für Musik* 103 (1936): 913–916.
Musaeum Hermeticum. Frankfurt, 1678; reprint, Graz, 1970.
Neumann, Werner and Hans-Joachim Schulze, eds. *Bach-Dokumente.* 4 vols. Kassel, 1963–1978.
Niedt, Friedrich Erhard. *Musicalischer Handleitung dritter und letzter Theil.* Ed. Johann Mattheson. Hamburg, 1717. Trans. Pamela Poulin and Irmgard Taylor as *The Musical Guide.* Oxford, 1989.
Nietzsche, Friedrich. *Human, All-Too-Human,* part II. Trans. Paul V. Cohn. New York, 1964.
Österreich, Georg. *Herrn Capell-Meister Österreichs Aufsatz von den gedoppelten Contrapuncten.* Manuscript. Staatsbibliothek zu Berlin, Mus. Ms. theor. 670.
Untitled manuscript. Manuscript. Staatsbibliothek zu Berlin, Mus. Ms. theor. 1038.

Select bibliography

Pagel, Walter. *Paracelsus*. Basel, 1958.
Palisca, Claude. "The Genesis of Mattheson's Style Classification." In *New Mattheson Studies*. Ed. George J. Buelow and Hans Joachim Marx. Cambridge, 1983, pp. 405–423.
Petzoldt, Martin. "Christian Weise d. Ä. und Christoph Wolle – zwei Leipziger Beichtväter Bachs, Vertreter zweier auslegungsgeschichtlicher Abschnitte der ausgehenden lutherischen Orthodoxie." In *Bach als Ausleger der Bibel: Theologische und musikwissenschaftliche Studien zum Werk Johann Sebastian Bachs*. Ed. Martin Petzoldt. Göttingen, 1985, pp. 109–129.
Pfeiffer, August. *Anti-melancholicus, oder Melancholey-Vertreiber*. Leipzig, 1691.
Potter, Pamela. *The Most German of Arts: Musicology and Society from the Weimar Republic to the End of Hitler's Reich*. New Haven, 1998.
Poyselius, Ulrich. "Spiegel der Alchemie." In *Eröffnete Geheimnisse des Steins der Weisen oder Schatz-kammer der Alchymie*. Hamburg, 1718.
Praetorius, Michael. *Syntagma musicum*. Vol. III. Wolfenbüttel, 1619; reprint, Kassel, 1958.
Syntagma musicum. Vol. III. Trans. Hans Lampl. D.M.A. dissertation: University of Southern California, 1957.
Printz, Wolfgang Caspar. *Phrynis Mitilenaeus oder Satyrischer Componist*. Quedlinburg, 1676; 2nd edn., Dresden and Leipzig, 1696.
Quantz, Johann Joachim. "Lebenslauf." In *Historisch-kritische Beyträge zur Aufnahme der Musik*. Vol. I. Ed. F. W. Marpurg. Berlin, 1754, pp. 197–250.
Sei duetti a due flauti traversi, op. 2. Berlin, 1759; reprint, Farnborough, 1967.
Versuch einer Anweisung die Flöte traversiere zu spielen. Berlin, 1752. Trans. Edward R. Reilly as *On Playing the Flute*. New York, 1975.
Rädlein, Johann. *Europäischer Sprach-Schatz ... oder Wörter-Buch*. Leipzig, 1711.
Reich, Wolfgang, ed. *Threnodiae sacrae: Beerdigungskompositionen aus gedruckten Leichenpredigten des 16. und 17. Jahrhunderts*. Das Erbe deutscher Musik. Vol. LXXIX. Wiesbaden, 1975.
Reimer, Erich. "Bachs Jagdkantate als profanes Ritual: zur politischen Funktion absolutischer Hofmusik." *Musik und Bildung* 12 (1980): 674–683.
Reincken, Johann Adam. *Erste Unterrichtung zur Composition*. In Jan Pieterszoon Sweelinck, *Werken*. Vol. X: *Compositions-Regeln*. Ed. Hermann Gehrmann. Leipzig, 1901; reprint, Farnborough, 1968, pp. 23–28, 49–58.
Richards, Annette. "Automatic Genius: Mozart and the Mechanical Sublime." *Music & Letters* 80 (1999): 366–389.
The Free Fantasia and the Musical Picturesque. Cambridge, 2000.
Riedel, Friedrich. *Quellenkundliche Beiträge zur Geschichte der Musik für Tasteninstrumente in der zweiten Hälfte des 17. Jahrhunderts*. Munich, 1990.
"Strenger und freier Stil in der nord- und süddeutschen Musik für Tasteninstrumente des 17. Jahrhunderts." In *Norddeutsche und nordeuropäische Musik*. Ed. Carl Dahlhaus. Kassel, 1968, pp. 63–70.
Rist, Johann. *Sabbahtische Seelenlust*. Lüneburg, 1651.
Rollenhagen, Georg. *Froschmeuseler der Frosch und Meuse Wunderbahre Hoffhaltunge*. Magdeburg, 1618; 2nd edn., Braunschweig, 1637.
Rosen, Charles. *Arnold Schoenberg*. New York, 1975.
Rosenberg, Hans. *Bureaucracy, Aristocracy and Autocracy: the Prussian Experience, 1660–1815*. Cambridge, Mass., 1958.

Select bibliography

Ruland, Martin. *Lexicon Alchemiae*. Frankfurt, 1612; reprint, Hildesheim, 1964.

Schäftertöns, Reinhard. "Johannes Brahms und die Musik von Johann Sebastian Bach." In *Bach und die Nachwelt*. 3 vols. Ed. Michael Heinemann and Hans-Joachim Hinrichsen. Laaber, 1997–2000, vol. II, pp. 201–224.

Scheibe, Johann Adolph. *Compendium Musices* (1736). Ed. Peter Benary. In *Die deutsche Kompositionslehre des 18. Jahrhunderts*. Leipzig, 1961.

Critischer Musikus. 2nd edn. 5 vols. Leipzig, 1745; reprint, Hildesheim, 1970.

"Rechtfertigung der Gegen Bach Erhobenen Vorwürfe." Hamburg, 1738. Reprinted in *Bach-Dokumente*. Vol. II, pp. 312–320.

Schenk, Erich. "Johann Theiles Harmonischer Baum." In *Musik und Bild: Festschrift Max Seiffert*. Ed. Heinrich Besseler. Kassel, 1938, pp. 95–100.

Schenkman, Walter. "Portrait of Mattheson, the Editor Together with His Correspondents." *BACH* 9/4 (October 1978): 2–9; 10/1 (January 1979): 3–12; 10/2 (April 1979): 2–8.

Schleuning, Peter. *Das 18. Jahrhundert: Der Bürger erhebt sich*. Reinbek bei Hamburg, 1984.

Johann Sebastian Bachs "Kunst der Fuge." Kassel, 1993.

Schmidt, Johann Michael. *Musico-Theologia, Oder Erbauliche Anwendungen musikalischer Wahrheiten*. Bayreuth and Hof, 1754.

Schoenberg, Arnold. *Style and Idea*. Ed. Leonard Stein. London, 1975.

Schulenberg, David. *The Keyboard Music of J. S. Bach*. New York, 1992.

Schünemann, Georg. "J. G. Walther und H. Bokemeyer." *Bach-Jahrbuch* 30 (1933): 86–118.

Schütt, Hans-Werner. *Auf der Suche nach dem Stein der Weisen: Die Geschichte der Alchemie*. Munich, 2000.

Schütz, Heinrich. *Neue Ausgabe Sämtlicher Werke*. Vol. V: *Geistliche Chormusik (1648)*. Ed. Wilhelm Kamlah. Kassel, 1965.

Gesammelte Briefe und Schriften. Ed. Erich Hermann Müller. Regensburg, 1931; reprint, Hildesheim, 1976.

Schweitzer, Albert. *Johann Sebastian Bach*. 2 vols. Trans. Ernest Newman. Leipzig, 1911.

Sheldon, David A. "The Galant Style Revisited and Re-evaluated." *Acta Musicologica* 47 (1975): 240–269.

Siegele, Ulrich. "Bach and the Domestic Politics of Electoral Saxony." In *The Cambridge Companion to Bach*. Ed. John Butt. Cambridge, 1997, pp. 17–34.

Snyder, Kerala J. "Dietrich Buxtehude's Studies in Learned Counterpoint." *Journal of the American Musicological Society* 33 (1980): 544–564.

Dieterich Buxtehude, Organist in Lübeck. New York, 1987.

Soltys, Adam. "Georg Österreich (1664–1735): sein Leben und seine Werke." *Archiv für Musikwissenschaft* 4 (1922): 170–193.

Spitta, Philipp. *Johann Sebastian Bach*. 2 vols. Leipzig, 1873–80. English trans. Clara Bell and J. A. Fuller Maitland. 3 vols. London, 1889; reprint, New York, 1951.

Stauffer, George. "Johann Mattheson and J. S. Bach: The Hamburg Connection." In *New Mattheson Studies*. Ed. George J. Buelow and Hans Joachim Marx. Cambridge, 1983, pp. 353–368.

Leipzig: Cosmopolitan Trade Centre." In *Music and Society: The Late Baroque*. Ed. George J. Buelow. New York, 1994, pp. 254–295.

Select bibliography

Steglich, Rudolf. "Friedrich der Große und Johann Sebastian Bach." *Zeitschrift für Musik* 106 (1936): 931–933.
"Nochmals: Friedrich der Große und Johann Sebastian Bach." *Zeitschrift für Musik* 106 (1936): 1368–1370.
Stinson, Russell. *Bach: The Orgelbüchlein*. New York, 1996.
Stoltzenberg, Stoltzius von. *Chymisches Lustgärtlein*. Frankfurt, 1624; reprint, Darmstadt, 1987.
Stölzel, Gottfried Heinrich. *Practischer Beweis / wie aus einem nach dem wahren Fundamente solcher Noten-Künsteleyen Canone Perpetuo ... zu machen seyn.* N.p. 1725.
[Strungk, Nicolaus Adam]. *Wiener Klavier- und Orgelwerke aus der zweiten Hälfte des 17. Jahrhunderts*. Denkmäler der Tonkunst in Österreich. Vol. II. Ed. Hugo Botsbiber. Graz, 1959.
Swack, Jeanne. "Flute Sonatas." In *Oxford Composer Companions: J. S. Bach*. Ed. Malcolm Boyd. Oxford, 1999, pp. 174–175.
Telemann, Georg Philipp. *XIIX Canons mélodieux, ou VI Sonates en duo*. Paris, 1738. Modern edn. in Telemann, *Musikalische Werke*. Vol. VIII. Ed. Günter Hausswald. Kassel, 1953.
Telemann, Georg Philipp, ed. *Der getreue Music-Meister*. Hamburg, 1728; reprint, Leipzig, 1980.
Theile, Johann. *Contrapuncts-Praecepta*. Manuscript. Staatsbibliothek zu Berlin, Mus. Ms. theor. 917, part II.
Curieuser Unterricht von denen doppelten Contrapuncten. Manuscript. Staatsbibliothek zu Berlin, Musikabteilung, Mus. Ms. theor. 916.
Gründlicher Unterricht. Manuscript. Staatsbibliothek zu Berlin, Musikabteilung, Mus. Ms. theor. 917, part I.
Musicalisches Kunstbuch. Manuscript. Staatsbibliothek zu Berlin, Musikabteilung, Mus. Ms. theor. 913.
Musicalisches Kunstbuch. Ed. Carl Dahlhaus. Denkmäler norddeutscher Musik. Vol. I. Kassel, 1965.
Unterricht von einigen gedoppelten Contrapuncten und deren Gebrauch. Manuscript. Staatsbibliothek zu Berlin. Mus. ms. theor. 913, part II.
Von dem dreyfachen Contrapunct. Manuscript. Staatsbibliothek zu Berlin, Mus. ms. theor. 910, part I.
Thilman, Johannes Paul. *Probleme der neuen Polyphonie*. Dresden, 1949.
Thorau, Christian. "Richard Wagners Bach." In *Bach und die Nachwelt*. 3 vols. Ed. Michael Heinemann and Hans-Joachim Hinrichsen. Laaber, 1997–2000, vol. II, pp. 163–199.
Tomlinson, Gary. *Music in Renaissance Magic*. Chicago, 1993.
Tralles, D. B. L. *De machina et anima humana*. Leipzig, 1749.
[Trisomsin, Salomon]. "Splendor Solis," in *Aureum vellis oder Guldin Schatz und Kunstkammer*. Trans. Joscelyn Godwin. Grand Rapids, 1991.
Valentinus, Basilius. "Vom grossen Stein der uhralten Weisen." In *Chymische Schrifften*. Hamburg, 1700.
Vaucanson, Jacques de. *Le mécanisme du fluteur automate*. Paris, 1738. Trans. J. T. Desaguliers as *An Account of the Mechanism of an Automaton, or Image*

Select bibliography

playing on the German-Flute. London, 1742; reprint of both French and English versions, Buren, 1979.

Verzeichniß des Naturalien-Cabinets, der Bibliothek, Kupferstiche und Musikalien ingleichen der mathematischen, physikalischen und optischen Instrumente des seligen Hofraths und Doct. Med. Herrn Georg Ernst Stahl. Berlin, 1773.

Vickers, Brian. "Analogy versus Identity: The Rejection of Occult Symbolism, 1580–1680." In *Occult and Scientific Mentalities in the Renaissance*. Ed. Brian Vickers. Cambridge, 1984, pp. 353–368.

Walch, Johann Georg. *Philosophisches Lexicon*. Leipzig, 1726.

Walker, Paul. *Theories of Fugue from the Age of Josquin to the Age of Bach*. Rochester, 2000.

Walther, Johann Gottfried. *Briefe*. Ed. Klaus Beckmann and Hans-Joachim Schulze. Leipzig, 1987.

Musicalisches Lexicon oder musicalische Bibliothec. Leipzig, 1732; reprint, Kassel, 1953.

Praecepta der musicalischen Composition. Ed. Peter Benary. Leipzig, 1955.

Sämtliche Orgelwerke. 4 vols. Wiesbaden, 1998.

Weidemann, Carla. *Leben und Wirken des Johann Philipp Förtsch (1652–1732)*. Kassel, 1955.

Werckmeister, Andreas. *Musicae mathematicae hodegus curiosus, oder richtiger musicalischer Weg-Weiser*. Frankfurt and Leipzig, 1686; reprint, Hildesheim, 1970.

Cribrum musicum, oder musicalisches Sieb. Quedlinburg and Leipzig, 1700; reprint, Hildesheim, 1970.

Harmonologia musica, oder kurtze Anleitung zur musicalischen Composition. Frankfurt and Leipzig, 1702; reprint, Hildesheim, 1970.

Musicalische Paradoxal-Discourse. Quedlinburg, 1707; reprint, Hildesheim, 1970.

Musicalisches Send-schreiben. Quedlinburg, 1699.

Williams, Peter. *The Organ Music of J. S. Bach*. 3 vols. Cambridge, 1980–84.

Wimmer, Gabriel. *Ausführliche Liederklärung (wodurch die ältesten und gewöhnlichsten Gesänge der Evangelisch-Lutherischen Kirche... erläutert worden)*. Altenburg, 1749.

Winckler, Johann Heinrich. *Die Frage, ob die Seelen der Thiere Verstand Haben?* Leipzig, 1742.

Winkler, Eberhard. *Die Leichenpredigt im deutschen Luthertum bis Spener*. Munich, 1967.

Wolff, Christoph. *Johann Sebastian Bach: Essays on his Life and Works*. Cambridge, Mass., 1991.

Johann Sebastian Bach: the Learned Musician. New York, 2000.

Kanons, Musicalisches Opfer: Kritischer Bericht. Kassel, 1976.

Der Stile antico in der Musik Johann Sebastian Bachs. Wiesbaden, 1968.

Wolff, Christoph, et al., ed. *The New Bach Reader*. New York, 1998.

Wustmann, Gustav. *Bilderbuch aus der Geschichte der Stadt Leipzig*. Leipzig, 1897.

Yates, Frances. *Giordano Bruno and the Hermetic Tradition*. London, 1964.

The Rosicrucian Enlightenment. London, 1972.

Select bibliography

Yearsley, David. "Alchemy and Counterpoint in an Age of Reason." *Journal of the American Musicological Society* 51 (1998): 201–243.
    "Towards an Allegorical Interpretation of Buxtehude's Funerary Counterpoints." *Music & Letters* 80/2 (May 1999): 183–206.
Zarlino, Gioseffo. *The Art of Counterpoint. Part Three of "Le istitutioni harmoniche," 1558*. Trans. Guy A. Marco and Claude Palisca. New Haven, 1968.
Zedler, Johann Heinrich. *Großes vollständiges Universal Lexicon aller Wissenschaften und Künste*. Leipzig 1732–52; reprint, Graz, 1961–64.
Zeller, Winfried. *Theologie und Frömmigkeit*. 2 vols. Ed. Bernd Jaspert. Marburg, 1971–78.
Zelter, Karl Friedrich. *Karl Friedrich Christian Fasch*. Berlin, 1801; reprint, Blankenburg, 1983.

INDEX

absolutism, 129–132, 135, 137, 166–171
  see also counterpoint and absolutism
Adorno, Theodor, 209–210, 235–236
Agricola, J. F., 33, 147
Agrippa, H. C., 57–58
alchemy
  and anatomical dissection, 73–74
  and counterpoint, 51–52, 65–78, 82–92, 235
  and Frederick the Great, 50, 62
  and Heinrich Bokeyemer, 48–52
  and J. G. Walther, 48–52
  and J. S. Bach, 49, 62, 64–65, 86
  and G. W. Leibniz, 50, 89–90
  and Isaac Newton, 50, 89–90
  and Lorenz Mizler, 62–64
  and music, 49–51, 68–72, 75–86, 90–92 *passim*
  and secrecy, 58, 62, 66–67, 76, 90–92
  see also artifex; J. S. Bach, reception of his canons/counterpoint; occult; magic
allegory, *see* counterpoint as allegory
Altnikol, J. C., 5
arbor philosophica, *see* Theile, *Harmonischer Baum*
Aristotle, 69
ars moriendi, 1, 6–12, 28, 36, 39–42, 224
artifex, 66–67, 68, 70–71, 72, 76–78, 88
  see also alchemy; artifice
artifice/artificiality, 36, 66–67, 69–70, 90, 95–96, 99, 101, 106–110, 120, 124, 126, 139, 151, 169, 176–178, 189, 193
  see also counterpoint, artificiality of
augmentation, 88–89, 113, 120, 123, 129, 148–149, 173, 189, 191–194, 236
autocracy, *see* absolutism
automata, *see* Vaucanson

Bach, C. P. E., 21, 101, 128, 137, 169, 183
  canons of, 123, 126, 187–188
  invertible counterpoint "device" of, 183–184, *185*, 186, 204, 207–208
  on J. S. Bach and his music, 4–5, 17, 33, 118, 126, 139, 143
  Sei sonate, dedicated to Frederick the Great, 132

Versuch über die wahre Art das Clavier zu spielen, 113, 117–118, 173
Bach, J. C.
  Lieber Herr Gott, wecke uns auf, 6
Bach, J. E., 62
Bach, J. S.
  and alchemy, 49, 62, 64–65, 86
  in Berlin, 128–130, 137–138, 157, 173–174, 230–231
  and biblical study, 6–7, 9–10, 12, 18, 36, 131
  bones of, *see* skeleton
  burial of, 210–211
  and coins/medals, 64
  and contrapuntal invention, 125, 186
  death of, 1, 5–6, 33, 35, 39–42, 130, 137, 188, 209–211
  and "Enlightenment," 96, 104, 106, 110, 119, 126–127, 235, 237
  exhumation of, 211–214
  festival of 1950, 222–225, 234
  and Frederick the Great, 128–131, 157, 170–173, 230–232
  funeral of, 6, 34, 210
  funeral music for, 6, 34–35
  and German nationalist ideology, 225, 228–235, 237
  grave site, 211–212
  honorary titles, obsession with, 97, 128, 134–135, 231
  keyboard playing of, 30, 173–174
  and materialism, 33, 180–181, 188–189, 205–206
  and Mizler's society, 24, 87, 110, 120, 136
  and the modern style, 87, 108–119, 125–127, 130, 138–147, 156–157, 165–166, 170
  and music criticism, xv, 58–60, 94–99, 102–103, 106–111, 115, 126–127, 170, 229, 237
  obituary of, 1, 8–9, 33, 209, 238
  politics of, 129–134, 170–172, 233
  portraits of, 87, 214, 222, 224–226, *226*, 227
  reception of his canons/counterpoint, 42–45, 47–48, 59, 62, 83, 87–92, 99, 143–145, 207–210, 228–238

Index

Bach, J. S. (*cont.*)
  selection as Thomascantor, 131
  skeleton of, 210, 212, *221*, 225, 237
  skull of, 212, *213*, *213*, 215, *216*, *217*, 218, *219*, *220*, 221, *223*, 225
  theological library of, 6–7, 12, 28, 36, 39, 170
  WORKS
  Art of Fugue (BWV 1080), 2, 4, 5, 39, 75, 90, 119, 238
    canons, 189–208
  Canonic Variations on Vom Himmel hoch (BWV 769/769a), 2, 33, 87, 88, 110–120, 124–127, 139, 181, 188, 193
  Canon a 4 ... perpetuus (BWV 1073), 48
  Canon a 2 perpetuus (BWV 1075), 82–83
  Canon: Concordia discors (BWV 1086), 60, 62, 70
  Canon doppio sopr'il soggetto ("*Fulde*" canon, BWV 1077), 87, 112
  Canon super Fa Mi (BWV 1078), 59–60, *61*, 189
  14 Canons on the "Goldberg" Bass (BWV 1087), 87–89
  Duetto in F major (BWV 803), 99, 101–110, 119, 126–127, 197
  Flute Sonata in E major (BWV 1035), 128
  Fugue in A major, *WTC I* (BWV 864), 45–46
  Goldberg Variations (BWV 988), 157, 189
    Quodlibet from, 120–124
  "Hudemann" Canon (BWV 1074), 26, 42, *43*, 44–48, 60, 83, 87, 89, 155
  Inventions and Sinfonias (BWV 772–801), 99, 101, 105, 109
  Liebster Gott, Wenn werd ich sterben? (BWV 8), 11
  Mass in A major (BWV 234), *156*
  Mass in B minor (BWV 232), 142, 156
  Musical Offering, A (BWV 1079), 75, 128–130, 132–133, 136–138, 142–172, 201, 229, 231–233, 236
  Orchestral Suite in B minor (BWV 1067), 139, *140*
  Organ Sonatas (BWV 525–530), 2
  Peasant Cantata (BWV 212), 230
  Prelude and Fugue in E♭ major (BWV 552), 99, 186
  Violin and Harpsichord Sonata in A major (BWV 1015), 139, *140*
  Vor deinenThron tret ich hiermit (BWV 668), 2, 3, 4, 5, 12, 17, 25, 33–34, 36, 40–41, 48, 181, 224
  Wenn wir in höchsten Nöthen sein (BWV 668a), 2, 33, 35, 37–39, 181, 188
  Wenn wir in höchsten Nöthen sein (BWV 641), 5, 35–36

Bach, Maria Barbara, 7
Bach, W. F., 5, 101, 112, 126
  account of J. S. Bach's arrival in Potsdam, 128–129, 156–157
  canons of, 154
Beer, Johann
  on status of counterpoint, 53
Beethoven, Ludwig van, 211, 230
Berardi, Angelo, 45, 195, *196*
Berlin, 5, 128–129, 133, 135, 138, 143, 155–157, 170–171, 173–174, 179–180, 224
Bernhard, Christoph, 15, 20, 73, 78
Bertouch, Georg von, 59
Besseler, Heinrich, 224–225, *226*, *227*
Birnbaum, J. A., 71, 94–95, 97, 110, 119–120, 125, 134–135
Blankenburg, Walter, 224, 234
body
  demise of, 7–8, 25, 26, 33, 36
  posthumous fate of, 1–2, 7, 212
  transfiguration of, 26, 30, 32–33, 36, 39, 211
  see also alchemy and anatomical dissection; Bach, exhumation of
Boeldicke, Joachim, 64
Bokemeyer, Heinrich
  and alchemy, 48–52, 65–74, 90
  allegorical conceptions of counterpoint, 24, 51, 67–68, 69–70, 73
  on canon, 24, 47–48, 52, 83, 87
  contra Mattheson, 52, 54–56, 65, 70, 72–73, 86
  see also "Die canonische Anatomie"
  correspondence with Walther, 13–14, 42, 43–44, 48–52, 74
  and J. S. Bach, 42, 45, 87–88, 90
Bordoni, Faustina, 136
Brahms, Johannes, 229, 233
Braun, Werner, 49
Bruno, Giordano, 57
Buffardin, Pierre-Gabriel, 136
Bünting, Heinrich, 64
Burgartz, Alfred, 232–234, 236
Buttstett, Heinrich, 31, 58–60, 64–66, 69, 73, 169
Buxtehude, Dieterich, 24, 66, 73, 75, 121
  Castrum doloris (BuxWV 134), 13
  Klag-Lied (BuxWV 76/2), 30–31, 36
  Mit Fried und Freud ich fahr dahin (BuxWV, 76/1), 13–15, 18, 30, 34, 36

Calov, Abraham, 36, 64, 171
canon
  artificialis, 70
  and alchemy, *see* alchemy and counterpoint

252

Index

and allegory, 18, 21, 24, 51–52, 70–72, 165, 171–172
codification/demystification of, 90–92
crab, 148–149, *150*, 151–155, 160
and *galant* style, 87, 139–143, 165–166
and heavenly music, 21, 24, 28, 31, 73
and invertible counterpoint, 20–21, 24–25, 44, 47, 53, 56–57, 67, 75, 83, 95, 100, 107–108, 153, 159–165, 193–195, *196*, 197–198, 201–207
methods of construction, 151–154, 160–161
naturalis, 70, 83, 87
and the modern style, 101, 112–116, 130, 142
and opera, 142, 155
perpetual, 21, 24, 52, 73, 83, 112, 143–148, 165, 193, 201, 206
per tonos, 171–172, 203
in performance, 111, 143–144, 147, 153
and secrecy, 44, 56, 65–67, 73, 91
and *stile antico*, 52, 54, 142
and trio sonata, 140–141, 143, 145–147, 165–166
as witchcraft, 56, 62
see also augmentation; counterpoint; diminution; inversion, melodic; retrograde
cantabile, 101–102, 105–106, 111–112, 115, 118
Carpzov, J. B., 8
contrary motion, *see* inversion, melodic
counterpoint
and absolutism/despotism/autocracy, 166, 168–172
as abstract, xv, xvi, 111, 118, 130, 138, 235, 237
and alchemy, *see* alchemy
as allegory, 18–21, 22, 23, 24–25, 52, 60, 67, 73, 84, *85*, *86*, 165, 171–172, 235, 237
artificiality of, 56, 73, 118, 122
automatic generation of, 183–188, 204, 207
as conversation, 101, 109, 143, 156, 166
and death, xv, 1, 12–20, 28, 31, 35–42, 48, 189
as diversion, xvi, 53, 143, 155, 183–184
as domination, 166
galant, 139–144
and *galant* style, 101, 108–119, 125–127, 130, 139, 142–145, 156–157, 170
and heavenly music, 20–21, 24–25, 28, 33, 39, 41
and pedagogy, 52, 54, 65, 168, 186
polemics concerning, xv, 52–56, 73, 160, 123, 166, 168–169
see also "Die canonische Anatomie"

and revolution, 168, 235
and rules, 44, 51, 60, 92, 96, 153, 197, 229, 237
and secrecy, xv, 44–45, 56, 66–67, 73, 90–92
see also canon and secrecy
and superstition, 55–56
as universal/truth in music, xvi, 20, 45, 47, 225–226, 228–230, 237
as witchcraft, 56, 62, 65, 90–91
see also alchemy and counterpoint; augmentation; canon; diminution; invertible counterpoint; inversion, melodic; retrograde; stretto

David, Hans, 159
death
and counterpoint, xv, 1, 12–20, 28, 31, 35–42, 48, 189
and chorales, 10–11, 25, 28, 41
definition of, 25
hour of, 7, 8, 13, 40–41
see also last words; *Todesgedanken*
preparation for, 5–8, *9*, 10, 28, 33, 35–36, 39–41
and the Reformation, 210–211
as sleep, 10, 25–26, 40
see also dying, Lutheran rituals of
Descartes, René, 90
"Die canonische Anatomie", 51, 55–56, 59–60, 67–73, 87, 94, 100, 119, 168, 237 *passim*
see also Bokemeyer, on canon; Mattheson, on canon
diminution, 5, 38–39, 186–188, 204, 236
double counterpoint, *see* invertible counterpoint
Dresden, 10, 44, 135–137, 143, 170, 234
DuMage, Pierre, 97
Dumoulin, Pierre, 174–175
dying, Lutheran rituals of, 1–2, 6–13, 39, 210–211
see also ars moriendi; death, and chorales; death, preparation for; Luther, Martin, on death

Emerald Table, *see Tabula Smaragdina*
enigmatic notation, *see* puzzle notation
"Enlightenment," the
and music criticism/theory, xv, xvi, 55–56, 62, 91–96, 104, 106–107, 110, 119, 125–126, 235, 237
and musical style, 104, 107, 109, 110, 126
see also Bach, J. S.; Heinichen; Mattheson; Scheibe
Erdmann, Georg,
letter from J. S. Bach, 131
Ernst, Johann, 47

253

Index

Faber, B. G., 59, 188
fantasy machine, 183
Fasch, J. C. F., 155–156, 187
Fasch, J. F., 140–141, 145, 165–166
Ficino, Marsilio, 57
Flemming, J. F. von, 132
Flor, Christian, 13
  Todesgedanken in dem Liede: "Auf meinen lieben Gott", 12
Flor, J. G., 12
Forkel, J. N.
  as Bach biographer, 5, 125, 128–129, 139, 207
  as Bach hagiographer, 127, 156, 225
  on Bach's humor, 207–208
  on Bach's keyboard playing, 173
  on fugue and *das Volk*, 232–233, 236
Förtsch, J. P., 24, 74, 91
Frederick the Great, King of Prussia, 175, 178
  and alchemy, 50, 62
  and autocracy, 168–172
  on counterpoint, 155–156
  on flattery, 158
  as *galant homme*, 151
  on liberty, 169
  meeting with J. S. Bach, 128–130, 137–138, 157, 170, 230–231
  as musical conqueror/hero, 135–138
  musical establishment of, 128, 133, 135, 143, 155, 187
  musical volumes dedicated to, 129, 132–133, 137, 157–158, 168, 172
  and Nazism, 230–232
  quasi-religious descriptions of, 132
  and the royal theme, 128–129, 157–158, 164–165
Frederick William I, King of Prussia, 136
Fredersdorf, M. G., 128, 138
freedom
  and compositional style, 54, 96, 99, 103, 118, 189–190, 206, 235–236
  in politics and music, 168–172, 232
  see also nature/naturalness; counterpoint, rules; Mattheson, on tyranny
Frescobaldi, Girolamo, 121
Friedrich August I, Elector of Saxony, 136
Friedrich August II, Elector of Saxony, 130, 132, 134–137
Fuhrmann, Martin, 30, 97–98
funeral sermons, 6, 8, 10–12, 25, 34
Fux, J. J., 59, 142

galant counterpoint, *see* counterpoint, *galant*
galant homme, 94, 98, 122, 125–126, 151, 156
galant style, 66, 97, 101, 110–116, 119, 122, 124, 138–139, 143, 156, 165–166, 170
Geier, Martin, 8, 10
Goethe, Johann Wolfgang von, 225
Graun, J. G., 128
Graun, K. H., 35, 128, 142, 155–156
Graupner, Christoph
  canons of, 46–47, 79, 140–141, 146, 165–166
Grigny, Nicolas de, 97
Gumpelshaimer, Adam
  cruciform canon of, 18, *19*

Haas, Robert, 222
Handel, G. F., 121, 230
Hasse, J. A., 35, 135–137, 143
Hasse, Karl, 233–235
Haußmann, E. G., 87, 214, 222
Haydn, Joseph, 230
heavenly music, 20–21, 24, 29, 31–34, 41
  see also counterpoint and heavenly music; Mattheson; Mizler; Schmidt, J. M.
Heermann, Johann, 6
Hegel, G. W. F., 130
Heinichen, J. D.
  and Bach, 58–59, 94, 97–98
  as critic of counterpoint, 55–56, 65, 90–91, 94, 122–123, 126, 168, 235
  and "Enlightenment," 56, 126
  on taste, 94, 98, 115, 120, 142
Herbst, J. A., 28
hermeticism, *see* alchemy
His, Wilhelm, 212–215, 217–223
Hofstadter, Douglas, 152, 155
Hudemann, L. F., 26, 42

infinite canon, *see* canon, perpetual
inversion, melodic, 5, 17, 38–39, 60–62, 78, 81–83, 107, 114, 124, 143–147, 159, 191, 236
invertible counterpoint, 13–17, 20–21, 24, 38–39, 53, 56, 74, 76–83, 92, 100, 108, 148–149, 153, 160–161, 183–185, 193–195, *196*, 197–198, 215
  see also counterpoint; canon and invertible counterpoint

Jung, Carl Gustav, 67

Kant, Immanuel, 211, 218
Kämpfer, Philipp, 234
Kauffmann, G. F., 114
Keiser, Reinhard, 55
Kennan, Kent, 151
Kesseldorf, Battle of, 135
Keyserlingk, Baron von, 157
Khunrath, Heinrich, 67, *68*

254

Index

Kircher, Athanasius, 21, 22, 31, 58
Kirnberger, J. P., 123, 126, 142, 155, 169, 184, 187, 204
Kuhnau, Johann, 30

La Mettrie, Julien Offray de, 173, 176, 180–181, 188
Lange, Fritz, 225
Last Day, 25–26, 27, 211, 222
last words, 2, 4, 10–12, 39–40
learned counterpoint, *see* invertible counterpoint and canon
Leibniz, G. W., 50, 89–90
Leichenpredigten, see funeral sermons
Leipzig, 1, 5, 8, 10–11, 30, 33, 46, 64, 75, 90, 94, 97, 129, 140, 180, 188, 212, 220, 222, 225
   occupation by Prussian troops, 137
   introduction of Reformation in, 210–211
   music criticism in, 98, 110
   musical resources of, 170
   political status of, 131
   Town Council, 98, 131–134, 213–214, 231
Leopold I, Emperor, 15, 75
Lessing, G. E., 40, 169
Luther, Martin
   death of, 1
   burial hymns of, 13, 25–26
   on death, 6, 25, 28, 36

magic
   and counterpoint, 55–56, 62, 73, 76–77, 83, 86, 89–92
   renaissance, 57–58, 90
   see also alchemy; Mattheson, distrust of occult/secrecy; occult; Scheibe, mechanical critic of
Maier, Michael
   Atalanta fugiens, 71, 72, 76, 84
Marchand, Louis, 132
Marenholz, Christian, 222
Marpurg, F. W., 5, 145, 184, 207
   Abhandlung von der Fuge, 91, 119, 140, 160, 153–154, 186, 194–195, 228–229
   as codifier/defender of counterpoint, 91–92, 228, 234
   on composing canons, 160–161
   as devotee/legacy-maker of Bach, 126, 228–230
Marx, A. B., 230
materialism, 33, 179–183, 188–190
Mattheson, Johann, 86, 95, 98, 110, 170
   on *Art of Fugue*, 228, 230
   on counterpoint, 31, 52–56, 60, 72, 90–91, 99, 142, 151, 190, 235
   on canon, 42, 43, 53, 100, 142, 147, 215
   canons of, 100–101
   on death, 39–40
   and Frederick the Great, 133, 135, 137–138
   distrust of occult/secrecy, 56–58, 72–73, 91, 93–94
   on heavenly music, 26–29, 31, 33
   humanistic conception of music, 93–94
   listener-oriented aesthetic, 65, 94, 99–100, 119–120, 123
   on musical freedom, 54, 100, 190, 235
      see also Mattheson, on naturalness
   on musical taste, 94, 119–120, 126, 142
   on musical superstition, 57–58, 73
   on naturalness in music, 53, 60, 70, 102–103, 105, 115
   personal motto of, 60, 63
   on revolution, 168, 235, 238
   on solmization, 59–60
   on titles and honorifics, 134
   on tyranny (musical and political), 168
   see also "Die canonische Anatomie"; nature and naturalness; *galant homme*
Meder, J. V., 66, 75
medicine/medical science
   and counterpoint, 73–74
   and death, 8–9
   and Bach, 9, 59, 188
   and the soul, 173–174, 188
   see also Stahl, G. E. (the elder); La Mettrie; Paracelsus
Meier, G. F., 31–32, 176, 180
Mel, Conrad, 11
Mirandola, Pico della, 57
Mizler, Lorenz
   and alchemy, 62–64
   his Corresponding Society of the Musical Sciences, 24, 87, 110, 120, 136
   as defender/admirer of Bach, 33, 98, 120, 126, 137
   and Frederick the Great, 135–137
   on heavenly music, 32, 62
   on metaphysics of the soul, 32
   thorough-bass machine, 182–183, 208
Moser, H. J., 229, 236
Müller, Fritz, 231–232
Müller, Heinrich, 7–8, 10–11, 25, 26, 28, 39, 212
Müller-Blattau, Joseph, 230
Münnich, Richard, 231
Musikant, 96–97, 130, 134–135
   see also Bach, J. S., honorary titles, obsession with

nature/naturalness, 20, 54, 60, 70–71, 72, 87, 89, 95–96, 99–100, 102–107, 109–112, 115, 118, 120, 124, 176–178, 189–190

Index

Nazism
    and Bach, 222, 224, 233–234
    and musicology, 222, 230–236
    and Frederick the Great, 230–232
Neoplatonism, 57–58, 62, 93
Niedt, F. E., 53–54, 56, 143

occult, the, 49–50, 56–58, 62, 64–65, 72–73, 92, 237
    see also magic; alchemy
Oley, Johann, 147
Österreich, Georg, 21, 23, 75

Pachelbel, Johann
    Musicalische Sterbens-Gedancken, 12–13
Paracelsus, 57, 73, 84
Parnassus Boicus, 90–91
perfection, 20, 24, 28, 41, 70–71, 83, 88, 127, 173, 178, 197, 232
permutation, 20, 25, 44–45, 47, 78–83, 88–90, 152, 184, 188, 237
    see also counterpoint; Bach, C. P. E., invertible counterpoint "device" of
Pfeiffer, August, 7–9, 12
philosopher's stone, 58, 62, 65–66, 68–69, 77, 79–80, 84, 90
    see also alchemy
phrenology, 215, 225
physiognomy, 215, 222, 224–225
Pirro, André, 234
Politzer, Adam, 215–216
prosopopoeia, 34–35
puzzle notation, 42, 43, 44, 46, 108, 111, 115, 143, 147, 151, 153, 159–160, 193
Pythagoras, 21

Quantz, J. J., 101, 104, 112–113, 115–116, 128, 132, 138, 143, 178–179, 188, 207

Radek, Martin, 15
Raphael, 211, 218
Reger, Max, 233
Reincken, J. A., 73
retrograde, 18, 44, 78, 81, 91, 124–125, 151–155, 186
Rist, Johann, 21, 23
Ritter, Christian, 59–60
Roentgen, Wilhelm, 218
Rosa, Salvator, 133
royal theme, the, 128–129, 147, 149, 153–154, 157–166, 171
    see also Frederick the Great
rules, *see* counterpoint and rules

Scarlatti, Alessandro, 143
Scarlatti, Domenico
    Essercizi, 122

Scheibe, J. A.
    contra Mizler, 182–183
    criticisms of Bach, 95–98, 103, 110–111, 118, 127, 134–135, 182
    humanistic conception of music, 95–96
    mechanical critic of, 182–183, 208
    music aesthetics of, 108–109, 115, 117, 119–120, 124, 160
    praise of Bach, 35–36, 115, 118
Scheibler, Christoph, 6
Schiller, Friedrich von, 211, 218
Schmidt, J. C., 59, 60
Schmidt, J. M.
    on Bach and heavenly music, 33, 189
    on Bach and materialism, 33, 180–181, 184, 188–189, 205–206
Schoenberg, Arnold, 236
Schumann, Robert, 230
Schütz, Heinrich
    as apostate of counterpoint, 230
    exemplary death of, 10
    as defender of counterpoint, 229
Schweitzer, Albert, 130, 133, 234
Second Silesian War, 135, 169
Seffner, Karl, 214, 218, 219, 220, 221, 222, 229
Selle, Thomas, 21, 23
Sivers, H. J., 30
soul
    of animals, 176
    of musicians, 31, 33–35, 41, 179–181, 183–184, 188
    metaphysics of, 25–26, 30, 32–33, 36, 173–174, 176, 179–181, 190
    posthumous status of, 2, 25, 28, 32–33, 36, 39, 41, 188
    see also body, transfiguration of
Spitta, Philipp, 108, 129, 133, 211, 229
Stahl, G. E. (the elder), 173–174, 188
Stahl, G. E. (the younger), 174
Steglich, Rudolf, 231–232
Stieve, Hermann, 224
Stölzel, G. H., 24–25, 55
stretto, 5, 37–39, 106, 109, 115, 156, 186, 201
Strungk, N. A.
    Ricercar sopra la Morte mia carissima Madre . . . , 16–17
Swack, Jeanne, 139
Swieten, Baron van, 157

Tabula Smaragdina, 69
taste, 94–96, 98, 106, 109, 115, 119–121, 126, 133–134, 138, 142, 155, 179, 182, 228
    see also Mattheson, on musical taste
Telemann, G. P., 35, 42, 55
    canons of, 101, 112–113, 119, 140, 145, 152, 154–155, 166

Index

Der getreue Music-Meister, 42, 124–125, 143, *144*, 148–149
Theile, Johann, 21, 24, 65–66
  Musicalisches Kunstbuch, 73–77, 78, 79–84, *85*, 91, 195
  Harmonischer Baum, 84, *85*, 86
Thilman, J. P., 234–235
thorough-bass machine, *see* Mizler
Tieck, J. L., 233
Todesgedanken, 11–13, 28, 35, 41
  see also last words
Todesstunde, *see* death, hour of
Tralles, D. B. L., 180–181, 184
transfiguration, *see* body

Valentinus, Basilius, 69
Vaucanson, Jacques de
  his flute-playing faun, 174–175, *176*, 177–181, 188, 190, 207–208
  his duck, 175, *177*, 181
virtuosity, 5, 107, 173, 189, 193, 203, 205–206, 208, 238
Voltaire, 169, 179

Wagner, Richard, 229–230, 232–233
Walther, J. G., 12, 13
  and alchemy, 48–52
  and J. S. Bach, 42, 45, 47–48
  on Buttstett, 66

correspondence with Bokemeyer, 13–14, 42, 43–44, 48–52, 73–74
  learned counterpoint of, 16–17, 52
  Praecepta der musicalischen Composition, 12–13, 45, 47
Webern, Anton von, 236
Weichtheile, 217–218
Weimar, 13–14, 47, 51, 225
  Kunstkammer, 47–49, 62, 64
Welcker, Hermann, 218–219
Wenzky, Georg, 33–34
Werckmeister, Andreas
  allegorical conceptions of counterpoint, 18, 20, 57
  and Neoplatonism, 57
  musical estate, 13, 47
Wimmer, Gabriel, 11, 13
Winckler, J. H., 176
Wolff, Christian, 32
Wolle, Christoph, 1
Wustmann, Gustav, 211, 214, 218, 222

X-rays, 218

Yearsley, David
  crab canon of, 154

Zarlino, Gioseffo, 45, 51–52, 74, 76, 229
Zelenka, J. D.
  canons of, 44, 148, 155

257

For EU product safety concerns, contact us at Calle de José Abascal, 56–1°, 28003 Madrid, Spain or eugpsr@cambridge.org.